Called To Be Saints

A Centenary History of the Church of the Nazarene in the British Isles 1906-2006

T. A. Noble

With reminiscences and character sketches by Hugh Rae and others

First Fruits Press
Wilmore, Kentucky
c2017

Called to be saints: a centenary history of the Church of the Nazarene in the British Isles 1906-2006.
By T. A. Noble, with reminiscences and character sketches by Hugh Rae and others.

ISBN: 9781621716990 (print), 9781621717003 (digital), 9781621717010 (kindle)

Digital version at place.asburyseminary.edu/academicbooks/23/

First Fruits Press
B.L. Fisher Library
Asbury Theological Seminary
204 N. Lexington Ave.
Wilmore, KY 40390
http://place.asburyseminary.edu/firstfruits

Noble, T. A. (Thomas Arthur)
Called to be saints a centenary history of the Church of the Nazarene in the British Isles 1906-2006 / T.A. Noble ; with reminiscences and character sketches by Hugh Rae and others. – Wilmore, KY : First Fruits Press, ©2017.
351 pages: illustrations, portraits ; cm.
Includes bibliographical references and index.
Reprint. Previously published: Manchester, England : Didsbury Press, ©2006.
ISBN: 9781621716990 (pbk.)
1. Church of the Nazarene--Great Britain--History. 2. Holiness churches--Great Britain--History. 3. Great Britain--Church history. I. Title. II. Rae, Hugh.
BX8699.N335 G75 2017 289.9

Cover design by Jon Ramsay

asburyseminary.edu
800.2ASBURY
204 North Lexington Avenue
Wilmore, Kentucky 40390

First Fruits Press
The Academic Open Press of Asbury Theological Seminary
204 N. Lexington Ave., Wilmore, KY 40390
859-858-2236
first.fruits@asburyseminary.edu
asbury.to/firstfruits

CALLED TO BE SAINTS

A Centenary History of the Church of the Nazarene in the British Isles 1906-2006

T.A. Noble

With reminiscences and character sketches by Hugh Rae and others

Manchester: Didsbury Press
2006

Published By
Didsbury Press,
The White House,
Dene Road, Didsbury
Manchester M20 8GU

Printed by:
MOORLEY'S Print & Publishing
23 Park Rd., Ilkeston, Derbys DE7 5DA
Tel/Fax: (0115) 932 0643
using text supplied on disk

In loving memory of

THOMAS GRAY (1872-1950)

and

JAMES NOBLE (1877-1962)

and of

ROBERT HUGH RAE (1890-1960)

and

MARGARET (SANDS) RAE (1894-1977)

TABLE OF CONTENTS

FOREWORD

Rev Dr Samuel W. Hynd, DSc, CBE

This is a very important book. It tells the story of the rebirth of a historical emphasis on holiness which needs to be proclaimed today, not only in Britain, but in the Christian community throughout the world. Many whose hearts may be failing them because of the prevailing spiritual and moral condition will be encouraged that God is still at work.

We all have our heroes, sung and unsung, whom we honour, and this book is full if them. It tells of those who had exceptional courage in the face of difficulties, opposition and outright warfare in the battle against evil as it manifests itself in spirit, mind and body. There are many such Christians today, both leaders and followers who willingly serve their Lord, even (as with some young pastors) to the point of collapse from hunger or fatigue.

It has been my privilege to meet many of those who played such a vital role in this ongoing saga, those who have kept burning the flame of spiritual renewal and revival in the church today. In the modern era, we look to the ministry of John Wesley, who felt his heart 'strangely warmed' at Aldersgate Street and lit the light for the church in Britain and to the ends of the earth.

For me, I can mention several of the 'saints' in this story, for since my childhood I have been very close to some of them. I have no hesitation in placing at the top of my list my own grandfather, Dr George Sharpe, founder of the Church of the Nazarene in Britain. I had a vague knowledge of his 'presence', having been born into the manse in Glasgow before we left as a family for Swaziland. My mother, Agnes Kanema, was the middle daughter of the Sharpe family, and I hold her and my father, Dr David Hynd, in high esteem.

At the close of World War II, I was able to go back to Glasgow to complete my medical training with a view to returning to Swaziland as a medical missionary, having been converted and called through the preaching of a Swazi pastor. My grandmother had died, and Dr Sharpe was now staying with his daughter and son-in-law, Isabel and Victor Edwards, who took me in as one of their own children. In the three years I spent close to my grandfather until his death, I discovered a true man of God. He was a giant amongst men. I witnessed what was a near perfect life in Christ and came to understand what 'Christian Perfection' meant. He had complete commitment to the cause of Christ in every way, whether in the home, the church or the community.

I witnessed how he was able to remain true to Christ whether under stress, or facing opposition in debate, whether in joy or other circumstances. His complete commitment to God, the church, the home never once failed. His leadership qualities were recognised beyond the confines of the British Isles when the denomination appointed him missionary superintendent for Africa, India and the Middle East. He opened the way for my father and mother to answer God's call to pioneer the medical, educational and church work in Swaziland. The foundation he laid for the church made possible the union with the International Holiness Mission, the Calvary Holiness Church and other holiness groups and colleges in Britain.

I have known the author of this book since his early childhood. He has never moved away from his commitment to his calling to serve God and the church to promote the work of the gospel. He has served as a teacher, leader and now as a writer, preserving our history. In this book he has written down a story which will be significant for generations to come, documenting what God has done for us as a group of believers and as a church.

As you read on, you will recognise a rich heritage that should touch the heart and soul of every Nazarene, particularly in the United Kingdom, and indeed of every Christian. To establish the work as it is today has not been an easy road. Behind each story there lie times of stress and strain. There have been problems in leadership, congregations with distinct histories, and varying traditions, all demanding a spirit of give and take. But there has also been a divine melting together that has ultimately won the day. The story recorded here can give us new strength to meet the challenges of the current breakdown of spiritual and moral values in the nations. It encourages us to believe that God will 'open the windows of heaven', making a reality of the vision of John Wesley for a world-wide parish, the fulfilling of the great commission of Jesus: 'Therefore, go and make disciples of all nations… in the name of the Father and of the Son and of the Holy Spirit.' Amen.

PREFACE

How long is a century? To the young it appears to be an eternity: but the old discover that it is not as long as they had thought. I am at that mid-point where it no longer appears quite so long! As I have written this centenary history I have become aware that my memory goes back to over half the decades covered. And Dr Hugh Rae, who has written so many of the reminiscences, can remember this history over seventy years.

Furthermore, some very remarkable women have lived throughout the hundred years from 1906 to the present. Mrs Bessie Wood, who died recently at the age of 102, was taken by her mother to the early meetings of the Holiness Mission held by David Thomas in Sydney Hall in Battersea. Mrs Jean B. Maclagan who died recently at the age of 103 was present with her mother in the first service held by Dr George Sharpe in the Great Eastern Road Halls in Parkhead, Glasgow on 30th September, 1906. And Mrs Isabel Edwards, the youngest daughter of Dr Sharpe, who was a little girl of three when her father told her about his eviction and about the new church, is with us as I write at the age of 102.

On the other hand, a century can seem a long time when we learn that there is at least one family, the Taylor-Irvine family, which has had seven generations active over the century in the Sharpe Memorial Church. The family tree (only including those who have attended the church) looks like this:

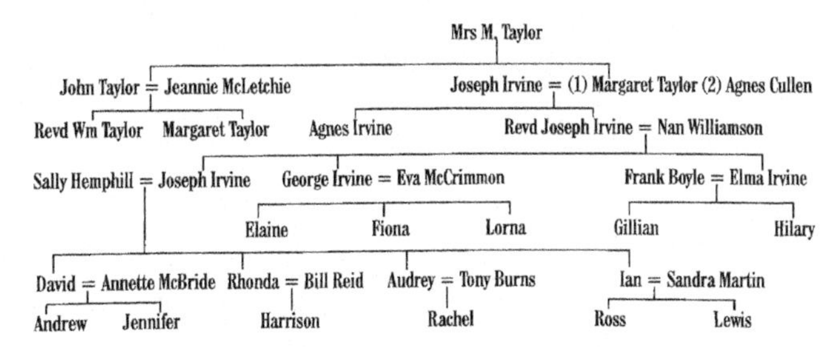

My own family can only claim four generations, but my cousin, Mrs Edith Fotheringham, her mother (my aunt), Mrs May Cullen, and our grandfather, Thomas Gray, can together claim unbroken regular attendance at Sharpe Memorial Church over the whole century, 1906 to 2006.

I hope this serves to make the point that the church is not all about preachers (although some preachers appear in the family tree above) nor about the leaders who dominate so much of this narrative. It is about people – ordinary people. They have sat in the pews, sung in choirs, counted the offerings, balanced the books, written the minutes, scrubbed the floors, plastered the walls, gone visiting door to door, taught Sunday school classes, given their tithes and offerings, sat on committees, given hospitality, washed the dishes, organized the missionary meetings, visited the elderly, supported the bereaved, welcomed the stranger, played the organ, given to the building fund, run the youth club, combated vandalism, opened and locked the door, testified at the open-air meeting, exhorted the sinner, and loved the lost. And I am just sorry that so many of the saints I have known and valued will not even have their names mentioned here. In fact, there are many preachers and district presidents and prominent lay people whose names are not mentioned here. I can just hear readers saying, 'You know, So-and-so really ought to have been mentioned!' And the closer we come to the contemporary scene, the more names have to be omitted. I really must apologize to them (including present Nazarene ministers, most of whom are my own former students), and remind them that even though the earthly historian cannot mention everyone, there is something in scripture to encourage us to believe that their faithfulness is known and remembered where it matters most.

Some may wish to question whether this is a centenary for British Nazarenes, for after all, the Scottish churches (with Morley) only united with the Church of the Nazarene in 1915 and most of the churches in England in the 1950s. But that is splitting hairs. The churches which took the name 'Church of the Nazarene' in 1915 or in the 1950s were exactly the same churches they had been before that. So 2006 is the centenary of those movements which today are known as the Church of the Nazarene in the British Isles. Conveniently, 1906 marks the beginning of both the work in Battersea from which the IHM and later the CHC sprang and the work in Parkhead. So this is our centenary.

Like any good history, this sets out to find its basis in objective facts arranged in roughly chronological order. However, as any student of history knows, facts cannot be separated from their interpretation. Even in selecting the facts to record, the historian is making judgements about their significance. All history is therefore written from a particular perspective, and that necessarily introduces an element of subjectivity. This history therefore is my perspective. While I try to be comprehensive, inevitably my perspective is biased by where I have lived and those whom I have known best. Further, while I depend on the researches of others, and have benefited from the views of others, every opinion expressed here, every comment, every assessment and every evaluation is not to be attributed to any official or board or committee. It is mine alone. Nazarenes (who are used to NPH books which express an 'official line') must remember that.

Furthermore, it seems inevitable that, although every care has been taken to secure factual accuracy, some minor inaccuracies and errors will have crept in. Eye-witnesses and those close to events are often annoyed by some misapprehension or misinformation in the written accounts. I may even have omitted some significant events or developments, especially in the hitherto unwritten story of the past thirty years. If so, I can only ask for forgiveness and for a letter correcting my version of events. At least the corrections can be made available to students at Nazarene Theological College, Manchester, who will no doubt use this book in the years ahead.

This has been an enjoyable task, to put down in black and white what is so much part of my own background and to incorporate so many scraps of information I have acquired since childhood by oral tradition as well as by reading primary and secondary documents. I must thank the Rev Colin Wood, the Rev Clive Burrows and Dr David McCulloch for their support and Dr Dwight Swanson acting for Didsbury Press. I am grateful too to Dr Samuel Hynd for finding time in his busy schedule and in midst of combating the scourge of AIDS to write the Foreword. I am particularly grateful also to Dr Rae for his inimitable reminiscences and character sketches, and to the other contributors from whom he and I collected fascinating memories. I'm afraid that the editor's pen has had to shorten what they wrote to keep the book at a reasonable length. And of course, it needs to be said that these articles in the 'As I Remember' series at the end of each chapter only tell us about *some* of the saints and worthies. I am sure that we could have written as many again!

To express my gratitude adequately to my wife, Elaine, would be impossible of course but I must thank her for tackling the chore of producing the index. Thanks for the index also go to my daughter, Elspeth, and to three N.T.C. students, Reuben Angelici of Rome, Joun Samara of Damascus and Colin Duffy of Lisburn.

I trust that all who read the history will find it informative and challenging. While these old saints had many faults and failings no doubt (dealt with kindly here, I trust) they certainly knew the meaning of commitment and sacrifice. And we today should be challenged to 'follow in their train'.

T.A.N.
Didsbury
1st January, 2006

Chapter One

THE HOLINESS MOVEMENT

Parkhead, 1906

Tempers had run high during an emotional meeting. It was Saturday 29th September, 1906, and the meeting of church members had been called in Parkhead in the east end of Glasgow to vote on the future of their minister, the Rev George Sharpe. He had first of all been voted out of the chair of the meeting, and then despite the attempts of his supporters, the majority had voted to sack him. Now as the unruly meeting broke up, one deacon took action. Robert Bolton was the Sunday school superintendent, a position of some standing and influence in the community, and he had seen the Sunday school and every other department of the church grow during Sharpe's ministry of just over a year. He called out: 'All who still want this man to be your preacher come underneath the gallery.' About eighty came. Someone put out the lights, but they sang and prayed together, and since Mr Sharpe would no longer have anywhere to preach the next day, they agreed to find a hall and to hold separate services.

News of the eviction spread like wild-fire through the community, and when George Sharpe went shortly afterwards to preach at the usual service held on a Saturday night at the street corner nearby, a huge crowd had gathered. With remarkable speed a hand-bill was printed and distributed:

GREAT EASTERN ROAD HALLS
Divine Service will be conducted
Sabbath First,
At the hours of 11 a.m. and 7 p.m.
In the above Halls, by the
REV GEORGE SHARPE,
late of
PARKHEAD CONGREGATIONAL CHURCH.
"We preach Christ crucified… Who
of God is made unto us Wisdom, and
Righteousness and Sanctification, and
Redemption."
ALL ARE CORDIALLY INVITED

Right from the start, the services in the halls were packed. People came from miles around to see the minister who had been put out of his church, and within a few weeks, a new congregation had been established with a court of deacons, a Sunday school, and land for a new building. What the locals called 'Sharpe's Kirk' had come to stay.

But what had caused the split? The controversy was about doctrine, and ironically about the doctrine of Christian sanctification. George Sharpe, born not far from Glasgow, near the steel town of Motherwell, had spent most of his adult life in the steel-producing area of upstate New York. There he had become a Methodist minister deeply influenced by the 'holiness movement'. It was this teaching on Christian holiness which had provoked such opposition in his native land.

Battersea, 1906

It was not that the emphasis on Christian holiness was unfamiliar in Britain, although it was perhaps more at home in England than in Scotland. The 'holiness movement' traced its roots to the great leader of the eighteenth-century revival and founder of Methodism, John Wesley, and by the late nineteenth century his teaching on Christian sanctification, allied to a new interest in the work of the Holy Spirit, had led to a movement across the Christian churches. One prominent leader of the movement in England was Richard Reader Harris, a leading London barrister. Reader Harris had had a colourful career as a railway engineer in Bolivia before becoming an advocate. Converted from agnosticism to Christian faith, in 1887 he had bought a large mission hall in Battersea, Speke Hall, filling its 1,400 seats for Sunday evening services. Influenced by two visiting preachers, G.D. Watson and F.D. Sanford, he had become an advocate of the holiness movement and had established an inter-denominational network, the Pentecostal League of Prayer.[1] The object of the League was to pray for the filling of the Spirit for all believers, revival in the churches, and the spread of 'scriptural holiness'. Its magazine, *Tongues of Fire*, soon had a circulation of twenty thousand.[2]

1 At this point, the word 'Pentecostal' referred to the revivalist wing of the holiness movement and did not have its later connotation of emphasizing the '*gifts* of the Spirit'.

2 It may have been as high as 40,000. See Geoffrey N. Fewkes, dissertation, 'Richard Reader Harris', 49.

In December, 1906, two months after George Sharpe had been voted out of his church in Glasgow, one of Reader Harris's mission workers, David Thomas, was to be seen holding a service at a street corner in London. It was a Sunday morning and it stood out clearly in the memory of his daughter:

> We were walking with him, as we thought, to the house of God where we usually worshipped. At the end of Falcon Road, near Clapham Junction Station, he stopped and said, 'I am going to hold an open-air meeting this morning. You children may go to the other service if you like.' We decided simultaneously to go with him, and accompanied him to a street corner, which afterwards became our rendezvous on Sunday and Wednesday evenings for many years.[3]

What a casual observer would not have known, however, was that this was a radical new departure. Thomas, a Welshman who owned his own substantial drapery business in Falcon Road, had had a significant disagreement with Reader Harris and was stepping out on his own.

This time the disagreement was not over doctrine. David Thomas completely agreed with the doctrine of Christian holiness taught by Reader Harris and retained the greatest respect for him. But after working with the League for fifteen years, Thomas had come to the conclusion that its inter-denominational approach was wrong. Although Reader Harris ran Speke Hall as an independent mission, he remained an Anglican, and was committed to working through the League to revive the churches. Members of the League were on no account to leave their churches even where the League's teaching on Christian holiness was criticized and rejected. They were to stay and work within the churches for revival. But David Thomas had come to disagree with this strategy. After years of witnessing the discouragement and loss of members of the League, he had come to the conclusion that new mission halls should be established up and down the country where the teaching of the holiness movement could be propagated without contradiction.

---

3 *David Thomas, Founder of the International Holiness Mission* (London: International Holiness Mission, [1933]), 106, where Mrs Ernest F. Harold (Lewiston, Idaho), contributes to a 'Book of Remembrance'.

Shortly after that first 'open air' service near Clapham Junction, Thomas began Sunday morning services in his drapery store, attended mainly by his own employees. In February, 1907 the services were transferred to Sydney Hall in York Road, Battersea, where the new 'Holiness Mission' soon had a Sunday school of two hundred and its own magazine, the *Holiness Mission Journal*.

But before we trace the development of Sharpe's Kirk and Thomas's Holiness Mission, we need to look a little farther back in order to see these new beginnings of 1906 in the context of the growth of evangelical Christianity which reached its climax in Britain in the Edwardian period.

The Edwardian High-point

The short Edwardian era began when King Edward VII succeeded his mother, Queen Victoria, in 1901, but is often thought of as extending four years after his death to the outbreak of the First World War in 1914. These years saw evangelical Christianity in Britain at the height of its influence in modern times. The eighteenth century had seen the church at a low ebb with the apathy of established religion and the scepticism of the intellectuals of the 'enlightenment'. The evangelical revival led by the Wesleys and George Whitefield had turned the tide. By the early nineteenth century this led to the growth of evangelical Christianity, not only in the newly established Methodist Church, but also among the Congregationalists and Baptists, and within the Church of England and the Church of Scotland. This in turn led to social and moral reform at home and missions abroad.

The evangelical MP, William Wilberforce, was influential at home as well as abroad. Along with his friends jointly nick-named 'the Clapham sect', he was not only successful in abolishing slavery throughout the British Empire, but also in abolishing much of the corruption in national life (including incidentally a national lottery). New standards of integrity were introduced to government and Parliament. Lord Shaftesbury and others introduced legislation to protect workers – miners, women and children employed in the new factories. The Sunday school movement increased steadily through the century, its moral and spiritual effect on young people aided by youth organizations such as the Boys' Brigade and the YMCA.

Temperance legislation tackled the scourge of drunkenness which blighted many families. The Salvation Army under William Booth tackled poverty.

In the 1870s, American revivalism became a major influence on the British scene in the 'campaigns' of Dwight L. Moody and his soloist, Ira Sankey. As a consequence of 'Moody and Sankey' many conventional church-goers became committed evangelical Christians. Evangelism was stimulated in deprived inner city areas through new 'city missions' and also among university students, especially in Cambridge where Moody held a memorable mission.

In addition to its effect within Britain, the long-term revival which began in the eighteenth century had also led to nineteenth-century 'foreign missions'. The Baptist William Carey left for the Bengal in 1793. The Anglican Henry Martyn, curate to the influential Charles Simeon of Cambridge, followed in 1805. The great Thomas Chalmers, the leader of the evangelicals in the Church of Scotland, promoted foreign missions. The greatest missionary hero of the century, David Livingstone, opened up the interior of Africa and advocated the spread of commerce to counter the slave trade he found there. In 1887 the 'Cambridge Seven' led by the cricketer, C.T. Studd, were the first of hundreds of young British graduates in the Student Volunteer Movement to go abroad as missionaries, adopting the famous watchword, 'The evangelization of the world in this generation.' By the turn of the century there were 17,000 Protestant missionaries world-wide and 9,000 of these were British.[4]

All this advance of evangelical Christianity reached its high-point in the Edwardian years. Church and Sunday school membership reached their highest point. In Parliament, the 'Nonconformist conscience' was well represented. Christian teaching was part of the school curriculum in all schools and Christian ethical standards were held throughout society. Divorce was virtually unknown, crime rates were lower than ever before, and illegitimacy was rare. True, not everything was as it appeared: a high moral consensus probably always produces hypocrisy. The immorality of King Edward, H.H. Asquith his Prime Minister, Lloyd

---

4 See Brian Stanley, *The Bible and the Flag* (Leicester: Apollos, 1990), 83

George, and other prominent people were known only to the charmed circle of the ruling class, and no doubt there was much hidden immorality, cruelty, and abuse at every level. But at least there was little dispute that Christian ethical standards were right: marriage was considered sacrosanct and there were high levels of integrity in government and business. Similarly, while the Darwinian debate had led to doubts among the informed and educated, there was as yet no mass atheism. Publicly and officially there was no serious challenge to Christian belief. Not all Christians were evangelicals, of course, and the High Church Anglo-Catholics were well represented in the Church of England and new 'liberal' or 'modernist' views in several denominations. But popular Christianity was broadly conservative and evangelical.

The Holiness Movement

It was against this background of the steady advance of evangelical Christianity, from the eighteenth century revival and through the nineteenth century, that the development of the holiness movement is to be seen. In the preaching and ministry of John Wesley, evangelism and Christian holiness were inseparable. Even before Wesley discovered the Reformation truth of 'justification by faith' through Luther and the German Moravians and became a great evangelist, he had been keenly concerned with Christian holiness. Through the influence of Anglican 'Arminians' like Bishop Jeremy Taylor and William Law, the medieval writer Thomas à Kempis, and early church fathers such as Clement of Alexandria, Wesley had become concerned with what they all called 'Christian perfection'.

The term 'perfection' is very misleading to the modern mind, but neither Wesley himself, nor any of these writers were advocating a 'sinless perfection'. The Greek word in the New Testament which is translated 'perfection' is better understood if we begin by thinking of it as 'maturity'. Wesley, following a whole tradition of Christian thought, understood the New Testament to imply that within this life, Christians could advance to that point of spiritual maturity where they fulfilled the Great Commandment and loved God with all their heart, soul, mind and strength and their neighbours as themselves. He referred to this point as 'entire sanctification', drawing on I Thess. 5:23, 'The very God of peace sanctify you wholly', but this is to be thought of as a qualitative and holistic 'wholeness' rather than a quantitative or legal perfection. Even the Christian who loved God and neighbour with an undivided mind still fell short in a thousand ways and must live in an attitude of confession and repentance.[5]

Wesley's Methodism was much more influential across the Atlantic than in Britain and grew rapidly to become the largest denomination in mid-nineteenth-century America. But the cultural context of America produced some changes in Wesley's teaching on Christian holiness. American revivalism had developed first of all in the Puritan Calvinist congregationalism of New England where great emphasis was laid on the necessity of the spiritual crisis of conversion. Since for Calvinists a truly converted person could never be lost ('once saved always saved') such a crisis of spiritual experience was vital. New England Puritanism therefore developed the 'revival'. The local minister or a visiting evangelist would hold 'protracted meetings' backed by long periods of concentrated prayer, when the unconverted would be invited to come forward to pray for conversion. The method had been modelled by the great Jonathan Edwards. This concentration on spiritual 'crisis' was now carried over into the Methodist doctrine of Christian holiness.

The significant figure was Mrs Phoebe Palmer, the wife of a New York doctor, who led a meeting in her own home for decades for the promotion of Christian holiness. Mrs Palmer (also the outstanding early advocate of women preachers) rejected Wesley's teaching that 'entire sanctification' had to come at the end of a long period of searching and self-examination and devised what she called 'the shorter way'. This focused on the idea of the 'altar': the Christian had to 'lay all on the altar', that is, completely consecrate herself to God. But scripture promised that 'the altar sanctifies the gift' (Matt. 23:19), and therefore the believer had to believe that because she had 'laid all on the altar', and because God had promised to sanctify such a self-offering, she therefore *must* be entirely sanctified. The seeker therefore had to rise and testify right away to 'the second blessing'.

5 The best short introduction to Wesley's doctrine of Christian Perfection is A. Skevington Wood, *Love Excluding Sin: Wesley's Doctrine of Sanctification* (Stoke-on-Trent: Wesley Fellowship, n.d.) reprinted in Paul Taylor and Howard Mellor, *Travelling Man* (Cliff College & The Wesley Fellowship, 1994), 59-80.

Some leading Methodists rejected Mrs Palmer's 'shorter way' as a valid interpretation of Wesley's teaching, but it was widely influential.

A second major modification in Wesley's teaching came from the 'new school Calvinism' of Charles Finney and Asa Mahan. Finney was the greatest revivalist of the mid-nineteenth century, a powerful and persuasive preacher who turned revivalism into a developed technique. Finney and Mahan, professor and president at the newly established Oberlin College in Ohio in the 1840s, became interested in Wesley's doctrine of Christian 'perfection', but they re-interpreted it in the light of their understanding of the 'baptism of the Holy Spirit'. Unlike Wesley (though somewhat foreshadowed by his colleague, John Fletcher), they developed the view that the apostles, already born-again Christians, were baptized with the Holy Spirit as a *second* spiritual crisis on the day of Pentecost, and that this was their experience of 'entire sanctification'.

This 'Pentecostal' interpretation of the Wesleyan teaching laid much greater emphasis on entire sanctification as a 'second blessing', and was accepted by Phoebe Palmer and other influential Methodists. Eventually the tendency of revivalism to accentuate great spiritual crises led to the virtual denial in the holiness movement of any gradual work of sanctification. Just as the unbeliever was invited to come forward in an 'altar call' to seek forgiveness of sins and the new birth, so now the believer was invited to come to 'the altar' to seek the 'baptism of the Holy Spirit' which brought entire sanctification. The new teaching was even given physical form in the kneeling rail now called the 'altar'.[6]

These two modifications which pragmatic American revivalism produced in Wesley's doctrine were influential on both sides of the Atlantic. The new emphasis on the Holy Spirit characterized much nineteenth-century evangelical piety. The British Methodists William and Catherine Booth were influenced by Phoebe Palmer (not least in advocating that women too were called to preach), so that when they launched the Salvation Army, it took as its motto, 'Blood and Fire'.

---

6 For a study of the American modifications to Wesley's doctrine, see John L. Peters, *Christian Perfection and American Methodism* (New York: Abingdon, 1956)

The blood of the cross was what brought forgiveness and cleansing from sin, and the 'fire' was a reference to the Pentecostal 'baptism of the Holy Ghost and fire', namely the 'second blessing'. Holiness, and specifically 'entire sanctification', was part of the doctrinal heritage of the Salvation Army.

Keswick

A little after the Salvation Army was launched to reach the poor, the influence of the holiness movement became evident at the other end of the social spectrum. In 1873 Robert Pearsall Smith, a Quaker glass manufacturer from New Jersey, visited England with his wife, Hannah Whitall Smith. The Smiths had been influenced by the Methodist holiness movement and had claimed the 'blessing'. Introduced into upper class circles through the evangelical Cowper-Temples, the Smiths spoke at a small conference at their country estate, Broadlands, followed by large conventions of a thousand at Oxford and eight thousand at Brighton! Pearsall Smith even had a series of large and remarkable meetings in Paris and Berlin. Their message was not particularly theological, and they certainly did not understand the nuances of the Wesleyan understanding of Christian holiness, but they were charming Americans, open and apparently genuine, and excellent communicators whose simple message that the Christian could live a 'victorious life' through faith and consecration had a remarkable effect on many Oxford and Cambridge students and Anglican clergymen.

The message that a Christian could pass from a life of defeat to one of victory over sin by a decisive act of faith and consecration became the keynote of an annual convention held in a tent at Keswick in the Lake District every year from 1875. It was summarized in lines of a hymn by Frances Ridley Havergal:

> Holiness by faith in Jesus,
> Not by effort of your own;
> Sin's dominion crushed and conquered
> By the power of grace alone.

One of the convention's notable converts was none other than the learned Bishop of Durham, Handley Moule, previously a Cambridge professor.

The Keswick movement did not claim to have a theology. It was an interdenominational convention for 'practical holiness'. Some of the notes of the Wesleyan teaching and indeed of the American holiness movement can be heard in its literature and hymnody - notably the emphasis on 'holiness' and 'sanctification', an early emphasis on the Holy Spirit, the language of 'consecration', the references to 'the blessing' as a distinct second moment in the Christian's spiritual journey when through faith he passes from a life of defeat to a life of victory. But this was all in a very modified, not to say 'genteel', form.

It was intentionally inter-denominational. In addition to the Anglicans, Baptists such as F.B. Meyer (and later Graham Scroggie), and Presbyterians such as Andrew Murray, were associated with it. It did not please everyone: if Bishop Moule was its most prominent advocate, Bishop J.C. Ryle of Liverpool wrote his book, *Holiness* to counter the Keswick emphasis. Seeing himself as standing in the Puritan tradition, he insisted that holiness *did* take effort! Active biblical verbs such as 'walk, run, fight, wrestle, struggle, endure' were also essential to the teaching of Christian holiness. But Ryle represented a minority. For the first half of the twentieth century, it was the Keswick version of Christian holiness which coloured British evangelicalism and most of the corps of thousands of British missionaries who planted the seeds of evangelical churches in the four corners of the globe.[7]

The Radicals

While the Keswick movement had this wide influence across the spectrum, the British Methodists still held officially to Wesley's doctrine. The leading Methodist theologian of the late nineteenth century, William Burt Pope of Didsbury College, Manchester, outlined the Wesleyan doctrine of sanctification judiciously in his systematic theology.[8] The Joyful News Mission, started by Thomas Champness, was handed over to the Methodist Home Mission Department in 1903 and led by Thomas Cook, who established Cliff College in Derbyshire to train evangelists. Cook and his successor, Samuel Chadwick, were notable exponents of Wesley's doctrine.

---

7 See John Pollock, *The Keswick Story* (London: Hodder, 1964) and J.C. Ryle, *Holiness* (London: James Clarke, 1952) first published in 1877

8 William Burt Pope, *A Compendium of Christian Theology*, 3 Vols, (London: Wesleyan-Methodist Book-Room, 1880)

Some smaller late nineteenth-century movements were (like the Salvation Army) more similar to the American holiness movement. In 1882 a young business man, John George Govan, was influenced by Moody's second visit to Glasgow to give himself to evangelism. Two years later he testified to having received the blessing of a 'clean heart' and two years after that launched the 'Faith Mission' for evangelism in rural areas. A training home was established in Rothesay in 1897, moving eventually to Edinburgh, and J.G. Govan, known as 'the Chief', continued to lead his 'pilgrims' in evangelism till his death in 1927.

In 1888, Francis Crossley, the Irish owner of an engineering works in Manchester, trusted God for a 'clean heart' through the preaching of the Salvation Army. He bought an old music hall, The Star, among the slums of inner-city Ancoats and established it as a mission, Star Hall, selling his beautiful home in the wealthy suburb of Bowdon to move into a flat in the mission. One of Crossley's achievements had been to alert Gladstone to the massacre of Armenian Christians by the Turks. When he died in 1897, fifteen thousand attended his funeral.

These along with Reader Harris, the leader of Speke Hall in Battersea and the Pentecostal League of Prayer, constituted the more radical wing of the holiness movement. Like William Booth, the most famous and outstanding member of this group, they were all committed to mission to the poor, and were more radical in their understanding of Christian holiness than the Keswick movement.

One of the particular points of contention was on the issue of 'eradication'. Although the Keswick preachers believed in a 'second' moment in the Christian life, when the believer moved from defeat to victory, they maintained that 'sin' (some called it 'the old nature' or 'the flesh') was present till death, so that the Christian's victory came because it was 'subdued'. To the radicals, reflecting Wesley's doctrine that 'inbred sin' was *destroyed* in entire sanctification, this was quite unbiblical. In a famous (or notorious!) pamphlet, Reader Harris promised £100 to anyone who could produce one biblical text which supported the Keswick contention that 'the old man' was 'subdued' and not 'eradicated'. No one replied!

It was to this radical wing that George Sharpe and David Thomas belonged. And their movements, both of which were to unite with the Church of the Nazarene, were – like all of these – committed to radical holiness.

The Rev George Sharpe, c. 1906

Chapter Two

GEORGE SHARPE AND THE NAZARENES

The Rev Mr Sharpe

George Sharpe was forty when he arrived in Parkhead in the summer of 1905. Born on 17th April, 1865 in the parish of Dalziel near Motherwell in Lanarkshire, he was one of thirteen children and the son of a miner who had risen to become a manager. The young George Sharpe became a clerk in Colville's steel works near his home, and although he continued to attend the church where his father was a Sunday school teacher, he was enjoying life with his fellow clerks and (he later wrote) 'sowing his wild oats'. Conviction of sin pursued him, however, till during a revival in Motherwell with marches and street meetings in the spring of 1882, he was converted in a dance hall. Two years later he had a sense of calling to the Christian ministry, but although his sister offered to pay his way at Edinburgh University to enter the ministry of the established Church of Scotland, he was attracted by another offer.

The Rose family had emigrated from Motherwell to Cortland in upper New York State in 1884. Charles Rose's brother owned steel works there, and on a visit home invited the young clerk to come to America to learn the business and help to begin a new factory in France. He sailed for America on 13th February, 1886, but the plans for a factory in France were abandoned and he settled down to work with the company in Cortland while courting Charles Rose's daughter, Jane. He became a member of the Methodist church and after some lay preaching, received an offer from his minister to pay his way through college to enter the ministry. He married Jane Brayton Rose on 17th November, 1887 and served in three churches in upper New York state at Depeyster, Hamilton and Chateaugay, all of which saw considerable growth.

While he was in Chateaugay, a Salvation Army preacher, Major L. Milton Williams, held special services, preaching on Christian holiness, particularly the Wesleyan doctrine of entire sanctification, each afternoon. After his wife had responded, George Sharpe made his total consecration, kneeling alone at the organ bench after a service. He later recorded his prayer: 'O Lord, I give Thee all: my spirit, soul and body, my time, my talents, my friends, all I have and all I ever will have, all I know and all I ever will know, to be anything and to go any where for Thee. Amen.' Sharpe was aware that some of the Methodist bishops were opposed to 'fanatical' preachers of holiness, but calmly and deliberately, in consecrating himself fully to God, he identified himself with the holiness movement.

In 1901 Mr and Mrs Sharpe and their two daughters, Katrina Elizabeth and Agnes Kanema, visited Scotland, staying with relatives in the west coast port of Ardrossan. Mr Sharpe was asked to preach in the Congregational church, then without a minister, and after four weeks was asked if he would consider a call. He was 'staggered' at the thought. The Scottish Congregationalists were a fairly new denomination, raised up only in the previous century by the preaching of the Haldanes, Scottish landowners and the Rev James Morison. They were evangelical and Arminian, preached for conversion, and strongly supported the Moody campaigns at a time when the three dominant Presbyterian churches in Scotland were somewhat more staid and still dominated by strict Calvinist theology.[1] But although Congregationalists were used to the evangelistic style of Moody and even used Sankey's American gospel songs (at least in their evening services), how would they take to the radical preaching and 'altar calls' of the holiness movement?

Sharpe accepted the call, and during his ministry of four years the church grew and a new building was built. In 1905 he accepted a call to Parkhead Congregational Church. Now with three daughters (Isabel, aged two, having been born in Ardrossan), the Sharpes moved to their own house, built by Mrs Sharpe's brother, Charles Rose. This large semi-detached red-sandstone villa in Muiryfauld Drive half a mile to the east of Parkhead Cross, right at what was then the outer

---

1 In addition to the Kirk, that is the Church of Scotland 'by law established' following the Glorious Revolution of 1688 as a Presbyterian national church, there were the 'seceders' (various more evangelical groups who had left the established Kirk from 1733 onwards, and now mostly in the United Presbyterian Church), and the Free Church of Scotland, formed at the Disruption of 1843 when the remaining evangelical wing of the Kirk left the establishment. In 1900, the year before the Sharpes returned to Scotland, the U.P. Church and the Free Church united to form the United Free Church of Scotland.

boundary of the city of Glasgow, overlooked Tollcross Park with its Victorian mansion and herd of deer. Parkhead itself had been a village of weavers' cottages clustered around the 'cross' where five main roads met. Magnificent new stone tenements, with flats finished to the highest standard of craftsmanship, had now replaced most of the cottages, and the city's modern bright new electric tramcars connected Parkhead with the city centre several miles to the west. Large steel works, Beardmore's forge, now dominated the area. Glasgow itself was a booming, prosperous international port and manufacturing city, the 'second city of the Empire' with magnificent stone Victorian buildings in its commercial centre and wealthy west end.

The Congregational church was one of a number of churches in Parkhead including the parish church of the established Church of Scotland, two other Presbyterian churches, the Methodists, the Scottish Episcopal Church, the Salvation Army, and, tucked down a back street, the Roman Catholic 'chapel' attended by poor immigrant Irish Catholics. Every family in the district was attached to some church and almost all Protestant children were sent to Sunday school. Mr Sharpe moved to his new church determined, 'first, that I should preach what I found in the Bible, second, that I should preach my experience and convictions.' He was later described as having 'an easy-going and placid temperament' in private, but

> his pulpit personality was robust and at times aggressive, voice and gestures brought effectively into play, his delivery varied and emphatic and often given colour and immediacy by the use of transatlantic expressions – for example, 'sidewalk', 'holler', 'gotten' – a habit which (as he no doubt knew) served on the whole to attract rather than antagonize...[2]

This powerful, uncompromising, expository preaching brought new life to the church: 'Every department in the church was ablaze with new interest. The membership grew every month while the growth of the Sabbath school was phenomenal.' This later assessment by Sharpe might appear inflated, but the statistics support his view.

---

2 Jean Cameron Whiteford, 'A Holiness Church in Scotland' (Glasgow: MTh thesis, 1996), 72.

But it is not surprising that his preaching also brought opposition. He obviously went determined to preach 'second blessing holiness' uncompromisingly as it was then understood by the holiness movement. That produced opposition, not only because theologically it would sound like 'sinless perfection', but also no doubt because the radical exposure of sin in the human heart always disturbs the spiritually comfortable. One must have some sympathy however for these committed Congregationalists: their new minister's dynamic preaching would sound both strange and provocative. They certainly soon demonstrated that they were provoked!

Parkhead Pentecostal Church

When the split came at the end of September, 1906, the minority who supported Sharpe quickly formed a new church of eighty-one charter members governed by congregational polity. Four of his deacons stood by him and formed the nucleus of the new deacons' court. Robert Bolton was a lithographer and became church secretary and superintendent of the new Sunday school; Andrew Robertson who was a foreman in the Parkhead forge was an experienced treasurer; William Barrie, formerly of the Salvation Army, was the only one who had been familiar with the 'holiness' teaching; Thomas Gray, who was an engine driver with the Caledonian Railway Company, was the youngest of the group. George Sharpe later wrote of them: 'No pastor ever had four truer men to stand by him and for him. How much these men have meant to the cause of holiness is known only in heaven.' They had their first meeting in the Sharpes' home in Muiryfauld Drive on 18th October and agreed to recommend four other men to the first quarterly meeting of members as deacons: James Jackson, John Berwick, Peter Mitchell and John Brown. They also nominated eight men to be managers to handle finance and property. This was the normal Congregational polity, ensuring that those who handled the pastoral oversight of the congregation were not distracted by business affairs. After the meeting the minister and four deacons joined their wives for 'a very handsome tea kindly and generously provided by Mrs Sharpe.'

The new church experienced something of a revival and the membership grew quickly. Within a few weeks land had been bought in Burgher Street near Parkhead Cross, the substantial sum of £350 being raised by the time the legal deeds were ready. Only one of the charter members, Alexander Stevenston,[3] owned his own business (a taylor's shop in Duke Street near Parkhead Cross), but in those days before Lloyd George's National Insurance scheme, the prosperous and thrifty working people of Parkhead apparently all had substantial savings. With a sense of responsibility and a determination to meet current expectations, they also paid their minister a stipend considered fit for his standing as a professional man and substantially larger than their own incomes. They shared the conviction that in a church of truly converted people, there was no place for sales of work and other such fund-raising expedients: the church should be financed by the free-will giving of God's people. Building began in May, 1907.[4] Sharpe crossed the Atlantic to raise funds and the new church was opened in the first weekend of December when the visiting preacher was Rev George J. Kunz, a Methodist colleague and friend from America. The total cost was £3,000.

The interior of the new church was an unusual shape, possibly based on one of Mr Sharpe's American churches. It was built to accommodate the maximum number of people on the site and its character helped to shape the character of the new congregation. The platform-shaped pulpit (which at first had the choir behind it) was placed on the long wall of the building and the pews built in a semi-circle around it. There were windows with stained-glass squares behind the congregation and roof-windows, but no windows on the wall they were facing. The gallery almost doubled the seating capacity and was shaped rather like the balcony of a small concert hall. Since it was the first building in the area to be lit by electricity, the new church no doubt attracted visitors for that reason alone, and made the surrounding streets and homes, lit by gas, seem dismal by comparison.

---

3 The Stevenstons gave the church a silverware communion service (still in use), and the original glass communion vessels were given to the original four deacons. The author has one of the original cut-glass plates given to his grandfather.

4 The writer has in his possession a small stone on which has been painted meticulously, 'This stone was taken from the first sod cut for the Parkhead Pentecostal Church. 20th May, 1907.' The foundation stones were laid by Captain Smith of Ardrossan and James Gardiner, a potato merchant from Perth. The engraved golden trowel used on that occasion is in the archives at Nazarene Theological College along with the golden key used by Mrs Sharpe to open the door of the new building in December, 1907.

It was essentially a preaching church, the semi-circular shape encouraging eye-contact with the preacher, a sense of close fellowship, and a good acoustic for congregational and special singing. The church was to attract many fine singers and became quite a notable singing congregation, usually drowning out the sound of the reed organ built under the pulpit.

A range of Christian traditions shaped the new congregation. Scottish church culture was of course predominantly in the Reformed tradition, rejecting liturgy for extemporary prayer and the singing of psalms, and emphasizing the priority of preaching. In Edwardian Scotland that also meant the enthusiastic singing of the great hymns of such writers as Horatius Bonar and George Matheson as well as the hymns of the older English hymn-writers, Watts and Wesley, Cowper and Newton. In common with all evangelical Presbyterians, Congregationalists, Episcopalians and Methodists, infant baptism was practised in the church with a view to the day when the infant would exercise its own faith and experience conversion. Following Congregationalist practice, they celebrated the Lord's Supper more frequently than the Presbyterians (generally once a month), yet in the Reformed tradition with the deacons sitting around the table and the congregation sitting in the pews to emphasize that this was a common meal and not the celebration of a sacrifice by a priest. But having been ordained in the American Methodist church, George Sharpe used Wesley's modified form of the Anglican *Book of Common Prayer*, kneeling at the table. The resounding liturgical phrases echoed in the memory of the people: 'Therefore with angels and archangels and all the company of heaven, we laud and magnify Thy glorious name…'

The kneeling rail around the communion table in the new church was therefore never used for communion services but rather served as an 'altar' in the American revivalist sense, where seekers would kneel when the invitation was given to 'come forward', usually at the end of the Sunday evening sermon. George Sharpe could not only conduct the communion service with great solemnity and preach expository sermons with the best Presbyterian, but he could conduct persuasive altar calls with the best revivalist. Long pews in the central section of the church soon had to be divided by a new central aisle to allow the many seekers to come forward more easily. When the congregation was dismissed after the altar call a large group would stay for the 'after-service' to pray and sing prayer choruses until the seekers were ready to stand and testify to what the Lord had done for them. There was a spontaneity and freedom about the services generally, with a chorus of 'Amen', 'Hallelujah' or 'Praise the Lord!' when worshippers wanted to respond. Sometimes the whole group at the after-service would finish the time of prayer and testimony with a 'glory march', marching around the church singing songs of victory: 'For the Lion of Judah will break every chain, and give us the victory again and again!' Although these altar services could be emotional, especially when seekers shared in their testimony how they had found forgiveness, new light on their problems, or the filling of the Holy Spirit, Mr Sharpe exercised firm and wise pastoral leadership, and the openness created strong bonds of fellowship and mutual support.

A full programme of weekly meetings was instituted beginning with an early prayer meeting on Sunday, followed by the morning worship service beginning with a psalm from the *Scottish Metrical Psalter*, hymns from the great tradition of British hymnody using the Scottish *Church Hymnary*, and an anthem from the choir. Prayer was extemporary, and sermons lasting at least half an hour were eagerly followed. On Sunday afternoon, the church would be filled with children for the 'Sabbath School'. Hymns were sung from the *Scottish National Hymnal for the Young*, teaching the children to sing harmony by the popular sol-fa notation. In later years, the Sunday school regularly won singing trophies awarded by inspectors from the Glasgow Sunday School Union. Sometimes an afternoon service was held, but there was always an evening service throughout the year when the church would be packed. Attendance was expected at least twice on Sunday (as in all evangelical churches) unless prevented by illness or caring for infants or the sick: to be present only once on a Sunday was a sign of a very lukewarm commitment or outright backsliding. As was also customary in evangelical churches in this era, the American gospel songs were sung in the evening, and Mr Sharpe soon arranged for song books in the holiness tradition, *Waves of Glory*. During the week a women's meeting (Monday), the prayer meeting (Wednesday), and a choir practice (Thursday) were regular fixtures. Saturday evening was originally devoted to the 'open air' service when a crowd would gather at Parkhead Cross. Later a

Saturday evening 'tea meeting' became common (as in many evangelical churches and missions in Scotland), with a 'deputation' of lay people from another church or mission hall to sing and testify and preach an evangelistic sermon.

In this era before radio or the cinema (far less television), churches were centres of the community, and meeting friends and relatives at church several times a week forged strong community bonds. Able and intelligent working people, with no opportunities to develop their talents through education and career, found in the church a place where they could exercise their gifts and serve not only their church community, but their Lord, in public speaking, Sunday school teaching, music, practical service or committee work. Because of George Sharpe's notoriety, crowds of visitors attended every service, and many, convicted by the preaching or caught up in the atmosphere of revival, stayed to become faithful members.

One visitor at the opening services in the new church was Mary Page Scott, taken by her cousin who ran the Partick Bethel, a mission hall in a poorer area at the west end of the city.

> When Mr George Hart, our cousin, took us to Parkhead Church, it would be Wednesday, 4th December, 1907. We were introduced to Mr Sharpe, and Mr Kunz of U.S.A. preached. Mrs John Taylor, then a young woman, went out to the altar weeping – it made an impression on me never to be forgotten. Then when Mr Sharpe preached, I thought Mr Hart must have told him all about me, for I was hit every time I heard him. He put his whole soul into the service, and my sin of unbelief found me out. Then on the last Sunday in January, 1907… the text Mr Sharpe preached on was, 'Adam, where art thou?' Mr Sharpe kept pleading so earnestly. I said, 'I shall prove tonight what is in this.' I put up my right hand. Dear Mr Bolton patted my back and said, 'It's the best thing you ever did, my lassie!' Pride said, 'The cheek of him! He doesn't even know me!' When I reached the front, I looked up at Mr Sharpe and said, 'What do I do now?' He said, 'Kneel down there.' His daughter, Miss Ina, knelt beside me and pointed me to Romans 10:9… when I closed my eyes to pray, I got a vision of the risen Christ. I could say

> with Paul, 'Last of all He was seen of me.' All my doubts fled away.

Molly Scott (as she was known) described the scenes at the altar services:

> Mr Sharpe could lead the singing. For altar work, he often called on me. Seldom a Sunday without someone out. Dear old Mr Barrie would start to sing, 'To Jesus every day I feel my heart is closer drawn.' We would all be marching round the church singing that and others. John Taylor always sang, 'I have given up all for Jesus.' Time did not matter. These men who started out were Spirit-filled men each one. We really had Pentecostal times.[5]

The Pentecostal Church of Scotland

With the large numbers of interested young people, George Sharpe launched the Parkhead Holiness Bible School in October, 1908. Twenty-four enrolled. They were taught in evening classes by Mr and Mrs Sharpe, their eldest daughter, Ina, and Joseph Robertson, the secretary of the Pentecostal League of Prayer in Motherwell.[6] At the end of that year, Mr Sharpe was invited by his brother-in-law, Charles Rose, to preach in Paisley, the large Renfrewshire town west of Glasgow dominated by its medieval abbey and the Coates and Clark thread mills. Some of the members of the choir in the church where Rose was choirmaster wanted to start a Pentecostal Church in Paisley and George Sharpe agreed to supply preachers from his Bible School for the meeting in the Good Templars' Hall. In February, 1909, a prominent preacher in the American holiness movement, Dr A.M. Hills, came to Britain for an extended visit and preached in Paisley in the Y.M.C.A. hall. Many of those who attended testified to entire

---

5 From a letter to the author written in 1975 shortly before Miss Scott died at the age of 90. After serving as head of the primary department of the Sunday school, she launched a Sunday school for the children of the fair ground families who used to spend the winter in Scotstoun in the west of the city.

6 The classes in Theology and Biblical Studies were presumably taught by Mr Sharpe himself. Jean Cameron Whiteford (whose father, Alex Cameron, attended the classes) examines the textbooks and curriculum and compares them to other colleges recently established in Scotland, the Baptist College (1894), the Theological Hall of the Congregational Union (1896) and the Bible Training Institute (1896). See 'A Holiness Church', 136.

sanctification and the Paisley Pentecostal Church was organized on 4th March with forty members and fifty children in its Sunday school. Sharpe appointed John E. Watson, a manager in Parkhead Church and a student at the Bible school, as the pastor.

Simultaneously in two villages east of Parkhead groups were forming. The Irish evangelist, W.P. Nicholson, had been holding meetings for the Lanarkshire Christian Union, and John D. Drysdale, a young barber who had a business in Blantyre, the birth-place of David Livingstone, was one of his workers. Drysdale formed a Bible class for the converts in the village of Uddingston, with up to forty meeting on a Sunday afternoon and also during the week for prayer, Bible study and 'open air' evangelistic services. Since Drysdale had testified to entire sanctification under the ministry of George Sharpe early in 1907, he took his group to Parkhead Church, six miles from Uddingston, for the Sunday evening services. In March, 1908, he also started meetings for miners' children in Blantyre with some initial help from W.P. Nicholson. On 15th March, 1909, eleven days after the formation of the Paisley church, George Sharpe organized the group in Uddingston into a small church with fourteen members. The group in Blantyre formed the Blantyre Holiness Mission.

With crowds flocking to Parkhead from miles around and new groups forming rapidly, Sharpe envisaged the need for some kind of denominational organization. Down in London, David Thomas had already broken away from Reader Harris's interdenominational strategy by forming the Holiness Mission. But George Sharpe was an ordained minister, and believed that with the revival he was experiencing, there was a need not just for mission halls, but for a new denomination with its own ordained ministry. The Welsh revival of 1904-1905 was also hitting the headlines and it seemed that the Spirit of God was moving. He sent out a call to 'the churches and missions existing to propagate holiness' inviting them to send delegates to a conference at Parkhead Pentecostal Church on 7th and 8th May, 1909. In fact only his own churches responded, with seventeen representatives from Parkhead, fourteen from Paisley, and three from Uddingston. Two representatives from the Blantyre Holiness Mission were given the status of 'corresponding members' of the assembly.

After a communion service at which Sharpe preached on I Cor. 3:11, 'For other foundation can no man lay than that is laid, which is Jesus Christ,' he read the wording of his call to the churches, and

> it was moved by Messrs R. Bolton, Watt and Turnbull representing the Pentecostal Churches in Parkhead, Paisley and Uddingston that the meeting now assembled be constituted the first Assembly of the Pentecostal Church of Scotland.

Miss M.A. Hatch, who led the work at Star Hall in Manchester along with Frank Crossley's daughter, preached at the second session of the Assembly on Daniel 11:32, 'The people that know their God shall be strong and do exploits.' Miss Crossley and Miss Hatch were launching a new paper, *The Way of Holiness*, and the new denomination adopted it as its official 'organ'. George Sharpe believed in proper organization, and various assembly committees were appointed including a standing executive committee with himself as president, John Watson as secretary, John Robb of Parkhead as minute secretary and Robert Latta of Uddingston as treasurer. A declaration of faith adopted by the Parkhead church some months earlier was also approved.

The Pentecostal Church of the Nazarene

Significantly the declaration of faith was taken from the handbook or 'manual' of a new holiness denomination in America, the Pentecostal Church of the Nazarene, formed by a union of three groups in 1907 and 1908. In California, a senior Methodist minister, Dr Phineas Bresee, had stepped out of the Methodist system of appointments in 1895 in order to establish a new church in Los Angeles specifically to reach the poor. It was to express that mission that one of his associates, Dr J.P. Widney, president of the University of Southern California, suggested that it be called 'The Church of the Nazarene' to express the humility of Jesus and his identification with 'the toiling...sorrowing heart of the world.' Bresee insisted that his new church was 'not a mission, but a church with a mission,' and soon planted other congregations. In 1898 they drew up a *Manual* based on the *Discipline* of the Methodist Church, but avoided the American Methodist use of the term 'bishops', deciding instead to have 'general superintendents'. By 1906 there were forty-five local churches with 3,385 members.

Meanwhile across America in New England, the Association of Pentecostal Churches of America was formed, a group in which the Rev H.F. Reynolds emerged as the leading figure. In the American South, two holiness movement groups united in 1905 to form the Holiness Church of Christ. The series of unions continued when the Californian Nazarenes united with the New England Association in 1907 to form 'The Pentecostal Church of the Nazarene', being joined the next year in an assembly at Pilot Point in Texas by the southerners. Bresee and Reynolds were the first two general superintendents of the united church and there was tremendous optimism that this union of the American East and West, and especially of the estranged North and South, would sweep the nation and restore the churches as a whole to true holiness.[7]

George Sharpe had left America before these unions of new 'holiness' groups took place, but the fact that he introduced elements of the Nazarene *Manual* into the Pentecostal Church of Scotland indicate that he had kept in contact with developments. He was at one with the Nazarenes in several respects. Most obviously, they believed that the time had come to unite in a distinct 'holiness' denomination fully organized with its own ordained ministry. The Americans felt that they had been discouraged and even rejected by official Methodism, and were suspicious of the spread of the fashionable 'modernism' which rejected the miraculous and the inspiration of Scripture.

But on the other side, the Nazarenes and George Sharpe both rejected a new development which appeared in the holiness or 'Pentecostal' movement, namely the sudden appearance of the gift of 'tongues'. In 1900, at a Bible College led by Charles Parham in Topeka, the state capital of Kansas, this phenomenon had appeared, but it first became widely known through a 'revival' held in 1906 in Azusa Street, Los Angeles, by a black preacher, Rev William Seymour. Seymour's preaching and emphasis on 'tongues' was rejected by Phineas Bresee as 'a most foolish and dangerous fanaticism',[8] and when Dr Campbell Morgan of Westminster Chapel, London, a leading British evangelical

---

7 See Mark Quanstrom, A Century of Holiness Theology (Kansas City: Nazarene Publishing House, 2004)

8 Quoted by Jean Cameron Whiteford (128) from the Nazarene Messenger (June, 1907), Vol. 2, 6.

preacher, visited Azusa Street, he too reacted against what appeared to be anarchy in the services. The phenomenon appeared in Britain in 1908, in Sunderland, encouraged by the vicar of All Saint's Church, the Rev A.A. Boddy, the local secretary of the League of Prayer. Reader Harris moved increasingly to repudiate the new interest in 'tongues'. In 1907 in an editorial in *Tongues of Fire*, he had declared that the teaching that it was the evidence of the 'baptism with the Holy Spirit' was an error, and while he was cautious about opposing it altogether, regarding it as in abeyance since the days of the apostles, he strongly condemned 'the rolling on the floor of men and women and other similar exhibitions.' 'Far be it from me to discount any real work of God,' he added, 'but I desire to avoid – and to warn others to avoid – *Satanic counterfeit*.' By 1908, he was linking the 'Tongues Movement' with other 'heresies and counterfeits' such as Spiritualism and Christian Science.[9] George Sharpe and the other British leaders of the holiness movement (as of evangelicalism in general) similarly rejected the new development, and were dismayed that a new meaning was being given to the word 'Pentecostal', diverting attention from the true gift of the Spirit, Christian holiness.

Miss Winchester and the Demand for Preachers

Although George Sharpe had much in common with the Nazarenes, it was the arrival of a remarkable American lady which was to establish close links. Olive M. Winchester was an heiress of the inventor of the Winchester rifle, a member of the Pentecostal Church of the Nazarene who had taught in the Collegiate Institute in North Scituate, Rhode Island, and was one of many women preachers in the American holiness movement. The holiness movement had been pioneers of women's ministry, but in 1909 women were still unknown in the professions generally and still did not have a vote. Miss Winchester had taken a Harvard BA in 1903 specializing in Hebrew and Arabic through Radcliffe College, newly established there for women students, and so arrived in 1909 qualified to enroll for the second degree of Bachelor of Divinity at the University of Glasgow, the first woman to do so. She became a member of the Parkhead church and started to teach in the Parkhead Holiness Bible School, which, with the

---

9 See Geoffrey Norman Fewkes, 'Richard Reader Harris' (MA dissertation, NTC, Manchester, 1995) 92ff.

establishing of the little denomination, became responsible for the education of its ministers. [10]

Each year, new congregations were being established. By the assembly of 1910 (held as always at Easter), the mission at Blantyre had been organized into Blantyre Pentecostal Church and it leader, George Dempsie, was 'given the right hand of fellowship'. By 1911, the membership at Parkhead had risen to almost 300 and the Buccleuch Holiness Church in Edinburgh had been established by George Kunz. A second church was formed in Marshall Street in Edinburgh with two further missions in Leith and another weekly meeting and several missions in Glasgow.

The first church was also established in England. In Morley near Leeds a quarry owner, George Pawson, built a new church after meeting George Sharpe at a convention in Star Hall, Manchester. As a Primitive Methodist, Pawson had testified to entire sanctification as a young man under the preaching of an American Methodist, James Caughey. Sharpe persuaded John E. Watson to leave Paisley and organize the new church on 14th August, 1910 with a membership of 62. George Pawson largely financed what became the finest building in the connection with its high pulpit, stained glass squares and pipe organ, and it was opened on 15th February, 1913. Within a few years the membership had risen to 190 and another church had been established in nearby Gildersome where Edmund Roach became its minister.

In Perth, the Pentecostal League of Prayer was active, led by the Episcopalian rector of St John's, the Rev C.E.D. de Labilliere, and holding conventions at which Oswald Chambers, among others, spoke. Five of their members, James Jack, Tom Macdonald, James Shaw, William Stewart and James Robertson, formed the Perth Holiness Mission on 2nd May, 1909, indicating that their link now would be with David Thomas. A number of them were railwaymen who supported the work of the Railway Mission, including Samuel Hynd who had now been appointed to a post at the railway junction of Carstairs in Lanarkshire. But three years later, on 21st March, 1912, the Perth Holiness Mission was organized into Perth Pentecostal

10 See Rebecca Laird, *Ordained Women in the Church of the Nazarene* (Kansas City: Nazarene Publishing House, 1993), 91-98.

Church. Their senior deacon, William Stewart, was 'given the right hand of fellowship' to welcome them into the Pentecostal Church of Scotland at the fourth assembly in 1912. A Canadian Methodist, Rev W.E. Smith, became minister.

The First Ordained Woman and a New College

Providing preachers for the growing number of churches was a challenge and the lay students of the Bible College continued to 'supply' pulpits. John E. Watson had been ordained by George Sharpe in 1909, and Andrew Robertson, the son of the Andrew Robertson who was treasurer of the Parkhead church, was lay pastor of the Uddingston church while pursuing his M.A. studies at the University of Glasgow. Two other young men from the Parkhead church, Peter Clark and Robert Purvis, were promising students at the Bible school. But to provide for the future, a proper College had to be established and the arrival of Miss Winchester seemed to offer an opportunity. Along with George Kunz, she provided much needed help in teaching in the Bible school. In 1912, he returned to the States, but in that same year she graduated as the first woman Bachelor of Divinity in the University of Glasgow.

At the assembly of the Pentecostal Church of Scotland, George Sharpe proposed her ordination. Remarkably, there was no opposition from the all-male assembly, and Olive Mary Winchester was elected to elders' orders and ordained on 11th May, 1912. The minutes of the assembly record this historic occasion – the first ordination of a woman in Scotland:

> A special service was held at 4 o'clock when Rev G.J. Kunz, Edinburgh, preached. His subject was 'The Common Salvation', his text was taken from Jude v.23: 'Earnestly contending of the faith,' etc. An interesting feature was the ordination of Miss Olive M. Winchester, BA, BD, as a minister of the Pentecostal Church of Scotland. After scriptural reading and prayer and assenting to the call of the church she was duly ordained by the laying on of hands. After praise, Bro. Kunz pronounced the benediction.

At the end of that year, George Sharpe arrived back from one of his periodic visits to America with the funds to purchase a large terrace house near the university in Glasgow's west end for £800, and 1 Westbourne Terrace, Kelvinside, became The Pentecostal Bible College. The Sharpe family moved into the house along with Miss Winchester, and the College was officially opened by Dr A.M. Hills, in Britain again for a preaching tour, on 16th August, 1913. It began its first academic session the next month with three residential students (housed in the large attic rooms), three day students, and one corresponding student. The Professor of Divinity at Glasgow University, the Rev Professor Henry Reid, honoured the new College with a visit.

In September, a new denominational journal was launched, the *Holiness Herald* edited by George Sharpe. The typesetting and printing was done by students in the basement of 1 Westbourne Terrace. Up to this point, all the churches had advertised in *The Way of Holiness*, but there had been some difference of opinion with Miss Crossley and Miss Hatch.

Union with the Church of the Nazarene

The Rev Miss Winchester (as she now was) had also been a strong link with the Pentecostal Church of the Nazarene. In 1913 she persuaded the assembly of the Pentecostal Church of Scotland to set up a missionary society and she was elected president with a view to co-operating with the Nazarenes. Enthusiasm for 'foreign missions' was at its height in the English-speaking world, and attention had been particularly focused on world evangelization by the World Missionary Conference in Edinburgh in June, 1910, generally considered an event of major significance for world Christianity. Miss Winchester corresponded with H.F. Reynolds, a general superintendent of the Pentecostal Church of the Nazarene and the main promoter of its foreign missions, but the Nazarenes were already well aware of the developments in Scotland, since Sharpe's work had been well-publicized in holiness journals in America and the Nazarene general assembly had voted in 1911 to establish a relationship.

It was 9th April, 1914 before Reynolds' colleague as general super-intendent, E.F. Walker, met with the executive committee and then the assembly of the Pentecostal Church of Scotland in Parkhead Church. He spoke of the close similarity in doctrine and spirit, and held out the hope of financial assistance to support a full-time superintendent in Britain. Since Parkhead church felt the absence of its minister in his duties as president of the assembly and principal of the College, this was a welcome offer. 'We have plenty of men and money,' said Walker, 'and such as we have we give to you.' The assembly appointed a committee to consider the question of union, and they recommended that the president should visit each church to present the arguments on both sides. The committee had already received a letter from the Morley church opposing the union, and it was clear that neither John Watson nor George Pawson were enamoured with the idea of joining an American church.

When Mr Sharpe met the executive committee again in July, 1914, he reported that the total votes in the meetings held in eight churches were 176 in favour of union and seven against. But that still represented a small minority of the total membership and George Pawson was reported to be executing a trust deed to ensure that the Morley property remained in British hands. There was also considerable feeling that the British churches should retain their deacons and managers instead of adopting the Nazarene offices of trustees and stewards elected only for one year at a time. At the next meeting of the provisional committee in October, 1914, H.F. Reynolds was present. A further problem arose when Reynolds informed Sharpe that the Nazarenes could only allocate funds to Britain equal to the amounts raised in Britain for foreign missionary work. Considering Walker's offer, Sharpe responded that he 'found it difficult to understand their attitude'. Nor did it seem appropriate to accept the generous offer of the local church in Kansas City to supply the finance for one year. Sharpe suggested that the denomination might be prepared to support an American appointed in his place, but the executive committee were not prepared to accept that.

Despite all these difficulties, at the invitation of the Nazarenes, the assembly of 1915 elected three 'fraternal delegates' to the forthcoming general assembly of the Church of the Nazarene, Mr and Mrs Sharpe and Mr George Pawson. Mr Pawson was unable to go, but the Sharpes were warmly received at the general assembly in Kansas City in October, 1915. The committee appointed to consider the matter recommended that the union should be consummated as soon as possible and that a sum of at least $1,000 dollars a year (approximately £250 in 1915) should be allocated to the work. The general assembly agreed to this at the afternoon session on Wednesday, 6th October and the Sharpes were besieged by well-wishers eager to grasp their hands. Back in Glasgow, the seventh assembly of the Pentecostal Church of Scotland re-convened on 5th November and unanimously approved the union. The secretary sent a cablegram the next day: 'Reynolds, 2109 Troost Avenue, Kansas City, Missouri UNION CONSUMMATED WRITING TURNBULL SECRETARY.'

Deacons and Managers of Parkhead Pentecostal Church, 1908. The deacons are seated in the front row with Mr Sharpe: 2nd from left, Alexander Stevenston: 3rd, Thomas Gray; 4th, Robert Bolton; 5th, Rev George Sharpe; 6th, Andrew Robertson; 7th, William Barrie. Charles Hunter is standing between Mr Sharpe and Mr Robertson

The Sharpe family with Miss Olive Winchester at their home in Muiryfauld Drive. Left to right: Kanema, Miss Winchester, Mrs Sharpe, Ina, Mr Sharpe, and in front, Isabel

Dr Olive Winchester

George Pawson

Chapter Three

DAVID THOMAS AND THE HOLINESS MISSION

The Welsh Draper

David Thomas was born on 29th September, 1860, in the farmstead of 'The Gors' in Llanllanwddog, Carmarthenshire, the eldest of eight children in a God-fearing family. His father, John Thomas, was a deacon in Peniel Congregationalist chapel and superintendent of a branch Sunday school near his home. Fond of history and excelling in mathematics, David nonetheless left school at fourteen to work on the farm. The Welsh farms were small and it took hard work to produce a meagre living. At seventeen, the young David Thomas was apprenticed to a cousin who had a draper's business in Swansea, and at twenty journeyed the two hundred and forty miles to London to look for a position. Almost reduced to his last penny, he was at last successful, and four years later launched his own drapery business at 55 Falcon Road, near the Clapham Junction railway station. In May, 1885, he married Elizabeth Lowth. They were to have five sons and four daughters.

Faithful in attendance at the Congregational church, teaching in Sunday school, upright in business and fair to his employees, the Welsh draper prospered. But at one of Moody and Sankey's meetings in Exeter Hall he was challenged to say whether he was a Christian and again whether he was 'saved'. He answered that he was, but he had been brought up to believe that it was presumption to say so, and went home under conviction that he had lied. Early in 1890, Reader Harris, Q.C., came to speak to the Sunday school teachers of Milton Hall mission Sunday school about the new birth. He invited all those who wanted to know that they were saved to raise their hands and David Thomas responded. Testifying to his brother John on returning home, he wrote, 'I felt the assurance of the coming of the Holy Spirit in my heart.' His Sunday school class was a group of a dozen lads, fourteen to sixteen years old and 'full of animal spirits'. In six months, through prayer and quiet personal conversations, every one had made their commitment to Jesus Christ.

He became a committed worker at Reader Harris's Speke Hall mission and despite his weakness through asthma taught in the Sunday school and participated in the evangelistic open-air meetings. In 1891, Dr G.D. Watson of Boston preached in Speke Hall on Romans 6:6: 'Knowing this, that our old man is crucified with him, that the body of sin might be destroyed, that henceforth we should not serve sin.' He emphasized that God could deal with sin in the heart, and under his direct preaching, David Thomas was convicted particularly about his hasty temper. He knew that he made cutting and harsh remarks to his young employees and went forward to the penitent form when the invitation was given. There he made his complete consecration of body, soul and spirit, business, wife, family and all that he knew. After his prayer, the elderly preacher shook his hand and said: 'Young man, if you keep true you will never need another consecration service, no, not if you live to be as old as Methuselah.' Dr Watson's text became for David Thomas the touchstone of the doctrine of holiness: the 'old man', the 'body of sin' or 'carnal mind' had to be *destroyed.* When giving testimony in later years to his experience of entire sanctification, he would often quote the Quaker, George Fox: 'Christ came in and took away out of my heart all that was uncharitable and would not keep sweet, and that was unlike himself, then he came in and shut the door.'

David Thomas's employees, some of whom lived on the premises in Falcon Road, noticed the difference, for the sharp and cutting words disappeared, and in time many of them were won to Christian commitment and a life of active service. Clearly those who knew him most closely in the practical tensions of living and working together were attracted to Christ through him, and that could not have been so if David Thomas had not exemplified daily the holiness he spoke about. When 'the Guv'nor' went to lead a mission for Reader Harris's League of Prayer in churches all over the country, he would take a band of them with him. And when after fifteen years of faithful service in Speke Hall and with the League, he felt he had to start the new Holiness Mission, it was his family and employees who formed the corps of workers. Soon after that first open-air service in December, 1906, over a dozen of them met for a Sunday morning in the 'upper room', a room already set aside for prayer in the large drapery store.

Reader Harris remained opposed to the new mission. He invited David and Elizabeth Thomas to meet him and his wife on three consecutive Tuesdays, persuading, praying and exhorting them to remain with the League. But the evening after the third of these meeting, Reader Harris thought that David Thomas was looking very ill under the strain this was causing. He took him for a walk and after some further conversation finally conceded: 'Thomas, I will set you free if you still feel the Lord is calling you to work outside the churches. Whatever you decide to do in after years, never say I hindered you from doing the will of God.'

Sydney Hall

In February, 1907, the new Holiness Mission found a home in Sydney Hall, a rather dingy brick building on York Road, Battersea, near the junction with Falcon Road and Battersea Park Road, previously the premises of the Fabian Club. Services were held on Sundays and on every night of the week except Fridays, when the hall was washed and scrubbed to make it fit for the weekend services. Sunday was a full day. It began with prayer meetings at 7.00 a.m. and 10.30 a.m. followed by a Bible study for adults when the group worked its way week by week through one of the books of the Old or New Testament. One of the workers spoke for ten minutes on a passage, followed by others who shared their thoughts on it along with scripture passages which had helped them during the week. Personal testimony mingled with reflections on Scripture and many of the expositions were extremely interesting, it is said, for their boldness and originality! Perhaps the claims being made to entire sanctification were not fully understood by those who made them, but the experience of the work of the Holy Spirit in their thoughts and conduct was genuine, and the mellow practical experience of David Thomas presiding over these meetings always gave encouragement to those young and immature in the faith.

From three o'clock to four, there was a Sunday school in an upper hall crammed with two hundred boisterous children from poor homes. From 5 o'clock to 5.45 there was an evangelistic open-air meeting strategically placed opposite the Prince's Head, a large pub at the corner, to invite the unconverted into the Gospel service at 6 o'clock. David Thomas was a typically fiery Welsh preacher at these meetings in the street. The mission workers would then march to the evening service past pavements thronged with passers-by. On one occasion, passing the queue waiting to enter a music hall, one of the workers, Brother Thatcher, stood and shouted invitations to the queue, and despite the ribald replies, two young men named Briggs and Clark, left the queue, came to the service and were converted. They were later to go to the Far East as missionaries.

In the evening gospel service the workers preached with power and conviction: heaven and hell were realities, and hymns were solemn and appealing. David Thomas would quote the last verse of 'When I survey the wondrous cross,' adding, 'The whole realm of nature will never be yours. All that any one of us here this evening is certain of, whether rich or poor, is six feet in Battersea or Wandsworth Cemetery,' and urging sinners to come to the penitent form and make their peace with God. Many came. The week-night meetings were for prayer, praise and testimony, and new converts would be warmly welcomed into the fellowship and encouraged to demonstrate the love of Christ in their homes and at work.

As can be imagined, the Holiness Mission was full of larger-than-life characters, especially among the older saints. There was old Mr Elden, a little man with big heart who went by the nick-name of Sankey because he would sing solos at the open-air services. Although he did not have a particularly good voice, he could communicate the message of the gospel songs in such a way that people would stop to listen. Brother Anderson, a Scot who had served in the Royal Horse Guards in the service of Queen Victoria, had been converted in the barracks at Windsor, and now found in the fellowship of the mission the one thing which helped him battle against depressing circumstances and grinding poverty. There was Miss Yeo, a tall old lady obviously of great beauty in her youth, who never missed a service, and Mrs Clements, a shy little woman from Wales who had brought up her family as a widow and was a mother to many new converts. There was 'Brother Murfin with his cheery, smiling face', the pleasing tenor voice and the sane advice in committee meetings, and 'dear old Mr White, naturally slow of speech' but grounded in the Word of God, whose expositions of a difficult passage often brought light and inspiration. An anonymous writer (probably W.S. Milbank) summed up his memories:

> Those dear old friends were quite the ordinary people one rubs shoulders with every day of the week. They served behind counters, or added up figures in ledgers, or spent their days in bending over steaming wash-tubs, but their lives had been made radiant by the Spirit of God. When meeting one of them there would come the kind inquiry of one's health, followed by an earnest, 'Well, brother, (or sister), how is it with your soul?' It was impossible to resent their inquiries: they were always courteous and never familiar. Their shake of the hand warmed the heart. It was as if one had met St Francis in the sordid markets of York Road.[1]

The Holiness Mission

In April, 1908, David Thomas launched the *Holiness Mission Journal*, an eight-page monthly which looked rather like a smaller edition of Reader Harris's *Tongues of Fire*. In his first editorial he outlined the object of the mission:

> The object of the Holiness Mission is to proclaim to a lost world the truth of Full Salvation, Regeneration for the sinner and the Baptism of the Holy Ghost and fire as the privilege of every believer, and that it shall be done effectually in every town and village throughout the land.

He invited anyone who shared this vision to join the new movement and offered to 'send workers who are filled with the Spirit to conduct the services free, without salary, simply to the glory of God.' Through preaching as a missioner for the League on the outskirts of London, in Somerset, Cardiff, Durham, Lancashire, Yorkshire and elsewhere, Thomas had contacts throughout the country, and by the time this first edition of the *Journal* was published, mission halls in Penn (Buckinghamshire), Southampton and Carmarthen had already associated themselves with the Holiness Mission. Their common intention, separating them from the League of Prayer, was to work outside the churches, which David Thomas dismissed in an early editorial as 'hopeless'. He asserted: 'The word of God tells us, and history confirms it, that if there is to be a Pentecostal revival there will

---

1 These reminiscences of Sydney Hall are drawn from *David Thomas* (London: I.H.M. [c.1933]), probably written mainly by W.S. Milbank.

be a split.' He referred to Paul, Luther and Wesley as precedents for necessary division. But he denied that the Mission was antagonistic to the churches: 'We love them and pray for them.'

In 1909 seven other missions were added: at Long Ditton, High Wycombe, Hitchin, Hammersmith, and Luton in the Home Counties, at Perth in Scotland and at Bargoed in Wales. The following year missions in Forfar, Eastbourne, Heacham and two in Bradford had joined with Thomas, and by the end of 1911 missions in Carstairs in Scotland, Seven Kings (north of Ilford in east London) and Hull. In 1912 missions were added in Leicester, Bridgewater, Leeds, Cleethorpes, and Stockton; in 1913 missions in Hoylake and Neston in the Wirral; in 1914 missions in Newick (Sussex) and Taunton; in 1915 more missions in the Wirral at Birkenhead, Bootle, West Kirby, one in Ilford; and in 1916 a mission at Portslade near Brighton. By that time eleven of these had withdrawn from association, including those at Perth (which associated with George Sharpe), Hammersmith, Heacham, Carstairs, Allerton, Forfar, Carmarthen, Little Neston, Penn, High Wycombe and Leicester, leaving twenty in association. Some of the missions were directly founded by David Thomas and his workers from Sydney Hall, but others had existed previously and knew of David Thomas through the wide network of the League of Prayer.

Clearly this expanding work required considerable organization, and this was provided by David Thomas and the leading managers of his drapery business. Jack Ford later described the 'four lieutenants' who shared his vision:

> His right-hand man was Leonard Wain, like his leader a countryman who had come to London to seek his fortune. Active, virile, shrewd, he was at the same time manager of his business and second in command in his religious enterprise. Harry Seekings, tall, fearless, with a distinct streak of humour and a flair for doctrinal discussion, was regarded as something of a theologian by his fellows. W.S. Milbank, whose cultured voice and facile pen commanded respect and forwarded the cause, was a regular writer in the *Journal.* B.H. Dunning, of Frome, Somerset, an able worker among children and young people, was already showing promise which was to find fulfilment in his work as secretary of the

South African Branch. These four, all members of his business staff, became known with David Thomas as 'the Five Men of the Holiness Mission'.[2]

The 'Five Men' were quite different in personality. Leonard Wain, with a neat pointed beard and spats, could be warm and humorous in company. But he was somewhat grim in the pulpit, warning of judgment and hell both at communion services ('He that eateth and drinketh unworthily…'), and in the pressure he applied during 'altar calls'. He would remind the congregation of what happened to Ananias and Sapphira when they 'lied to the Holy Ghost', and ask those who were 'saved and sanctified' to stand so that the others would be exposed! Walter Milbank was a quietly thoughtful preacher and a gifted writer. He worked for David Thomas, Ltd, for over forty years and eventually became the buyer in a very successful new department with furniture, carpets, linoleum and china. Bert Dunning, who saw himself as the most liberal of the five, was the avuncular superintendent of the large Sunday school and, as 'Uncle Nebo', wrote the children's column in the *Holiness Mission Journal.* He conducted a 'Young Preachers' Meeting' every Monday and was a great encouragement to many an aspiring speaker. He was later to become managing director of David Thomas, Ltd. Harry Seekings, who was disfigured by an enormous cyst at the back of his neck, was also a buyer for David Thomas, Ltd., a genial personality who later, after some tension with Leonard Wain, ran his own business in St Leonard's.[3]

There were also a number of active local leaders. George Wooster was a Buckinghamshire farmer who testified to entire sanctification after David Thomas had preached for the Pentecostal League in January, 1904 in the Methodist church he attended. Frustrated by the opposition he encountered, he withdrew from the church and started meetings in his home, Pennbury Farm, opening a mission hall in the village of Penn in January, 1907. He held a tent campaign in the nearby town of High Wycombe and asked the American preacher, Rev Charles

2 Jack Ford, *In the Steps of John Wesley* (Kansas City: Nazarene Publishing House, 1968), 98.

3 For these character sketches, see Colin H. Wood, 'Personalities and Powers', MA dissertation, Manchester, 1996) 8ff.

Stalker, to open a mission hall there in January, 1909. Another tent campaign in Leicester led to a Holiness Mission in Mere Road, opened by Rev George Kunz in January 1912.

Frank Lucas was a Strict Baptist in Southampton who was informed that he had embraced error when, under the influence of Leonard Wain, he testified to entire sanctification. He withdrew with some others from the church and held meetings in the open air, until he found accommodation in a hall five years later. In 1908 the group acquired their own premises in St Mary Street, Southampton and David Thomas donated two hundred chairs.

Alfred Place was a miner, converted in 1886 as a result of evangelistic open-air services held by Hunslet Carr Methodists near Leeds and was taught to read by one of the members. He came to think that the Wesleyan Methodists were too 'worldly' and held house meetings, moving into several premises including one above a bakehouse which he called 'The House of Prayer'. He taught 'the blessing of a clean heart', regarding John Wesley as his chief authority. About 1901 his mission moved into a hall in Dewsbury Road, Leeds, and in conjunction with two other small missions in Hull and Dewsbury, drew up a doctrinal statement and rules of membership. Through the influence of W.G. Anderson (a contributor to the *Holiness Mission Journal*) the three missions allied with David Thomas's connection in 1912.

George Dempsie left the Pentecostal Church of Scotland in 1913 and went to the Wirral, raising up missions at Hoylake, Neston, Bootle, Birkenhead and West Kirby, but in 1917 went abroad.

The I.H.M.

Clearly the wider connections of the holiness movement helped the quick development of David Thomas's Holiness Mission in the years before the First World War. Reader Harris and the Pentecostal League of Prayer felt that they should work in an interdenominational way and that an independent mission outside the churches was a mistake. This remained the League's position after Reader Harris died in 1909 and his widow took over the direction of Speke Hall and the Pentecostal League. Their leading preacher was now the Rev Oswald Chambers, who opened a Bible College in nearby Clapham. But others in the holiness movement took a different view. Not only the Americans George Kunz, Charles Stalker and A.M. Hills, but also Miss Crossley and Miss Hatch of Star Hall, Manchester, were supportive. David Thomas led a convention meeting at Star Hall in the autumn of 1909 and his brother, Rev John Thomas, was briefly superintendent of the Star Hall mission.[4]

David Thomas began an Easter Convention in Battersea in 1914. Over 300 were present, and this became an annual event, a rallying point for the members of the different missions around London and the home counties. It soon had to move to Battersea Town Hall. At the same time there was also the development of an ordained ministry in what began as a lay movement. Perhaps one of the most striking features of the whole evangelical world in the late-Victorian and Edwardian era was the large number of lay preachers. Certainly in the holiness movement, John George Govan, Frank Crossley, Reader Harris and David Thomas were all laymen. What was also significant in the holiness movement of course was the leadership of laywomen such as Miss Crossley and Miss Hatch, but the development of lay ministry was seen across the evangelical spectrum following the Moody and Sankey campaigns. With the spread of mission halls in working class districts of the large cities, the leading lay missioner sometimes took the title 'pastor', especially when he was a full-time worker supported by the mission. But although that title conferred a certain standing, in British usage (unlike America or Germany) it did not imply a professional man educated for the ministry and duly ordained - a proper 'minister'. But it is also significant that David Thomas came from a Congregationalist background and was used to a church polity in which ministers were ordained not 'from above' by bishops but 'from below' by the lay elders and deacons of their own congregations, and where, on principle, a layman could preside at the Lord's Supper. Ordination was a purely pragmatic matter for Congregationalists. Baptists too were congregationalist in church polity, and it was a

4 The Rev John Thomas became a missionary to Korea with the Oriental Missionary Society and founded what is now Seoul Theological University. Later still he settled in the United States. See Gweneth Thomas Zarfoss, *Faith as a Grain of Mustard Seed: The Story of John Thomas Welsh Evangelist in Korea* (Lampeter: Cae'r Nant, 1995).

Baptist minister who was the first to join the ranks of the Holiness Mission.

The Rev W.J. Willis, minister of St James Road Baptist Church in Watford, attended a holiness meeting early in 1913 and testified to 'the blessing' of entire sanctification. On 22nd February, 1914, he spoke at the Sunday services in Sydney Hall, and he was one of the speakers in April, 1915 when the mission moved from Sydney Hall and opened the new Holiness Mission Tabernacle on Battersea Rise. Between then and the end of 1916, he led over twelve weeks of evangelistic campaigns for the Holiness Mission, and his testimony was printed in the *Journal* in the April and May issues of 1916. In the January issue of 1917 it was announced that he had been appointed as 'the first Superintendent Minister of the International Holiness Mission', with 'a practically free hand to go as the Holy Ghost leads him to proclaim this great truth of Bible Holiness'.

The other change announced in the same issue of the *Journal* was that the Holiness Mission had now become the *International* Holiness Mission, a change which resulted from developments in South Africa. It was as early as 1908, just two years after the Holiness Mission began, that David Jones and William Clements had sailed for Port Elizabeth with no training and no promise of support, but with David Thomas's blessing. Clements had returned home, but David Jones's successful mission to the mine workers was officially adopted by the Holiness Mission in 1914. A Board was set up, including the 'Five Men' along with Frank Lucas and Harry Trigg from Southampton, George Walker of London and William Tyler of Luton. David Thomas was president and Wain and Lucas were vice-presidents. Evangelism rather than education was to be the main focus of the South African work and strong emphasis was to be laid on separation from 'worldliness', total abstinence from tobacco and alcohol, and the importance of entire sanctification.

By 1916 this new development, the creation of formal structures of government, was extended to the work at home in Britain. A constitution of what was now to be the 'International Holiness Mission' created a self-perpetuating executive council. Individual missions were invited to apply for affiliation, and the representatives of those accepted by the executive council would form a general council which would meet annually. The executive council could also terminate such affiliations, but each mission was to be 'entirely self-governing and self-supporting'. The superintendent minister would be appointed and paid by the executive council.

These developments, formal structures of government and a supported ministry, were not to the liking of George Wooster, and the Buckinghamshire missions withdrew. In the Wirral, John D. Drysdale of Blantyre and Ardrossan, was now pastor of the Birkenhead Holiness Mission, and that mission, along with Hitchin in Hertfordshire and Newick in Sussex also withdrew. The *International* Holiness Mission began its career then with nineteen missions in the home country.

Incorporation and an Ordained Ministry

The trend to formal organization went further in 1920 when the executive council was incorporated as a limited liability company under the Companies Act. The Articles of Association included a statement of doctrine:

> The Trinity, Unity and Equality of the Godhead
> The Divine Inspiration, authority and sufficiency of the Scriptures
> The utter depravity of human nature as a result of the Fall
> The Incarnation of the Son of God, His complete atonement on Calvary, His Resurrection, His Ascension, His Pre-Millennial appearing and His earthly reign[5]
> The absolute necessity of the New Birth, through which the repentant sinner is justified by faith and brought into the family of God
> The privilege and obligation of every believer to receive the Baptism of the Holy Ghost and fire, purifying the heart through faith, and filling with the Holy Spirit (Acts xv. 8,9)
> The immortality of the soul, the resurrection of the body, the judgment of the world by the Lord Jesus Christ, the eternal blessedness of the righteous and the eternal banishment of the unrighteous.

---

5 There was no such commitment to millennialism in the Pentecostal Church of Scotland or the Pentecostal Church of the Nazarene.

But the twenty members of the incorporated mission were the members of the executive council, all laymen. In fact it was stipulated 'that no member of the Council of Management or Governing Body of the Mission shall be appointed to any salaried office of the Mission.' That kind of safeguard against anyone making personal profit out of a charity no doubt has much to commend it, but in this case it meant that none of the ministers now beginning to serve with the I.H.M. could serve on the council.

W.J. Willis resigned as superintendent minister in February, 1920 to go to Korea as a missionary with the Oriental Missionary Society. Since the previous October he had been pastor of the new Manchester Holiness Mission Tabernacle, formed when Miss Crossley and Miss Hatch retired from Star Hall. According to Francis Crossley's will, the property was handed over to the Salvation Army, but a number of the members wanted to continue the work of the mission and arranged a meeting with David Thomas. In a conversation on a Manchester tramcar, he discovered that Brunswick Street Presbyterian Church near the university was empty and arranged a meeting with the trustees. The building was purchased and re-decorated in time for its first Holiness Convention, and the congregation brought with them from Star Hall the silver communion goblets sent to Francis Crossley by Armenian Christians in gratitude for alerting W.E. Gladstone to the Armenian massacres.[6] According to Jack Ford the purchase of the Manchester Tabernacle was something of a new departure: 'Its stately spire, stained glass windows, pipe organ and ordained minister were far removed from the original vision of plain buildings and unsalaried workers.'

When Mr Willis left for Korea, the Rev H.E. Jessop succeeded him as superintendent minister in March 1919. Jessop had exercised faith in God to sanctify him fully under the ministry of David Thomas at a meeting of the League of Prayer in Sheffield in May, 1906, and had served as minister of the Church of the Nazarene in Morley following the union of 1915. He was now to serve as superintendent minister of the I.H.M., publishing 'Our Superintendent's Letter' regularly in the *Holiness Mission Journal*. To some (as Dr Ford later commented) it

---

6 The goblets are still used by the same congregation, now the Longsight Church of the Nazarene.

became as authoritative as David Thomas's editorial, 'laying a more ample and informed conception of holiness before the readers.' Jessop advocated a closer union of the various groups in the holiness movement. He invited Samuel Chadwick, the Principal of Cliff College, to preach at the Tabernacle and in return preached at Cliff College and at the Methodist Southport Convention.

Two months after Jessop began his ministry in Manchester, the I.H.M. recognized a third ordained minister as pastor of the Bristol mission. Norman Woods Melling, a minister of the Independent Methodist Church, had come to Bristol in 1914, supporting himself by selling home medicines. Through contact with the Holiness Mission, he began mission work, an open-air meeting and a weekly 'holiness meeting' at the YMCA, leading to the founding of a Holiness Mission associated with the I.H.M. in the Railwaymen's Hall in Mead Street in 1919. By that time, one of Melling's surprising adherents was the curate at St Silas Church, Bristol, the Rev E.A.J. Bolt. Melling was a natural open-air speaker, standing on a little box playing his concertina and enjoying repartee with hecklers as he preached. He later recounted that day: 'At the close of the meeting the curate responded to an appeal by raising up his arm, indicating his spiritual need and his desire to seek Full Salvation.' Mr Bolt gave the inner story:

> I was in possession of the light, had many times preached about the truth, had earnestly sought the experience itself, but without effect. There were hindrances in me which I had not realized. But now, before the end of 1918 the long-desired and much sought for blessing became actually mine. God led me to a Holiness Meeting at Totterdown, Bristol, having entirely and eternally laid myself and my all on the altar, to claim, and by faith to receive, 'the Baptism of the Holy Ghost and Fire'. God in response to faith made the work real in my heart, and I knew that I had indeed entered into 'the land of rest' from 'inbred sin'.[7]

Within a short time, Bolt was instrumental in the conversion of some thirty people, but he was to pay the price for his bold preaching of entire sanctification. His curacy was terminated and he was banned

---

7 L.C. Shepherd, *Into the Unknown* (Bristol, 1999), 6f.

from preaching in the diocese of Bristol. But on 30th April, 1920, he was inducted as minister of the Bristol Holiness Mission.

Later that same year, Joseph E. Griffiths, who had served on the staff of Star Hall for eight years became pastor of the Hull Holiness Mission. He moved to Luton in 1926 to be succeeded at Hull by Edmund Roach. Roach had been a member of the Star Hall congregation, had entered the ministry of the Pentecostal Church of Scotland, serving in Gildersome in Yorkshire. James Bedwell was listed among the I.H.M ministers as early as 1922. He had been a lay preacher with the Primitive Methodists, had trusted God to sanctify him fully under the preaching of Reader Harris and joined the I.H.M. in 1919. Dan Philips of the Manchester Tabernacle prepared for ministry by studying at Cliff College, was accepted as a probationary minister in 1926 and appointed to the Grimsby Holiness Mission in 1928. Thomas Food, who had worked for six years with George Wooster, became a probationary minister in 1927.

Home-Call

In 1924, the I.H.M. was shocked by the sudden death of E.A.J. Bolt. Norman Woods Melling resumed his ministry in the Bristol mission. In 1929, H.E. Jessop resigned to accept an invitation to be guest pastor for one year at the Northwest Gospel Tabernacle in Chicago. In time, as Dr Jessop, he became president of the Chicago Evangelistic Institute and later of Vennard College, ending his ministry and career in the 1960s in the Church of the Nazarene. He was to publish several books, including *Foundations of Doctrine in Life and Experience: A Student's Handbook on Holiness*. He was succeeded at the Manchester Holiness Tabernacle by one of the up-and-coming young preachers, Maynard James.

David Thomas collapsed at a Sunday school outing in June, 1929, and never quite recovered his strength. He wrote in his last editorial:

> We desire the prayers of God's people that the Holy Ghost shall guide and control in the coming days concerning a great campaign that is going to take place all over the country. The object is to spread Scriptural Holiness in every place possible, especially where the truth is not proclaimed or taught. If we might be asked what is the

greatest need of this country, our answer would be a great spiritual revival, and we should say that it is the only hope of our land as the whole trend of the country is towards materialism.

A few days later, despite his weak condition, he took the opening services of a convention at Wellingborough and died a few days later on Monday, 16th June, 1930.

The tributes published later were remarkably honest.[8] One of his children wrote that he was no great orator. H.E. Jessop wrote similarly, recalling the occasion when he had first heard him speak:

> To say that he 'preached' would be to do violence to homiletics: but he did more, he brought to my heart a message straight from God Himself. I have since heard him preach something like that same sermon scores of times from as many different texts. No one else could have got away with it, but he did. His only concern was to get what he believed to be the truth of God to the people before him, and neither repetition nor reputation mattered in the least, and God marvellously honoured the word.

But Jessop added:

> His special genius was in the leading of the meeting and the directing of the altar call. No one could lead like David Thomas, and none could handle an altar call like he... Somehow he seemed to know just what to say at the moment and how to say it. And yet what did he say? It was all so ordinary. There was nothing new, yet somehow, when he said it, it was different.

Jessop also recalled his directness. When a testimony had been vague and not clear enough, he would call the witness back and cross-question him. Yet he was remembered by all as an outstanding encourager. He poured his money into the mission, and he emphasized strongly that 'death to sin' was part of his clear understanding of Christian holiness. Jessop recalled one specific occasion when the

8 For these tributes, see *David Thomas* (c.1933), 99-129.

preacher at an afternoon meeting of a convention had been rather vague on this, and David Thomas was very disappointed.

He could not remain for the evening meeting, and I was to preach. But before leaving he placed his hands on my shoulder and in his severest tones gave me this injunction: 'Jessop, my boy, if you don't preach the destruction of the old man to-night, I'll never forgive you.' Then he said, 'What are you preaching on?' I replied, 'Romans 6:6, sir.' His eyes glistened as he said, 'God bless you, my boy. Go on!'

David Thomas

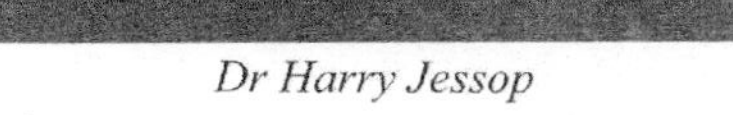

Dr Harry Jessop

David Thomas… as I remember him
David Lowth Thomas

Extracts from David Lowth Thomas's recollections of his father in a memorial volume published in 1931

When David Thomas, in the early days of his Christian experience, made that memorable covenant with God, his consecration was entire and complete. A frequent expression of father was: 'Let God have all there is of you. Let God have your whole life without a single reservation.' Many were the temptations of the enemy in the early days to compromise. The old lie would be trotted out that religion and business did not go together. Time and again the thought would come that if he kept strictly to the promise given to God at the time of consecration, business would not prosper, and that he would go to the bankruptcy court. One Saturday evening, on looking out of the shop door, father noticed a man selling stockings on a stall in the street. Like a flash the enemy asserted that if he continued to trust God, circumstances would change, and he too would have to take a coster's barrow and sell goods in the street. Strong as was the temptation, stronger was the determination that if every word of the enemy came true, and he lost every penny, he would obey God, whatever the cost. Subsequent events have shown that the Word of God is true and the devil to be a liar.

When the plan unfolded for father to take a leading part in the work of God, no one was more surprised than himself. Naturally of an extremely nervous temperament, together with none too robust health, the implicit obedience he gave to this call of God reveals his courage and strong character. Humanly speaking he was no orator, yet his sincere and earnest manner often carried his congregation where a more gifted speaker might have failed. In the testimony meeting and Bible class he was particularly used of God, the much needed word of encouragement to the young Christian to give a word for the Master was never left out, the eager exhortation to the wavering to stand firm often went home, and many a discouraged one took fresh heart.

He had a wonderful gift in employing others in the service of God, and in many a successful meeting it would be hard to say what the leader really did himself, but he brought out the talents of others. God endowed him with a grace and insight to recognize in others what he lacked himself. The greatest gift of all was his power in drawing in the net in the after-meeting. Patiently he would wait, relying on the Holy Spirit for the word in season, bringing souls to a decision seemed to be a service for which he had been specially set apart.

We who knew him in the home know that what he preached on the platform he practised in daily life. It is said of some that they were men of dual personality, but with father, he was a man of one purpose. True religion was to him his very life. Any discussion at home on family affairs or a suggested business venture would not continue long before he would say, 'Before we go further we will pray and get to know the mind of God.' Although a warrior, he was a happy warrior. In times of difficulty and struggle his happy smile and cheering word encouraged all about him. Sorrow and bereavement came into the home – first the youngest, Joseph, was taken, then Rachel and Miriam. Their long sickness and weakness he felt keenly. Under such heavy trial and grief, father was able to comfort with that comfort with which he had been comforted of God.

In the home the family altar was never neglected. No matter how early a member of the family had to leave in the morning, or how pressing other matter might be, the day was not commenced without reading and prayer. Every member of the family can testify to his godly life. Truly, he walked with God.

David Thomas… as I remember him
George D. Holmes

From the same memorial volume.

I well remember visiting him at Heathfield with two purposes in view, viz. to attend meetings and teach him to drive a car. I felt safe under his guidance in a meeting, but in a motor-car with him at the wheel I began to tremble. One day in his early driving stages he turned the wheel the wrong way and up a stone heap we went. The car nearly overturned, and there was I hanging on like grim death. 'What is the matter?' said Mr Thomas. 'Matter, guv'nor?' said I. 'You may be able to guide people to heaven, but we are not safe under your guidance in a motor-car!'

Once I remember going to the Keswick Convention with him, and we wanted to go to Borrowdale. So I said we would go up Derwentwater. He said, 'You had better not take me in a boat or something is sure to happen. It always does.' 'Come along,' said I. I picked a real good motor-boat, we all got in and away we went. Before we had gone very far our rudder fell off. 'There, I told you so,' were his words. We returned to the landing stage to get another boat. I told him that if anything went wrong this time we should count him a Jonah, and that would mean his being pitched overboard! But all went well and we reached our journey's end.

But I must record my last journey with him to hold a meeting in the north. We left his home in Battersea after praying for God's guidance. We got just beyond Norman Cross on the Great North Road, and we stopped for lunch, which we had taken with us. We sat on the footboard of the car and after asking God's blessing on the meal, we began. Presently I heard a voice, and I learned afterwards that it was a man offering us something for sale, but I never found out what it was. Mr Thomas interrupted by telling the man in the name of Jesus we could offer him something without money and without price. After a little talk we invited the man to take lunch with us, and invited him to accept God's salvation. We turned the footboard of the car into a penitent form, and there on our knees we all prayed, and as cars went rushing by God saved John Pitman of Woolwich.

Chapter Four

THE BRITISH ISLES DISTRICT, 1915-1940

The Disruption of the War

The First World War no doubt affected the work of the International Holiness Mission to some extent, but the leading laymen were all beyond the age for conscription, which began in 1916. The Pentecostal League of Prayer was affected when Oswald Chambers closed the Bible College in Clapham and went off to Egypt as a Y.M.C.A. chaplain. There his preaching had an immense impact on the troops, but he died tragically of peritonitis in 1917. His widow, who had taken short-hand notes of his addresses both in Clapham and in Zeitoun Camp outside Cairo, was later to publish many of them, including the spiritual classic which still sells widely, *My Utmost for His Highest*.[1]

But the effect of the war was more evident on the Pentecostal Church of Scotland, which in November 1915 became the British Isles District of the Pentecostal Church of the Nazarene. Even before the war, growth was not as great as might have been expected, the three original churches at Parkhead, Paisley and Uddingston staying much the same size from 1909 to 1915. Crowds flocked to the services at Parkhead and many were converted or testified to entire sanctification. But as they came into membership, others left. Some left to emigrate to the United States or the Dominions of the British Empire, notably the Young family from Ireland, charter members in Parkhead church, who settled in Cleveland, Ohio, and the Gatherers, whose daughter, Elsie, became a Nazarene minister in the United States.

Some members were lost because the rules in the Nazarene *Manual* opposed membership in oath-bound secret orders, and there were a number of the Parkhead men who were Ulster Protestants and belonged to the Orange Order. The Irish Catholic majority were campaigning for 'Home Rule' for Ireland, thus breaking up the United Kingdom, and Scottish Protestants, along with the Scots-Irish Protestants of Ulster (Northern Ireland), were strong 'Unionists'. The

---

1 See D.C. McCasland, *Oswald Chambers: Abandoned to God* (Grand Rapids: Discovery House, 1993).

Orange Order, an oath-bound order named after the Protestant champion of two hundred years before, William of Orange, was strong in Glasgow and the West of Scotland. Some Orangemen left the church when George Sharpe preached against secret orders, but others left the order and stayed with the church.[2]

The other Nazarene rules, including total abstinence from alcohol and tobacco and the avoidance of all 'worldliness' (including dancing, music halls and the theatre, and later the cinema) were not a problem. Given the appalling social problems caused by drunkenness in Scotland, there was already strong support for the temperance movement, and the children's organization, the 'Band of Hope' encouraged children to sign the 'pledge' that they would never touch alcohol. And no evangelical Christian would be seen in a pub, a dance hall or a theatre. As for 'Sabbath observance', the Scots were probably more Sabbatarian than the Americans. As to the generally puritanical life-style in evangelical churches then, the Nazarenes were only different in that (at the insistence of the American southerners at the union of 1908) these were *written* rules of church membership.

Some no doubt left because they felt they could no longer testify to the entire sanctification which they had claimed. The message was preached in very stark black-and-white terms, and perhaps, after they had 'laid all on the altar' and claimed 'the blessing', some could not square their experience with the doctrine. One such was Thomas Purvis, whose very honest letter, written in January, 1914 after he had emigrated to Canada the previous year, was recorded in the minutes of the Parkhead members' meeting of 26th March. 'I believe I professed a higher state of grace than I attained,' he wrote. But he still believed in the doctrine of holiness: 'Perhaps you will think that these confessions hurt the cause of holiness. I used to think so too,' he added, but the Lord had taught him differently. He had to be honest, but he had now determined to take up his cross and 'live for Jesus as never before.' His letter suggests that the problem was not the doctrine of Christian holiness as such, but the pressure to make premature claims which resulted from the 'altar theology' and 'shorter way' which the holiness movement had inherited from Phoebe Palmer.

---

2 The author's grandfather, James Noble, who had signed the Ulster Covenant in 1912, was one of the latter group.

A further reason why the Parkhead membership settled back to about 250 after a brief rise to almost 300 was no doubt the many calls on George Sharpe's time and energies with new churches, assembly business, a Bible College, and eventually a journal to edit. But a membership of 250 highly committed members, plus a large group of adherents and a large Sunday school for children meant that the strength of the church was in fact equivalent to many a Scottish parish church which had three or four times that membership on their official roll. The membership of the Paisley church grew rapidly in its first year, but dropped again after John Watson left for Morley and his successor, J.H. Farmer of Star Hall, was plagued by poor health. Uddingston was a small but solid church, handicapped by the position of the old dance hall they had procured in an obscure back-court, but including some mature and able people, notably William Turnbull, a business man who became secretary of the Pentecostal Church of Scotland, Robert Latta who became the denomination's treasurer and Robert Collins who succeeded him as district treasurer in 1920.

But if there were difficulties before 1914, these were compounded once the war began. Miss Winchester had returned to America in June, 1914 and students and other young men left for military service. George Sharpe continued doggedly tutoring his last college student, William Nicholson, until he was called up in June, 1916. Nicholson was gassed in the trenches and returned home to die in Stobhill Hospital on 25th September. That same night there was an air raid on Glasgow when thirty were killed and 110 injured. Robert Collins' son and two of Robert Latta's sons also died in the war. Eventually in May, 1918, the house in Westbourne Terrace was sold and the Sharpes moved back to Muiryfauld Drive, Parkhead.

From April, 1916 the annual assembly was now the 'British Isles district assembly' of the Pentecostal Church of the Nazarene and George Sharpe, who presided, was now the 'district superintendent'. But apart from the nomenclature, not much seemed to have changed. The total membership of the churches declined throughout the war and its aftermath. No assembly was held in 1918, the last year of the war, by which time conditions were very hard. But the statistics for 1919 showed that total membership in all the churches had dropped in four years by almost a third, from 655 to 464. The number of children in

Sunday school had remained at about 840, and there had been a growth in Bible classes for young people, with over a hundred enrolled by 1919.

The Call to the Ministry

But whereas the I.H.M. was led by mature laymen, the British Isles district of the Church of the Nazarene depended on recruiting young people to its full-time, ordained ministry. John E. Watson had moved from Morley to Edinburgh by the assembly of 1917, but later in that year he left to become a Baptist minister and soon afterwards the Edinburgh church closed. H.E. Jessop, who succeeded him in Morley church in 1916, left to work with the I.H.M. in 1919, although remaining an ordained elder of the Church of the Nazarene. Edmund Roach, previously of Star Hall, assisted George Sharpe at Parkhead and then served in Blantyre and Gildersome before joining the International Holiness Mission. When J.D. Drysdale left Ardrossan in 1916 to lead the Holiness Mission in Birkenhead on the Wirral, the Ardrossan group was organized as a Nazarene church, and Robert Purvis of Parkhead, who had studied at the original Parkhead Bible school, became minister. W.L. Telford was ordained in 1915 and served as minister of the Paisley church. William Turnbull of Uddingston gave up his business to enter the ministry, being ordained in 1916 and serving in nearby Blantyre. Peter Clark, also one of the early students at the Bible school, was ordained in 1919 and after an attempt to plant a church in his native Forfar, served as minister in Gildersome.

Andrew Robertson, Jr., served the Uddingston church as lay pastor while pursuing his studies at Glasgow University, but when he graduated he became a schoolmaster.[3] His older brother, Bob Robertson married Ina Sharpe and they emigrated for a time to the

---

[3] It is not entirely clear why this able and gifted man later left the denomination. He was a good friend of his fellow-student David Hynd, and an able classicist (the author has his Greek lexicon). He continued to defend the doctrine of the holiness movement and mark the annual district Bible exam, and his wife (one of the Latta sisters) and children continued to attend the Uddingston Church. One minor contributory factor was (according to his own account given to the author's father) his love of opera, regarded by some narrow-minded souls as 'worldly'.

U.S.A. Ina's younger sister, Kanema, gifted as an artist like her mother, studied at the Glasgow School of Art in the new building designed by the notable architect, Charles Rennie Mackintosh. Miss Winchester had had a considerable influence on Nema and she had moved on from art school to Glasgow University in 1912 with a view to teaching in her father's Bible College. In addition to Andrew Robertson, Jnr, and Nema Sharpe, a young man originally from Perth who joined the Parkhead church in January, 1916, David Hynd, was also a student at the university, following with the others the rigorous three-year course in Classics, History and Philosophy for the degree of M.A.

The First Ordained Scotswoman

With the shortage of candidates for the ministry in the middle of the war, Mrs Sharpe was drafted into service. Jane Brayton Rose (as she was before her marriage) was a woman of strong character and artistic abilities. She had filled her husband's Methodist pulpit in an emergency when they were in upper New York state, and thereafter was in demand as a speaker. Some said that she was a more able preacher than her husband. She had her own views on certain matters which he did not always share, including the bizarre but quite popular British-Israelite theory (also entertained by Reader Harris) that the Anglo-Saxon race was descended from the lost ten tribes of Israel. And many remembered for a long time her fascinating illustrated lectures on the Tabernacle which were no doubt an elaborate scheme of typology.

Following a spontaneous proposal at the district assembly of 1917, Mrs Sharpe was ordained on 7th April by the elders (Watson, Telford, Jessop and Turnbull with her husband presiding), making her the first Scotswoman to receive ordination to the Christian ministry. Thereafter Mrs Sharpe was never minister of any congregation (except temporarily during a vacancy), but was of great assistance to her husband as he travelled a great deal in his duties as district superintendent, visiting his churches from Perth to Yorkshire. One occasion on which she conducted a wedding however was followed by a distressed bride at the manse door to report that the registrar maintained that a marriage conducted by a woman was not legal!

As the war ended, other prospects appeared. David Hynd and Nema Sharpe were married in January, 1918. Like most other students during the war, they had suspended their studies to help the war effort. David Hynd had worked in the munitions department of the Parkhead forge becoming a foreman, and his wife had undertaken book-keeping in a business office. After their marriage he went off to do his military training in North Berwick, east of Edinburgh, having enlisted in the Highland Light Infantry. But Mrs Sharpe had drawn the attention of the young couple to an advert in the new Nazarene missionary magazine, *The Other Sheep*, asking for a doctor with British qualifications to go to Swaziland, the British protectorate in southern Africa, and they decided together that, at the end of the war, David would start a medical degree at Glasgow in order to do just that. The Sharpes provided a home for them and their little daughter, Isabel. David Hynd went back to university for the five year course, and as well as being a top medical student and picking up an extra degree in passing (B.Sc.), he was very active in the church, leading a large Bible class for young people, serving on the church board, singing in the choir, preaching from time to time, and playing his concertina at the large open-air services.

David's younger brother, John, who had been a student at Glasgow Technical College, proved to be a gifted public speaker, and, pressed to find ministers for his churches, George Sharpe put remarkable trust in the young man, and sent him off to act as lay pastor of the Morley church while pursuing studies for the ministry. James Jack, originally from Perth, was released from military service and became pastor of the Ardrossan church, and two other young preachers of promise appeared. James Maclagan was an orphan attending the Parkhead Sunday school. Put out of his uncle's home when he was converted, he was apprenticed to a cobbler, and came into church membership in January, 1919, soon professing a call to the ministry. In 1921, Mr Sharpe visited many parents, interviewing them about the possibility of their sons being called to the ministry. That same year a young man in Parkhead church, Tom Pritchard, invited a wild young friend to church. The nineteen-year-old George Frame, who had run away to volunteer for the army when he was fourteen years old and had since been in some trouble with the police, was converted under the forthright and uncompromising preaching of James Jack. Frame and

Maclagan started the course of study for the ministry under Mr Sharpe's direction. With other young men, they formed a 'deputation party' called the 'Glory Band' and went around Glasgow's numerous mission halls and 'open-airs' singing and testifying.

The General Assembly of the denomination was now to take place every quadrennium, and the British Isles district was represented accordingly by George Sharpe at the next General Assembly in 1919 in Kansas City. In order to disassociate the denomination from the spreading 'tongues movement', which was attracting some notoriety, that assembly voted to drop the word 'Pentecostal', used widely in the holiness movement for sixty years. From now on the name was to be simply 'The Church of the Nazarene'.

The Pawson Estate

In March, 1921, George Pawson died. He was the only wealthy member of the Church of the Nazarene in Britain and he left his entire estate (mainly extensive property in Morley) to the church. Not surprisingly his family contested the will, and it took George Sharpe several years of patient negotiation before the matter was settled out of court. The Pawson estate became the property of the church, but the members of the family were each to receive an annuity for life. One of these was still being paid at the end of the century! Half of the estate went to Nazarene missions and half was invested by the Support Investment Company in the United Kingdom which was set up to provide the district superintendent's stipend.

Other new recruits to the cause appeared in the early 1920s and Mr Sharpe re-launched classes for prospective ministers. The Rev J.D. Lewis, an inspiring Welsh preacher who had been an evangelist with the Faith Mission, stirred the district assembly of 1920 with his preaching, and was received as an elder the next year. Kenneth McRitchie of Parkhead and John Hutton Hynd received minister's licences that year, and James Jack became assistant minister at Parkhead to release Mr Sharpe for his district work and succeeded him as minister in 1921. Something of a stern legalist and a hell-fire preacher, James Jack nonetheless had an impact in a short ministry.[4] In 1921, for the first time since the union, a general superintendent, Dr H.F. Reynolds, presided at the district assembly. That year the membership statistics reached their lowest point, but by 1922, with J.D. Lewis at Paisley, Robert Purvis in Ardrossan, John Hynd in Morley and Peter Clark in Uddingston, 150 new members had been added. These figures included two new churches, one at Bellshill in Lanarkshire and one at Dunfermline in Fife. The Dunfermline church began when a young man from the town, James Macleod, an ex-soldier who had graduated in Civil Engineering from Edinburgh University, was brought to the New Year convention at Parkhead. He responded to the call to holiness, and introduced his brother and sister to the church along with his cousin, Peter Ferguson. Kenneth McRitchie became their minister, and was to marry James's sister, Jean. Sadly, William Turnbull, the Uddingston businessman who had entered late into the ministry and had had a short but fruitful ministry in Blantyre, died in May, 1922. In 1922, Mr Sharpe re-launched the *Holiness Herald* and took over the direction of an annual convention which the Ardrossan church had started. From 1924 this became a camp meeting.[5]

The Missionary Superintendent

George Sharpe had now given over twenty years of his life to ministry in his native Scotland. He had invested the decade of his forties in establishing the Pentecostal Church of Scotland and, seeing the dangers for the future for a little denomination so dependent on his leadership, he had guided it into union with the Church of the Nazarene. That same year, he had his fiftieth birthday. For most of the next decade of his life, he had persevered to bring his churches back to the strength they had had before the ravages of the First World

---

4 Mrs J.B. Maclagan once recalled to the author how, when the congregation was dismissed after the altar call, and the saints gathered round the seekers to pray, James Jack would address those leaving the church warning them that they were going to hell!

5 The author's father re-called going to the camp meeting with his good friend Joseph Irvine. The two lads were not wearing ties and had their shirts unbuttoned at the neck. On the way there they met James Jack who promptly reproved them for going to a meeting improperly dressed. Those were the days!

War. But now, on the verge of sixty, a wider field of ministry seemed to open out to him. In October, 1923, the General Board of the Church of the Nazarene appointed him one of three missionary superintendents, and put under his care the Nazarene missions in Africa, India and Palestine.

At this point, there were about a hundred Nazarene missionaries in eleven 'fields': Africa, Argentina, Peru, the Cape Verde Islands, Central America, China, Western India, Eastern India, Japan, Mexico and Palestine, with a total of just over 3,000 members.[6] It made sense to have a British superintendent for India, Palestine and Africa, where all the mission fields except the Cape Verde Islands were part of the British Empire. George Sharpe set off to tour his mission fields in 1924, and the Rev Peter Clark succeeded him as district superintendent in the British Isles. All three American groups who formed the Pentecostal Church of the Nazarene at the union of 1908 already had missionaries in India, the first arriving in 1897. There were mission stations to visit at Igatpuri, Buldana and Chikli near Bombay (now Mumbai) and in Calcutta. Nazarene missions in Africa had begun when the American Harmon Schmelzenbach had trekked by ox cart with his wife and child to Swaziland, arriving in 1910. The mission to Palestine had begun only three years previously in 1921 with the arrival in Jerusalem of the Rev Samuel Krikorian, an Armenian who had survived the Armenian massacres as a child and had studied at Pasadena College, the Nazarene College in Pasadena, California.

In Swaziland Harmon Schmelzenbach had discovered that giving medical aid was the key to opening the hearts of the Swazi people to the gospel. At his instigation, a small hospital had been opened at Pigg's Peak, a settlement high in the western hill country on the edge of the high veldt, and a former American army surgeon, Dr Charles West, had arrived to supervise it. But the British administration of the little protectorate would only accept a doctor with British qualifications for permanent settlement, and that had led to Schmelzenbach's advert in *The Other Sheep*. Land had now been obtained on a hillside near Bremersdorp, a little town of white settlers at the heart of the protectorate, down in the middle veldt, and on this visit in 1924 George Sharpe knelt in the long grass along with

6 J.B. Chapman, *A History of the Church of the Nazarene* (Kansas City: Nazarene Publishing House, 1926), 69.

Schmelzenbach, his assistant Josefa Mkhwanazi, and the missionary C.S. Jenkins, and prayed a prayer of dedication that God would use this place for the healing and salvation of many.

That same year David Hynd graduated with his medical degrees, having already obtained an M.A, and a B.Sc. and having completed, along with his wife, studies for ordination. They were ordained at the district assembly that year, the Rev Agnes Kanema Hynd thus becoming the third woman to be ordained in Scotland, all three in the Parkhead church. David Hynd had graduated from the Medical Faculty as one of three students gaining honours in a very large post-war class, a success which opened the door to a career at the top of his profession. But after a year in which he served as a surgeon in Barnsley and completed a Diploma in Tropical Medicine and Health in London, he was ready for Africa.

The whole family sailed for Africa on 22nd May, 1925, after a great farewell at the district assembly in Parkhead: Dr and Mrs Hynd and their two small children, Isabel and Samuel, Mr and Mrs Sharpe and their youngest daughter, Isabel. The missionary superintendent visited the work among the Africans employed in the mines in the Transvaal around Johannesburg, and the whole family drove from Johannesburg to Swaziland over the open country where the roads were almost non-existent. Mr Sharpe presided at the second annual council meeting of the Nazarene missionaries in Africa, hearing reports of the work in Portuguese East Africa (now Mozambique) as well as Swaziland and the Transvaal. The Sharpes then left the Hynds to settle in to Bremersdorp and visited the mission fields in India and Palestine.

But before the end of the year, one of their periodic financial crises had struck Nazarene missions, and the General Board of the church, meeting in Kansas City, had decided they would have to terminate the appointment of all three missionary superintendents. By the British Isles district assembly of 1926, Mr and Mrs Sharpe reported to the assembly as 'elders without charge'.

John Hutton Hynd

Peter Clark and Robert Purvis had both become members of the Parkhead church in March, 1907 while the services were still being held in the Great Eastern Road Halls. They had been students together in the Parkhead Holiness Bible College and had entered the ministry, Clark being ordained in 1919. His ministry in Uddingston had seen a great step forward when an attractive church was built near the heart of the village. Succeeding George Sharpe as district superintendent in 1924 was a considerable challenge, especially since a difficult problem arose concerning the district secretary, the Rev John Hutton Hynd of Morley.

John Hynd was every bit as intellectually able as his older brother. Sent to Morley in 1919 as lay pastor, he had completed studies under Mr Sharpe's direction and been ordained along with Robert Purvis in 1923. Elected district secretary in succession to William Turnbull, he had signed his older brother's ordination certificate the following year. Wanting to continue his studies, he had taken classes in Theology at the University of Leeds, and there a whole new world opened up to him. He found himself struggling with questions in the study of Theology which none of his fellow-Nazarenes had encountered at first hand.

The wider social background to this was the revolution in the world of thought and fashion following the First World War. The churches in Britain encountered widespread agnosticism and even atheism for the first time, at least among men. The propaganda of the new agnostic humanism spread by popular writers such as the novelist H.G. Wells and the dramatist George Bernard Shaw persuaded many in the younger generation at least, that science had disproved 'religion', and that to be 'modern' and 'up-to-date' one had to reject the 'old-time religion'. In the 1920s this led to a polarization between generations. The word 'Victorian' became a term of abuse, and it became fashionable in the 'jazz age' for the young smart set in high society to mock the legalism and hypocrisy of 'establishment' Christianity. King George V and his eldest son, Edward, Prince of Wales, embodied the contrast and rivalry between 'Victorian' values and the rather loose life-style of the young rebels of 'modernity'.

Theological 'Modernism' was the attempt of some Christians to bridge the gap and be in tune with 'modern' times and thought. In Switzerland and Germany the war seemed to produce a more conservative reaction against Liberal theology led by Karl Barth, challenging so-called 'modernity' with a return to the Bible and the

Reformation. But in Britain and especially in the U.S.A., post-war developments led to the Fundamentalist-Modernist controversy. Fundamentalism was the sadly inadequate attempt by conservative Christians to defend old ways and old values, and it was seriously out-thought and out-manoeuvred. Modernism strongly defended Christian moral values, but it called for a 'modern' adaptation of doctrine.

Perhaps if John Hynd had had the breadth of his brother's university education in philosophy and science, he would not have been so quickly carried away with the new 'Modernism'. But having been given a year at the time of the district assembly of 1926 to think through his position, he wrote to the district advisory board within a few weeks resigning from the church. 'I have honestly tried to understand the Christian religion in the light of modern thought,' he wrote, and he explained that he had tried to read the *Manual* statements (the Articles of Faith) 'between the lines,' that is to say, 'mystically rather than dogmatically.' He understood 'inbred sin' for example as 'a reference to the principle of evil' which he thought was 'necessary in the scheme of things.' He continued:

> Sin is submission to the evil principle. The test in the Garden of Eden is going on every day. Man's greatest happiness and his highest self is realized in the overcoming of evil. This is Holiness. And when a man's mind is in a certain attitude then the Eternal Mind and Spirit comes to his aid. There is a conscious 'baptism' of moral and spiritual power. There may be an instantaneous work, but not a complete work. As God has successive stages of evolution in the physical life, so does he work in the spiritual life, for the same God is in all and through all and over all.[7]

Within the framework of a kind of Hegelian Idealism, John Hynd was trying not only to re-interpret the Fall and sin, but also the specific doctrines of the holiness movement.

Everything was done to give John Hynd a dignified and friendly farewell at the Morley church. In later years he came under the influence of Stanton Coit of the South Place Ethical Society in London,

---

7 A copy of John Hynd's letter to the advisory board in the archives at Nazarene Theological College.

eventually becoming leader of the Ethical Culture Society in St Louis and President of the American Humanist Association. His going was an enormous loss to the holiness movement and the Church of the Nazarene, for John Hynd had the ability to be an outstanding leader of the church.

Perhaps it was the sadness of losing another of his promising young men which led George Sharpe to reflect on his first experience of 'Modernism' thirty years before in America. He recalled a young preacher who, after undergoing his theological education, had denied the miracles and the deity of Christ and taught that 'much that was written about him was mythical and should be treated as fairy tales'. 'That was the beginning of the Modernist crusade,' Sharpe wrote: 'It has gone a long way since then, until today this leaven has eaten into the very vitals of the organized church. The fundamentals of the Christian faith are being shattered and broken in the very place where they should be expected to live through all time.'[8]

Peter Clark as District Superintendent

John Hynd was not the only loss in the opening years of Peter Clark's superintendency. Edmund Roach had gone back to England to join the I.H.M. before the 1925 assembly, and W.L. Telford had gone to Birkenhead to assist his brother-in-law, J.D. Drysdale, who had started Emmanuel Bible College in Birkenhead, before the 1926 assembly. But there were gains as well as losses. The Rev J.M. Cubie was described by Jack Ford as 'an able and energetic Scotsman who had entered the Church of the Nazarene in America.' He became minister of the Perth church in 1925 and the next year, the Independent Holiness Mission in Perth which had been associated with George Wooster of Buckinghamshire and included such stalwarts as James Shaw and John Thatcher, united with the Perth church. Both of them had been radical supporters of the 'holiness' work in Perth for some years, but it seemed to take them a while to accept the idea of an organized church with paid ministry. George Frame served as a licensed minister in Gildersome, meeting and marrying the deaconess, Emily Edginton, who was a member of the Morley church. He was

8 From the introductory paragraph of George Sharpe, *A Short Historical Sketch of the Church of the Nazarene in the British Isles* (Glasgow, 1926).

ordained in 1926. J.B. Maclagan married Jean Willox of the Parkhead church and the young couple set up home in Blantyre where 'J.B.' was serving as a licensed minister.[9] He was ordained in 1927. James Macleod from the new Dunfermline church was given his minister's licence in 1928.

The denomination launched a new organization for its youth in 1923, the Nazarene Young People's Society. In keeping with the democratic congregationalist ethos, the young people were to elect their own officers, and run their own affairs, and the elected president of each local society would be a full member of the church board. This gave the young people a strong sense of identity and responsibility. But rather wisely, the age range was from 12 to 40, resulting in a mixture of adolescents and young adults in the society. The elected officers were generally in their twenties and the inclusion of young adults gave the societies a stability and continuity that was missing in many church youth groups. There already was a Bible class for youth which had been led in Parkhead church by David Hynd, followed by James Cunningham and Joseph Irvine. An N.Y.P.S. was formed there in 1926 with Robert Cullen as president. When the Rev Mrs Susan Fitkin from Brooklyn, New York, the general president of the Nazarene Women's Missionary Society visited Scotland on her way to Swaziland, she gave each of the young people one of the sterling silver N.Y.P.S. lapel badges with the reference of the motto text inscribed, I Timothy 4:2.[10]

Churches were also planted in Port Glasgow and Motherwell. Port Glasgow, a seaside town built on a sloping hillside looking out over the waters of the Firth of Clyde, had been established as a port before the river was widened and deepened up to Glasgow itself. It had several of the ship-yards which gave the Clyde the largest ship-

---

9 Part of the dedication of these young couples was the poverty they accepted as part of their call. Jim and Jean Maclagan once walked from Blantyre to Rutherglen to speak at an afternoon women's meeting. Receiving no expenses to cover the fare on the tramcar, they had to walk to Parkhead to take an evening meeting, and receiving no expenses there, had to walk home to Blantyre – a total distance of 22 miles.

10 'Let no man despise thy youth; but be thou an example of the believers, in word, in conversation, in charity, in spirit, in faith, in purity.' The author has in his possession the badge which his father received from Mrs Fitkin.

building industry in the world. A little church was begun there in 1925, but it flourished when the young James Maclagan arrived in 1926 on his bicycle with a hundred pounds from his old friend Tom Gray to support him. Maclagan was a short, stocky young man, an enthusiast with a magnetic personality, a heart-warming smile on his up-turned face and an outgoing manner, and his confident and definite doctrinal preaching attracted a strong following. Smartly dressed (like all his contemporaries in the Nazarene ministry) in a black clerical suit and hat and white clerical collar, his habitual over-accenting of the final consonant of every word made him easy to mimic! But it was the trade mark of a much loved 'character'. His leading of the singing with his concertina at an open-air service or street march was infectious. An 'iron church' was constructed on railway land at the end of a short cul-de-sac which was cut off from the shore by the main railway line to Glasgow. The steam engines pulling the carriages could be heard puffing and shunting past the wall behind the pulpit. But the little band of committed Nazarenes, the Barclays and Fergusons and Mackintoshes, could drown out any steam engine with their enthusiastic singing!

In Motherwell, George Sharpe's home town in Lanarkshire, a church was begun when a similar 'iron church' or 'tin kirk' was acquired. These buildings, little chapels constructed out of corrugated iron, were commonly used by most denominations in Scotland from the Victorian era to start home mission churches, and at this point not only the Nazarene congregations in Port Glasgow and Motherwell but also those in Blantyre and Perth had 'tin kirks'. W.L. Telford had a fruitful ministry in the new Motherwell church, but then some dissent had scattered the congregation, and Mr Sharpe himself became minister to rescue the situation when he set up home in Motherwell in 1926.

George Sharpe's other new task, at the request of the assembly of 1926, was to re-establish a College. He began classes in his Motherwell home, The Grange, and enrolled three residential and three day students. But the shortage of students, lack of financial support and illness in his family made this a short-term venture. The Sharpe and Robertson families suffered a severe loss in September, 1927, when Bob Robertson, the husband of Ina Sharpe, was killed in a road accident. At Easter, 1928, the district assembly had an indecisive election for district superintendent when no candidate received the necessary two-thirds majority in several ballots. The matter was placed in the hands of the presiding general superintendent, Dr Reynolds, who decided to appoint the one with the highest total of votes. Peter Clark had 203, Kenneth McRitchie, who had succeeded John Hynd as district secretary, had 362, and Mr Sharpe had 386. After considering the matter, he accepted appointment as district superintendent and the College closed in June. Peter Clark wisely decided to transfer to the Church of the Nazarene in Canada, taking a church in Alberta.

In 1929, at the request of the district assembly, Olivet Nazarene College in Illinois conferred the honorary degree of Doctor of Divinity on Mr Sharpe. At this period it was a common practice for the Scottish Universities to confer honorary doctorates on prominent Presbyterian ministers in recognition of their scholarship and service,[11] and the assembly saw this as fitting for their founder as he approached retiring age. But Dr Sharpe did not retire! During three years as district superintendent, churches in the Govanhill district of Glasgow and the Renfrewshire town of Kilmacolm were closed, but new churches were established in Troon, a seaside town on the Clyde coast, and again in Edinburgh, and new groups were formed in Leeds and in Greenock, the town on the Clyde coast next to Port Glasgow. But in 1931, after seven years at Parkhead, J.D. Lewis resigned. His preaching was as inspiring as ever, but his administrative and pastoral skills were not of the same high order, and he was appointed district evangelist. When Dr Sharpe met with the church board as district superintendent to consider who should be the next minister, several of his old colleagues, including James Cunningham and the blacksmith, Charlie Hunter, asked the pointed question: 'What about you?' He accepted.

Robert Purvis

Robert Purvis succeeded Dr Sharpe as district superintendent. He is described by Jack Ford as 'a man of imposing appearance and

---

11 1929 also saw a significant event in Scottish church history, the union of the established Church of Scotland (the 'Auld Kirk') with the larger United Free Church of Scotland to form an established church that was truly national and yet kept its spiritual independence from the state. A small minority stayed out of the union and formed the continuing U.F. Church.

attractive personality' with 'an acceptable pulpit manner', 'gifts of organization' and 'a shrewd mind'. His parents and his older brother, Thomas Purvis, had been charter members of Parkhead church. He had had good ministries in Ardrossan and Morley, and during his nine years as district superintendent, the membership of the district increased from 744 to 1001 and the number of churches from sixteen to twenty-five. Churches were organized in 1932 in Inverness and Irvine by Dr Sharpe, and in Leeds, and in 1933 in Greenock and in Birkenshaw near Gildersome. The work in Inverness was led by John Thatcher of Perth. In Irvine a group from the Railway Mission held meetings, had a tent campaign led by J.D. Lewis and the minister of the new Troon church, George Cooke, and acquired a hall in Fullarton Street where Tom Wilson served as their first pastor.

In 1934 the Ardrossan camp meeting was moved further south on the Clyde coast to the county town of Ayr, leading to the formation of a new church there the next year. In 1935, in the mining village of Twechar in Dunbartonshire, north-east of Glasgow, a group led by Walter Neil and his extended family were formed into a congregation. Walter Neil had taken a large group to the Ardrossan camp each year, and over the next four years this group of miners dug and blasted solid rock to lay the foundations of their new church building. In 1936 a new church was organized in Govan, a ship-building community in the south-west of Glasgow on the south bank of the Clyde, following a tent campaign led by the 'blue-shirts' (the trekkers) under Maynard James. In 1937, after contact with J.B. Maclagan, minister of the Perth church, the Cherryfield Mission in Dundee led by Robert Deasley united with the Church of the Nazarene and the Perth congregation were able to give particular support to the Deasley family when Mrs Deasley died. The Uddingston church launched a branch church in nearby Viewpark and churches were also formed in Carlisle and Workington, just across the English border in the county of Cumberland. A significant new advance too was the founding of the first two churches in Ireland. The Rev and Mrs Frank Clark, originally from Perth, opened a church at Lurgan in 1937, and two years later another was organized at Skegoneill Avenue in north Belfast.[12] The *Holiness Herald* was re-

---

12 James Noble, who had become a member of the Parkhead church in 1911, retired back to Ireland to his native Carrickfergus in 1938 and became a pillar of the Belfast church.

named *The Way of Holiness* after the old magazine from Star Hall ceased publication.

Two new missionaries left for Swaziland in 1931. Mary Tanner, brought up in the Parkhead church, graduated from Glasgow with her medical degrees and set off for Bremersdorp in February, 1931. In July, the school teacher Margaret Latta of the Uddingston church sailed for Swaziland to take charge of the mission schools. Since the general board of the denomination could not afford to pay her, her sisters together with several district laymen agreed to support her.

Dr Sharpe's second ministry in Parkhead was a fruitful one. In 1932, his daughter and son-in-law, Dr and Mrs Hynd, were able to come home from Swaziland for their first furlough, leaving Dr Tanner in charge of the new hospital. That same year, Dr Sharpe travelled to Wichita, Kansas, with the Hynds, Robert Purvis and Thomas Gray, the chairman of the district Sunday school board, for the Nazarene general assembly. Two promising young men in Parkhead, the cousins William Taylor and Joseph Irvine, sensed a call to the ministry. The Sunday school flourished with many children voluntarily sitting the long-established annual Sunday school exam, a written test of Bible memory work lasting two or three hours.

Sadly, the two promising young men did not live long. William Taylor, who was a graduate of Glasgow University, fell on some sharp railings while at the camp meeting and his injury was eventually fatal. He died in 1938 while minister of the Morley church. Joseph Irvine, who did not have the same academic opportunities as his cousin, was a warm personality and born leader, and had a very significant ministry in the Troon church, later becoming assistant and successor to Dr Sharpe at Parkhead. But he contracted tuberculosis and died in 1942.

From 1931, an annual convention was held in Parkhead at New Year. Since the 1560s when the Scottish Reformers had abolished the celebration of Christmas, New Year had been the traditional Scottish winter holiday, and Parkhead church would be packed for afternoon and evening services on 1st and 2nd January, with two speakers at each service. It was crammed full again at Easter time for the district assembly and again in October for the church anniversary. The lively

Nazarene gospel songs were heartily sung, often songs of testimony: 'The Saviour has come in his mighty power and spoken peace to my soul', or 'He abides! He abides! Now the Comforter abides with me', or 'He brought me out from the miry clay, he put my feet on the rock to stay.' Whether it was the 24th Psalm to the old Scottish tune, 'St George's, Edinburgh', beginning morning worship on the 'Sabbath', or a Charles Wesley hymn, or the Welsh hymn, 'Guide me, O Thou great Jehovah' set to 'Cwm Rhondda', or one of these lively gospel songs sung at a convention meeting, a congregation packed into the Parkhead church could lift the roof off!

Dr Sharpe greatly appreciated good singing and he had many fine soloists in the congregation, notably Marion Robertson, the daughter of one of his four original deacons. With a pure soprano voice of operatic quality, she could deliver a song of testimony with all the skill and drama of an accomplished actress. But it was no mere act! One of her favourite solos on the theme of Christian assurance asserted that her experience of Christ was 'real':

Oh, how well do I remember how I doubted day by day,
For I did not have the witness that my sins were washed away;
When the Spirit tried to tell me, I would not the truth receive,
I endeavoured to be happy and to make myself believe.

After several verses describing the search for spiritual reality, the turning point came:

But at last I tired of living such a life of fear and doubt,
For I wanted God to give me something I would know about;
So the truth would make me happy, and the light would
clearly shine,
And the Spirit give assurance that I'm His and He is mine.

So I prayed to God in earnest and not caring what folks said;
I was hungry for the blessing; my poor soul it must be fed;
When at last by faith I touched Him, and, like sparks from
smitten steel,
Just so quick salvation reached me; O bless God, I know it's real.

The congregation could almost see the 'sparks of smitten steel', and the chorus then rose to a great climax of assurance and ended in praise, greeted by a dozen cries of 'Amen!'

But it's real, it's real, Oh, I know it's real;
Praise God, the doubts are settled,
for I know, I know it's real.[13]

The other solo which she sang with great operatic power, and for which she was long remembered, was 'The Old, Rugged Cross'. She was quite possibly the first to introduce this American gospel song to Britain, and it became a popular national favourite.

These were undoubtedly 'popular' expressions of faith reflecting the somewhat sentimental popular culture of the early twentieth century. Looked at critically, the gospel songs could not match the theological and poetic depth of Charles Wesley or any of the classic hymn writers. But they express an intense spiritual experience which was transformative. And in addition to those whose vivid experience and deep commitment to Christ and to a life of holiness made them stand out as radical Christians, there were hundreds of others who attended Nazarene Sunday schools or youth meetings or conventions whose world-view and life-style were shaped by the impact these made upon them. There was certainly something unforgettable about a convention meeting at Parkhead church.

Dr Sharpe eventually retired in 1937 at the age of seventy-two. James Cubie returned to the United States, but Peter Clark came back to Scotland from Canada in 1937 and took up the duties of district secretary after Kenneth McRitchie's sudden death in 1938. J.B. Maclagan had a memorable ministry in Perth, and was called to Parkhead, his own home church, to succeed Dr Sharpe. The thirties, the years of the great depression, had seen considerable advance under Robert Purvis, but the storm clouds were now gathering again for war with all the social and economic changes that would bring.

---

13 A typical example of the American gospel song, the words and music were by H.L. Cox and the copyright of 1907 is held by the Lillenas Publishing Company, which became the music department of the Nazarene Publishing House.

The District Assembly of 1920 outside the Parkhead church. Front Row: 8th from left: David Hynd. Second row: J. Jack, J.H. Hynd, E. Roach, Will O. Jones (an American evangelist), E.G. Anderson (secretary of the Nazarene Board of Foreign Missions), G. Sharpe, Dr H.F. Reynolds (general superintendent), W. Turnbull, R. Collins, P. Clark, R. Purvis, K. McRitchie. Back row: 2nd from left, T. Gray; 5th, J. Noble; 6th C. Hunter, 7th, W. Robertson, 9th Mrs David Hynd holding her

George Sharpe ca. 1930

James Jack

Robert Purvis

John Thatcher

On left - Rev & Mrs James Jack; centre – Rev & Mrs Robert Purvis; right – Rev & Mrs Frank Clark; centre back – Rev James McLeod

Leaders at the Ardrossan camp meeting
Back, l. to r.: James Cubie, L. Ravenhill, G. Frame, J. Thatcher, J.B. Maclagan; Front: l. to r.: Victor Edwards, unknown speaker, T. Wilson, J. Macleod

Kenneth McRitchie

Joseph Irvine

J.D. Lewis

Tom Wilson

Sharpe, John Hynd, Pawson and Anderson in Morley

Emily Edginton and Sarah Bedford

George Sharpe ... as I remember him
Hugh Rae

My first contact with Rev Dr George Sharpe was on an October Sunday evening in Troon in 1929. Having moved a few days earlier from Glasgow, my mother was invited to send us to Sunday school in the Church of the Nazarene, then eighteen months in existence. Knowing nothing of this strangely named church she took me as an eight-year-old with her to the evening service. The location was an upstairs hall belonging to the Co-operative Society in Portland Street. My memory is of a tall elderly gentleman in a frock coat and white tie preaching with power to that small congregation. As we made our way home my mother's words were very simply, 'Hugh, these are my people.'

In 1945 he preached in the Central Halls in Bath Street in the centre of Glasgow. His text was Psalm 48: 12–14: *Walk about Zion, go round about her: tell the towers thereof. Mark you well her bulwarks, consider her palaces; that you may tell it to the generation following. For this God is our God forever and ever: he will be our guide even unto death.* His description of the gathering around the throne of God in heaven was one which those who heard it would not easily forget. Suddenly as if on a voice of command the entire congregation rose to its feet in an act of silent acclamation. Sharpe had few peers in his preaching ministry.

I had the great privilege of having a Homiletics class with Dr Sharpe for one term. He laid down some very basic principles for the preacher, one of which was that early preparation was essential and he suggested that the pastor should prepare six weeks ahead of delivery. This allowed the original outline to mature and would make the preacher much more open to the guidance of the Holy Spirit.

He was an active man to the end of his life. Two memories remain with me. I had just come to College in April, 1946 and conscription was still in force. I had been exempted while an engineer but was now called up for my medical. This eighty-one year old man came with me to the medical board to seek an exemption on the grounds that I was preparing for ministry. In the event it was not required. The other memory is of his coming to class and asking permission to sit while he lectured. This was because he had given an 'elderly' man his seat on the bus while he stood for the four or five miles. Now that I have passed his age I have even more admiration for him!

An Early Recollection
Peter Clark

This article by the Rev Peter Clark was published in The Way of Holiness, *Vol. II, No. 9 (June-August, 1948), a memorial edition following the death of Dr Sharpe.*

In the early days of my Christian experience, had a sincere desire to have all that God had for me. In the process of seeking, I came in touch with the Pentecostal League, and learned through that company of praying people that there was a minister in the east end of Glasgow who was preaching scriptural holiness. One Sunday morning I found my way to the church, but the service was somewhat disappointing. The Rev George Sharpe was not in the pulpit, the atmosphere was very cold, and I literally shivered as I sat up in the gallery. Then a strange thing happened. A man, I presume a deacon, stood up and read: 'They went out from us, but they were not of us; for if they had been of us, they would no doubt have continued with us; but they went out, that they might be made manifest that they were not all of us' (I John 2:19). I discovered afterwards that the Rev George Sharpe had been evicted on the Saturday evening, evicted from preaching the great and glorious truth of scriptural holiness. I had come a day too late.

Robert Purvis... as I remember him
Hugh Rae

Robert Purvis was born in Magherafelt, Co. Londonderry, and his family were charter members of the Parkhead church. Like Peter Clark, he was an early student in the first College. He supplied the Paisley congregation for a brief time and then seems to have worked as a layman. In 1923 he was ordained to the ministry and became pastor of the Ardrossan congregation. He was a tall, very fine looking man and a very successful and much loved pastor. After a time he moved to the Morley church and was there until his election in 1931 as district superintendent.

I remember his coming to Troon as district superintendent for an annual general meeting in 1936. The pastor, who had been appointed by the district superintendent but not yet licensed, asked him if he was not due to have a recall. (He misunderstood the constitution.) The district superintendent asked the church secretary to pass round ballot papers and then took them away uncounted. We never heard the result, but that pastor was moved away!

When Mr and Mrs Purvis celebrated their silver wedding anniversary in 1940, Mrs Purvis, who usually never spoke, told of her struggle when her husband was elected district superintendent. It meant his being absent from home often, and they had no family. God had given her a word from the passage dealing with the raising of Lazarus: 'Loose him and let him go!' Robert Purvis quipped: 'Well, I have been loose all these years and did not know it!'

When he laid down the responsibilities of district superintendent in 1940, he was appointed as pastor of Vancouver First Church, British Columbia. After six months it was discovered that his wife was suffering from cancer and they returned home to Scotland where she passed away. He finally accepted a call to the United Free Church of Scotland in Newton-on-Ayr and then moved to the Chryston United Free Church. A second marriage (to the widow of J.D. Lewis) was not successful and he spent the remainder of his years in South Africa as an evangelist. In 1979, at ninety-five years of age he died in Bromley in Kent at the home of Mrs Christine (Whitehurst) Ferguson, who was the niece of the first Mrs Purvis.

His influence upon my home and my life were significant and I had the privilege of speaking at his memorial service. His Irish wit made him a great favourite and I recall his love of people. His loss to the denomination was particularly unfortunate. For more than thirty years he had been a force for good in the life of the church.

George Frame… as I remember him
Sarah E. Bedford

George Frame arrived in Yorkshire as a bachelor to be minister of the little church in Gildersome in 1923. John Hutton Hynd was minister of the larger church in nearby Morley where Emily Edginton and Sarah Bedford were the first two consecrated deaconesses in the British Isles district. Sarah Bedford wrote this account for a 'This is Your Life' celebration when Dr Frame retired in 1972:

A home had to be provided for Mr Frame. The Edginton family opened their doors, giving him a Yorkshire welcome for the time being. Miss Emily Edginton was my dearest and closest friend. We worked together in all activities of the church, ever seeking to fit ourselves for future work for God. As time went by I noticed a change in my friend. One part of Sunday I always had fellowship in her home. One Sunday walking down the road Emily turned to me and said, 'Where are you going now, Sarah?' I replied, 'Don't you want me, Emily? I'm going home. Good night!' To me this was a keen blow. I soon saw my mistake. Two are company, three too many – when two are in love. Shortly after, George and Emily became engaged. I was more proud of her than ever. George Frame received a priceless jewel, a saint of God, a woman who helped him to rise to be the man whom God has honoured.

I spent my last holiday with her before her marriage. To a coastal town we went. One day, walking along the beach we found a quiet spot where we could swim or paddle. Shoes and stockings off, we paddled about enjoying the sea breeze and God's beauty around. Suddenly a sound I heard. It was the voice of Emily, saying, 'George Frame is walking around.' Forgetting myself, a shock I got. My clothes were drenched. Never shall I forget the day George Frame walked the beach seeking his friend, his bride-to-be.

Pastor George Frame spent three happy years in Gildersome. Morley church and Gildersome church were very helpful to each other, ever seeking to spread the gospel of full salvation. As a young minister, he was missionary-minded. He wrote a missionary play, Morley people along with Gildersome people taking part. It was a success, a church hall being filled for the occasion… At the end of three years' ministry, he married the Yorkshire lassie, Emily Edginton.

George Frame and J.B. Maclagan as I remember them Jean B. Maclagan

Mrs Maclagan wrote this account on 17th January, 1972 in a letter to the author as part of the preparation for 'This is Your Life', an evening to mark Dr Frame's retirement.

He [Dr Frame] and Jim [Maclagan] were very close, and in the early days went on deputation work together. I was not able to join them since I worked until 9.00 p.m. on a Saturday, but I was told many times of how in their endeavours to preach and testify to heart holiness in the various churches and missions it was not unusual for someone in the audience to rise up and challenge them. Sometimes their first visit was their last one. When I did manage occasionally to go with them I remember I was so embarrassed because they would get on the top deck of the tramcar. Jim would play his concertina and they would sing and testify sometimes to the annoyance of the passengers and the conductor would threaten to put them off. I and the other girls would sit downstairs and pretend not to know them.

I can recall Miss Frew of Uddingston and Mrs Hynd starting classes in the Parkhead Church and Mary [Tanner] and I decided we would do the ministerial course too. The men (Jim and Dr Frame) were so cock sure they would beat us hollow. They along with others would come to my home to study Field's Theology and I can hear them yet as they tried to repeat from memory: 'Evolution thus described by Tyndall, strip it naked and you stand face to face, etc.' I would be ironing or doing some other jobs but they would go over things so often they were fastened on my mind, and when it came to the exams the girls were top. They were humbled.

I cannot remember much of his early pastorates, but I do remember when he was pastor at Bellshill he had to preach with his coat on as the seat of his trousers was patched. There is another incident that stands out in my mind. In 1927 he married Emily Edginton. We were in Port Glasgow at that time, and while on their honeymoon they came to visit us. Charles Hunter and his youngest son were also in the home that day and someone suggested we hire a boat and cross over the Clyde to Cardross. Jim managed to get a rowing boat but on the way to the boat Charlie said, 'Something tells me I shouldn't go with you today.' Little did we know how true his words were to prove?

The trip across was very enjoyable and we had a walk and tea in a small café. When we got back in the boat the sea was a bit rough and I said to Mrs Frame, 'I am a bit scared.' When we got into the channel where the big ships go up and down – well, we were sure every next wave would capsize the boat. By this time the women and children were hysterical and Dr Frame was shouting to Dad that we were going far past where we had come out. I can see Dad yet. He got hold of an oar and told us all to be quiet or else.

By this time we were caught in the cross currents. The man who owned the boat said we would never see land and people were lined up on the shore expecting each large wave to swamp us. The coastguards were alerted, but once out of the channel Jim decided to let the current guide us and we ultimately landed in one of the Greenock shipyards and had to hunt around for the night watchman to let us out as the gates were all locked. Charlie had a [glory] march round Parkhead [church] the next Sunday!

John Thatcher...as I remember him
George Frame

An extract from Blood Brother of the Swazis *(Kansas City: Beacon Hill Press, 1952), Dr Frame's missionary biography of Dr David Hynd*

Holy John of Perth stepped out of a deathbed in Perth Infirmary... He described himself as an 'old sweat', a soldier with forty-two convictions against him in the army for drunkenness. His old life had caught up with him in another bout of *delirium tremens*, in which he was half-crazy and dying. A lady visitor from Sandes Soldiers' Home came to his bedside and told him about what Jesus Christ could do for him. He immediately believed and was instantaneously and miraculously transformed.

The next day while reading the New Testament that she had given him, he came across James 5:15: 'And the prayer of faith shall save the sick.' God had saved him the day before, so God would surely heal him now in answer to prayer again. His prayer for healing was immediately followed by a request to the startled staff for his clothes, as God had healed him. With the doctor's warning that he was going out to his death ringing in his ears, John Thatcher walked out to life for thirty years as a radiant Christian and successful soul-winner.

He was the most lovable, effervescent, and unpredictable character I have ever met. A walk down-town with John was an adventure or an ordeal according to one's temperament. A casual meeting with the parish priest or minister not infrequently ended with the startled cleric being pulled to his knees on the pavement while John fervently prayed for his salvation. A crowd of any kind was a challenge and opportunity for him to proclaim the wonders of the Christ he loved so passionately. The joy in his heart was liable to spill over at any time and in any place and find expression in a shout or a dance.

John Thatcher ...as I remember him
Hugh Rae

John Thatcher's miraculous conversion and healing when he was dying in the last stages of alcoholism in Perth Royal Infirmary is a remarkable story. He was a remarkable man of God, fearless in his advocacy of God's power to destroy the works of the devil. In 1932 I went as a boy with my father to a Saturday service in Troon at which John Thatcher was the evangelist. My father was not entirely sober. When the preacher began to talk in a rather dismissive way about other denominations, my father, who was Irish, rose to his feet and challenged him: 'Preacher, if you have a gospel to preach, preach it and leave them other boys alone.' He sat down and I will never forget the preacher's response: 'My friend, I have a gospel to preach and I will preach it.' That was the first step on the road to my father's conversion.

J.D. Lewis... as I remember him
Hugh Rae

J. D. Lewis had been serving as an evangelist with the Faith Mission and had been ordained prior to his coming into the Nazarene ministry in 1920. He was a fiery, fast-speaking Welshman whose ministry was to bring many into the kingdom. He was an evangelist at heart and systematic pastoral work was in some ways irksome to him, but he was an inspiring preacher. The Parkhead people remembered him preaching fluently for an hour, and then saying, 'Well, that is the introduction. I shall have to preach the sermon another time.' In his excitement, he would sometimes jump up on the large chair in the pulpit! In 1931 he became district evangelist and as a ten-year-old boy I was greatly impressed by this shiny-headed Welshman who brought fire to his ministry. A ten-day tent campaign in Troon was my first introduction to a man whose stature grew with the years.

In 1939, in his early fifties he married the Tasmanian evangelist, Beryl Devine, and they served in Morley and then in Port Glasgow, but this marriage of the much younger woman to the more elderly man was not a success. His influence on all who knew him was considerable. He taught Biblical Studies at the newly-opened Hurlet Nazarene College in his own inimitable manner. When returning exam results he would polish his shining head with his handkerchief and announce, 'You have all passed - some better than others.' He lived very frugally and was a great encourager to us all. 'J.D.' took ill and died in March 1952.

James and Ina Macleod ... as I remember them
Helen Williamson

We have all heard the 'rags to riches' story. Well, my Dad, James Macleod, decided to do it the other way round. When God called him into full-time ministry, he left his wealthy home behind, got on his bicycle with his Bible and concertina, and began his new life of living by faith.

He was born on 14th October, 1895, in Dunfermline, Fife, the second son of the owner of an iron foundry. When war was declared in 1914, he joined the Argyll and Sutherland Highlanders and spent the next four years in France as sergeant of a machine gun troop. Many days he went 'over the top' with his troop and came back alone. Later he would testify that he believed he had been spared through his mother's prayers. When the war ended, he matriculated at Edinburgh University to study Civil Engineering. He attended a special service at the local Baptist church and raised his hand for prayer when an Irish evangelist pleaded with those who were not Christians to 'give Jesus a chance in your life.' A friend took him to a New Year convention at Parkhead Church of the Nazarene where for the first time he heard the message of holiness and responded immediately. He introduced his brother and sister to the message and they formed the nucleus of a new church in Dunfermline. Kenneth McRitchie became their first pastor and married James's sister, Jean.

When he was called to full-time service, he was invited by J.B. Maclagan to come and work with him in the new Port Glasgow church. J.B. could not offer him any money, but he could live in the Maclagan's home. This began a life of faith. After some time, he felt called to work in the slums of Greenock. Conditions were bad with a shortage of work in the shipyards and a great deal of drunkenness. A tent was erected and a service held every night with many conversions, some of notorious characters. The tent served also as his home, and the district NYPS pledged half-a-crown per week in support.

While working in Port Glasgow and Greenock, James got to know the young Ina Barr, one of Maclagan's young people. Brought up like James to attend the parish church every Sunday morning, at the age of fifteen she had been drawn by the announcement of a woman preaching in Greenock Town Hall. This was the 'Maréchale', the daughter of William Booth, and Ina heard the gospel for the first time in her life. She responded and made her way to the inquiry room where she was led to Christ. The counsellor directed her to the 'tin kirk' where J.B. Maclagan was the pastor. Here she found a whole new family – something lacking in her life as an only child whose mother had died when she was six weeks old. Having been told that she should never have been born, she had discovered that before she was born God had loved her!

She felt that God was calling her as a missionary and on her day off work, she would visit the sanatorium in Bridge of Weir, often accompanied by James Macleod. They would cycle there together. He was seventeen years older than her and she was shocked when he told her that he felt that God wanted them to get married. She told him that his proposal was ridiculous. James asked her to pray about it, to which she replied that she wouldn't waste her breath! Finally, six months later, she said yes.

Since the happy couple planned to go 'up the Amazon' as missionaries there were to be no wedding presents but instead donations could be sent to the district missionary treasurer, Miss Frances Collins of Uddingston. When neighbours came to see the bride leave for the church, they discovered that she had already left for the pre-wedding prayer meeting! In preparing the church for the wedding, the pews had been given a fresh coat of varnish, but had not fully dried in time, and when the congregation rose to sing there was a great 'ripping' sound! The happy couple cycled off to their honeymoon for a week of camping at the Keswick Convention. Then it was back to the slums of Greenock where there weren't too many home comforts since James lived like a pioneer missionary in a Spartan two-room tenement flat.

Four children were born to them in Greenock, Flora, Billy, Helen and Catherine.

Throughout his ministry James never took a salary, receiving instead a free will offering in the Sunday morning service which often did not amount to much. When he had dedicated himself to God's service, he chose vows of piety, purity and poverty. Ina would often remind him that if you took vows of poverty, everyone was happy to help you fulfil it! Some colleagues took him to task for not providing for his family, but God faithfully provided for us in amazing ways and all our needs were met. When James's father died the foundry business was sold and the estate divided between the family. Typically James decided that he did not need this considerable fortune, and having bought himself a raincoat he needed, he gave the money to missions.

My mother trained as a midwife and also studied for the ministry. She remained a licensed minister for the rest of her life and preached regularly, but they never did get to go up the Amazon. In later life she would say that he got her on false pretences! In the years following their marriage the finance was not available, and after the war he was over fifty and considered to be too old. Since British doctors were more acceptable in the British Indian Empire, he was asked to study medicine to go to the Nazarene hospital there, but after prayer did not feel that that was what God wanted him to do.

After James had served twenty-five years in Greenock, James and Ina and their four small children moved to Dromore in Northern Ireland to plant a new church. They spent twenty-seven years there until he was forced to retire 'prematurely' through ill-health at the age of eighty-two! In 1980 he slipped away peacefully with his family around him. Ina died in her sleep four years later, having been busy and active to the end. They both donated their bodies to medical science, and James was delighted that the 'tent' he had lived in would be of use when he had finished with it!

A hymn my parents often sang was:

> He was not willing that any should perish:
> Am I his follower, and can I live
> Longer at ease with a soul going downward,
> Lost for the lack of the help I might give?

... Banish our worldliness, help us to ever
Live with eternity's values in view.

Jim Macleod ... as I remember him
Hugh Rae

At the 1936 district assembly Jim Macleod managed to get the assembly to pass a resolution to the effect that they should fast one lunch as a group. When the time came, it was evident that some put a different construction on what fasting included. Dr Sharpe was reported to have come prepared with a bag of apples. Two ladies slipped out to the nearby City Bakery restaurant for a cup of tea and were surprised to see the general superintendent, J. G. Morrison, and the district superintendent, Robert Purvis, having lunch. The news of this reached the ears of Jim McLeod and he took the matter up with Dr Morrison. A lengthy correspondence was carried on in which Jim insisted that the good doctor was under the jurisdiction of the assembly, but the good doctor replied that on the contrary, the district assembly was under *his* jurisdiction, and if he were subject to the vagaries of district assemblies it would be impossible to operate. I suppose the district superintendent simply saw himself as a host looking after the needs of his guest.

On a rare occasion during the Second World War, Jim was the preacher in an afternoon session of the New Year convention. Although he had fought in the First World War, he was now an ardent pacifist and although there were servicemen in the congregation, this featured in the sermon. The redoubtable Miss E.S.L. (Lizzie) Baxter, whose brother, Tom, was in the forces, started to demonstrate against the sermon. Sitting downstairs in the last pew in front of the aisle, she spoke out and shook a closed fist at the preacher. But he carried on unmoved!

On one occasion when I was a student at Hurlet and Jim McLeod came to give his weekly class in Theology, there was a visitor from Italy speaking in chapel who had a mouthful of gold fillings. We all knew that Jim was against all adornment. (Although he had a lovely pocket watch, it was held by a pleated shoelace!) Knowing that he had not as yet met the preacher, we asked what he thought about gold fillings, expecting condemnation. He replied, 'I think that they last longer and so they would be all right.' You can imagine his broad smile when he met the preacher and saw where we had been leading him!

He never seemed to go anywhere without his trusty concertina. He used to sit in the front seat in Parkhead church at district assemblies and help the organ along. When his niece, Margaret McRitchie, was married in the chapel at Glasgow University, he brought his concertina with him, intending no doubt to help the pipe organ along. But somehow it mysteriously disappeared! (His dear wife possibly had something to do with that.)

Jim Macleod, a true Scot ... as I remember him
John Paton

From the district superintendent's report of 1991

It was pointed out that bodily exercise profited little. The Rev Jim Macleod said: 'That's true, but never despise profit no matter how little it is!'

James McMillan, David Wallace and Hugh McLaughlan...... as I remember them Hugh Rae

Among the outstanding laymen of the district was James McMillan who was organist of the Ardrossan church and served on the district advisory board for many years (followed decades later by his son, Lyle). The Paisley church produced staunch laymen like David Wallace who became not only a children's leader of great ability at the local level but also at the district level. In 1934 he was presented with a framed illuminated certificate signed by the district superintendent, Robert Purvis, and the district Sunday school chairman, Thomas Gray, marking twenty-five years of work in the Sunday school. Another Paisley layman was Hugh McLaughlan, father of the late Ina McLaughlan, who also served on district committees. Two stories about him are worth recording. He was attending a committee meeting held at the Mount Vernon home of Dr Sharpe. Late in arriving, he was admitted to the home and went round the room shaking hands with all present before sitting down. He felt a little strange when nothing was said and after some time a door opened upstairs and the committee members filed out. Unknown to Hugh he was sitting with the patients in the waiting room of the homeopathic doctor who had his clinic on the ground floor. On another occasion his minister, Rev J. D. Lewis, was visiting the home for tea, and while Mrs McLaughlan prepared tea the two men spent time in the sitting room on their knees in prayer. When called to tea their appearance caused amusement. They had been kneeling at the old horsehair chairs and had been pounding on the chairs excessively so that the accumulated dust in those days of coal fires left them looking like miners who had just come from the coalface! The story, while amusing, does indicate the fervency of both men in prayer.

Tom Wilson...as I remember him
Hugh Rae

In the 1930s there were new recruits to the ministry. Tom Wilson from Perth and Joe Irvine from Parkhead came to Irvine and Troon churches respectively. They were in their early twenties and were eager to build up their churches where they were the first full-time ministers. Murdoch Luke had been a very brief time in Troon and George Cooke and his wife had given oversight to both churches.

Tom Wilson was a small man and appeared very shy but he gave steady ministry to the Irvine church for ten years before moving to Skegoneill Avenue, Belfast. He married Jessie Whitelaw, an Irvine girl. After some years in Belfast he moved to Morley in 1946 and served there till accepting the call to Uddingston in 1950. There he followed Arthur Fawcett who had served the church for ten years and was an outstanding preacher. Tom Wilson felt that he was unable to live up to the strong ministries that had preceded him and resigned from the ministry in 1955. He later returned to the church in Perth but was never to serve again as a minister.

Joseph Irvine...as I remember him
Hugh Rae

Joseph Irvine was brought up in the Parkhead church and was greatly influenced by his mentor, Dr David Hynd, becoming leader of the Bible class which David Hynd had led. He married Nan Williamson, who had brought her family (parents, three brothers and four sisters) to the church. The coming of Joe Irvine to Troon in 1932 was a turning point in the life of the church. His enthusiasm was contagious and his preaching ministry was of a high calibre. That he felt less well-equipped for ministry is indicated in a letter he wrote to Dr Hynd. He felt when he met other ministers in the town that their preparation for ministry was so much better than he had received through the home study course. Nevertheless in the three short years that he ministered in Troon he left an indelible impression on all whose lives he touched. It was under his ministry and through his counselling that I became a Christian and was led to the point of sensing God's call on my life. We talked about it as we were out walking, till he said to me, 'Hugh, I still have a key to the church. Let us go in and pray that the Lord will keep his hand on your life.' Joe Irvine was never a robust man and the early sign of the disease that took his life at the early age of 33 was already in evidence. He returned to be assistant minister at Parkhead, his home church, and then for a brief period after the retirement of Dr Sharpe he served the church as pastor. His spirit was always strong as was his faith, but his body did not allow him to serve for long and he died in 1942.

Frank Clark...... as I remember him

Frank Clark was from the Perth church, a brother of the long-serving layman, Hugh Clark. After a brief ministry in Gildersome he pioneered the work in Lurgan, Northern Ireland. Later, with his son William, who had been a student at Canadian Nazarene College (then situated in Red Deer, Alberta) he pioneered the second church at Skegoneill Avenue, Belfast. But soon after his ordination William resigned from the church and moved into the Congregational ministry and then the Army Chaplaincy. Soon afterwards his father also moved into the Congregational church. Some years later Frank Clark with his wife and daughter went to Canada and he served there for some years in the Nazarene ministry.

John Dyson and Peter Connolly...

John Dyson and his wife had been long standing members of the I.H.M in Leeds (now the Leeds South church). In 1934 he became pastor of the church in Dunfermline. He was a very gentle man and was older when he came into full-time ministry. They then moved to Motherwell. Mrs Dyson belonged to the 'old school' of holiness and gave wholehearted support to the work of her husband. In retirement they settled back in Dunfermline where he served a nearby United Free Church. Peter Connolly had been an outstanding evangelist, well-known along with Jock Troup in evangelistic circles. On Maclagan's moving from Perth to Parkhead in 1938, the Perth church called Peter Connolly and he was there for several years. He was ordained at Parkhead at the assembly and was elected a delegate to the 1940 General Assembly. He finally went back to evangelism and took up permanent residence in the United States - an outstanding preacher with a very remarkable testimony.

J.B. Maclagan ... as I remember him
William Still

The Rev William Still, who had a long ministry at Gilcomston South Church, Aberdeen, and a profound influence on many in the Church of Scotland, was in hospital in Glasgow in 1944 with a broken ankle. He was a divinity student, but unsure of his future. He wrote the following account of his hospital visitors in his autobiography, Dying to Live *(Fearn: Christian Focus, 1991).* .

The Fitches from Troon and their friends, the Roberts, also came, as did an exceedingly devout Nazarene pastor, Mr McLaggan [*sic*] ... That dear man brought a breath of God to my little side-room, and I could believe it was possibly after he had prayed with me and for me that my mind clarified and my heart was at rest, and I determined that I would simply be the Lord's servant, wherever he took me.

Charlie and Marion Hunter...
...as I remember them T.A. Noble

Charlie Hunter was an ebullient Irish blacksmith who became a member of the Parkhead church in 1907. I can only just remember him since he died when I was a small child. But I do remember going to visit the Hunters in their villa in Ardlui Street, Shettleston. They had the luxury of a garden (we lived in a Dennistoun flat), and I can remember sitting in the old kitchen with its brightly polished 'range' where, much to my childish fascination, the old man drank his tea in the old-fashioned way from the saucer. 'Aunt Marion' (as we called her) had been my mother's Sunday school teacher, and was the daughter of the Andrew Robertson who was a founding deacon of Parkhead church along with my grandfather, Thomas Gray. She was an outstanding soprano singer, and my mother used to say that she loved to stand beside her to sing the hymns in Sunday school since when she sang the high notes 'she took you up with her!' My mother also remembered her drilling the children in her fierce schoolmarm way to participate in the annual Sunday school soirée (pronounced 'swarry' in Glasgow). They had to articulate their recitations or songs so clearly that she could hear every word from the back of the gallery. Charlie had been widowed three times when he married Aunt Marion and her family were opposed to the marriage. But when she was widowed, she told my mother that those had been the happiest years of her life.

There are many stories about Charlie Hunter. He was an 'out-and-out' Christian who loved to 'shout and sing' and let the world know about his Saviour. If he saw a young Christian across the street or at the other end of a tramcar, he would be sure to shout in his Irish brogue, 'Are ye still lovin' Jesus?' People were known to 'jeuk up a close' if they saw him coming![1] He certainly believed in the right of free speech at a district assembly, and was known on one occasion, to tell the chair, 'You houl' yer tongue! I was on my feet afore ye!' He loved to shout 'Glory!' when he really felt blessed in a meeting, and to participate in a 'glory march'. He wasn't in favour of preachers entering the ministry without doing the appropriate study, and would ask at the district assembly, 'Is this man coming in the front door or the back?' He used to chair the Saturday evening 'tea meeting' at Parkhead and when the 'deputation' had been particularly lively, he would take the chair again with the words: 'We've had a high-larious evening!' It was one of his great joys in his last years that he had been over forty years on the church board at Parkhead and had never been voted off.

My grandfather, James Noble, wrote to tell Dr Hynd in Swaziland about his last visit to Charlie in the hospital. As he left the ward he turned to wave, and Charlie waved back and shouted, 'Glory!' Grandpa added: 'Now he'll be shouting glory with the saints above!'

1 'Jeuk', 'deuk' or 'jouk' (pronounced dyook) in the Scots language means to duck or to dive, and a 'close' is the passageway open to the street (in Glasgow tenements) which leads to the stairway.

Chapter Five

MAYNARD JAMES AND THE CALVARY HOLINESS CHURCH 1930-1940

The Holiness Mission Trekkers

Maynard James was converted in the Bargoed Holiness Mission as a boy. In 1920, when he was seventeen, he renewed his commitment to Christ under the preaching of Leonard Wain, and claimed entire sanctification by faith at the Easter convention at Battersea a few weeks later. His account of this event emphasizes that he almost missed his 'Pentecost' by relying too much on 'emotional surges', but 'a Manchester business man' who counselled him pointed him to simple faith in the promise of God.

> I did not hear the sound of a rushing mighty wind. Neither did a cloven tongue of fire rest upon my head. Nor was it given to me to speak in another language when the Holy Spirit came in. But my Christian life was revolutionized from that hour. Carnal fear was cast out by perfect love. Frustration was exchanged for a life of victory in the Holy Spirit. Prayer became an intense delight and the Bible was my veritable meat and drink. More wonderful than all was the unveiling of Christ to my longing heart. He became the loadstone of my affections. His beauty and grace ravished my happy soul. And something happened that I had never known – the Holy Spirit melted me to tears when praying for needy humanity. Truly the love of God had been shed abroad in my heart by the Holy Spirit.[1]

The young man was a junior research chemist, working at the Cardiff Mental Hospital, and in 1923, the year he became 21, he was made the lay leader of the Cardiff Holiness Mission. In January 1927, when he was 24, he enrolled at Cliff College, the Methodist College for evangelists, with the encouragement and financial support of George D. Holmes, a business man in the Hull Holiness Mission. The principal, the Rev Samuel Chadwick, recognizing his gifts of

1 Maynard James, *I Believe in the Holy Ghost* (Nelson, Lancs: Coulton, 1964)

leadership, appointed him student chairman. At this point, Chadwick was at the height of his influence in Methodism, and recognized as one of the leading evangelical preachers in the country. The war-time Prime Minister, David Lloyd George, regarded as the greatest orator of the time, came to hear him preach, and, striking up a friendship, came to Derbyshire to address the students.[2] Undoubtedly the great Methodist evangelist with his clear Wesleyan view of Christian holiness had a deep influence on the young man from Bargoed.

Cliff College had created the 'Methodist Friars', groups of young men who would tramp from place to place with their sleeping bags and basic supplies on a two-wheeled cart, preaching in market places and street corners and holding evangelistic meetings in mission halls and Methodist churches. Maynard James saw the possibilities of this 'trekking' for the Holiness Mission and persuaded three of his fellow-students, William Henson, William J. Maslen and Albert E. Hart, to join him. They began with special services in two of the established mission halls, in Fenton Holiness Mission in Stoke-on-Trent, beginning on 28th June, 1928 and in the I.H.M. headquarters in Battersea. There they were joined by Kenneth Bedwell, the son of Pastor James Bedwell, and the five 'trekkers' set off in August, 1928 to conduct campaigns in each of the I.H.M. missions, completing the task by September, 1929. En route they picked up a new recruit in Hull in May, 1929. This was Jack Ford, who had been brought up as an Anglican in Hull and converted through an Anglican lady, but attended the Holiness Mission and had recently trusted God for entire sanctification at a conference of the Japan Evangelistic Band at The Hayes Conference Centre in Swanwick. When the trek ended, he entered Cliff College in September, 1929. This long trek of 1928-29 created enthusiasm for two trekking parties in 1930, one in the north of England and Wales and one in the south led by Jack Ford, and two efforts in 1931, a trek from Manchester across to Sunderland in the north-east of England, and a tent campaign in Bolton in Lancashire.

---

2 In those days when the privacy of the great was respected by the press, Chadwick clearly did not have any information about Lloyd George's private life! On Samuel Chadwick, see Norman G. Dunning, *Samuel Chadwick* (London: Hodder & Stoughton, 1933) which has a foreword by Lloyd George recounting his visit to Cliff College.

'Trekking' certainly caught the attention of the towns and villages the teams visited in the industrial north. The word 'trek' came from South Africa, like the idea of the Boy Scout movement founded by Baden-Powell, and the trekkers wore a uniform not unlike the scouts, a fashion also borrowed in the 1920s and 1930s by the various fascist movements such as the 'brown shirts' in Germany and the 'black shirts' in Britain. The trekkers had quite a different aim of course! But following the fashion of the time, they wore blue shirts with a badge - a lighted torch with the motto, 'Aflame for God', and printed underneath, 'Holiness Mission'. Their cart, an ambulance trolley reconstructed by William Henson, had slogans on the side, 'Back to the Bible', and 'Holiness unto the Lord'.[3]

Revival and Healing Campaigns

The tent campaign at Daubhill Crossing in Bolton was led by Maynard James and Dan Philips, a fellow-Welshman, also a former Cliff College student and I.H.M. pastor, aided by various trekkers. This was a new development, different from 'trekking' from place to place. James had been impressed with the way the brothers Stephen and George Jeffreys had raised up Pentecostal churches by 'revival and healing campaigns'. There was no existing Holiness Mission in Bolton, and the tent campaign was prolonged through the summer with the express intention of establishing one. About a thousand people professed conversion and there were some cases of faith healing. Local shopkeepers reported that long-standing debts had been paid by those professing conversion. A prefabricated building seating four hundred was built by Albert Lown, one of the trekkers who was a joiner, and since Samuel Chadwick took ill, the Rev Norman G. Dunning deputized for him at its dedication in October, 1931. One of the trekkers, Arthur Fawcett, remained as pastor.

The following year, 1932, a similar 'revival and healing' campaign was held at the Holiness Mission in Leeds when the Mission hall was filled to overflowing and two hundred people professed conversion. The tent was then set up in new territory in Oldham for a campaign in

---

3 Paul James gives an account of all this in *A Man on Fire: The Story of Maynard James* (Ilkeston: Moorley's, 1993). See also the accounts in A.J. Lown's pamphlet, 'The Story of Trekking' and Beryl P. Allam's Leeds dissertation, 'The Outreach and Mission of the Holiness Movement'.

which all previous records were broken. A building seating seven hundred was secured and opened as the Holiness Tabernacle in October. In 1933, the tent was put up in Salford at the end of July and another Holiness Tabernacle established in a disused mill. Another team of trekkers led by J.T. Henson began a campaign in a hall at Atherton near Bolton in August, and again a strong church was formed.

In the spring of 1934, a new mission was established in Shaw near Oldham and another in Queensbury, a village near Bradford. The peak was reached in Dewsbury in a campaign from 9th June to 5th August. On the final evening, there were 2,000 people in the Playhouse Cinema and a further 1,000 overflowed a simultaneous meeting hastily arranged in the tent. A smaller campaign followed in Keighley, also establishing a new mission.

This remarkable success in establishing several strong new missions in such a short time was unprecedented. At the human level, explanations could be looked for in the social and economic conditions of the time. The great depression had thrown thousands out of work particularly mill-workers in the industrial areas of Lancashire and Yorkshire in the north of England. Masses of people still lived in the small Victorian terrace houses built in the decades following the Industrial Revolution, crowded together in narrow streets, shopping together in little privately owned shops close to their homes, using public transport, crowding on to trams and buses and trains together. With large families in small houses, the street life was vibrant! There was often no place to go for privacy, everyone knew everyone else's business and the sense of community was very strong. The cinema had appeared and radio, but in working class areas there were no televisions or cars and few telephones, and community life took the form of clubs and societies, mission halls and chapels. 'Open-air' meetings and marches, both religious and political, were quite common.

There was also a general respect for Christianity and an assumption that to be British was to be Christian. In a society where most people had attended Sunday school as children, and gave lip-service at least to Christianity and accepted Christian morality, the trekkers were not evangelizing raw pagans. The background knowledge of the Bible and respect for Christian standards was there, and indeed most would be familiar with some form of working-class Christianity, a small chapel or mission hall or Salvation Army citadel, if not the Anglican parish church. Although there was a minority influenced by secularism, particularly among men in reaction to the sufferings of the war, this was not yet the general mood of society.

But the social conditions do not alone explain the remarkable success. The principal explanation must be found in the trekkers themselves. While all of them were capable preachers, and some (such as Arthur Fawcett and Albert Lown) were to become notable, at this point Maynard James was the outstanding orator, a powerful preacher with a pungent style and a touch of the Welsh 'hwyl'. To his natural fluency and eloquence he added an unrivalled knowledge of the Bible and he knew how to captivate an audience. No doubt some of his themes were somewhat sensational and even scary for a generation not yet accustomed to being scared out their wits by the suspense or horror of the movies. To people living quiet, hum-drum, fairly parochial lives, a pre-millennialist view of the imminent second coming of Christ, followed by the Last Judgment, proclaimed by an authority figure like a preacher, could create alarm in the guilty consciences of young and old alike. He would announce sermon titles such as 'Will Christ Come in 1931?', 'The Greatest Sinner in Bolton' (a sermon on John 16:9), or 'A Night in an Eastern Ballroom' (a sermon on Belshazzar's feast). The drama of faith-healing and the drama and emotion of the altar call no doubt also attracted fascination. But behind all that, there was a deep moral earnestness and a spiritual power which all recognized as the anointing of the Holy Spirit. And hundreds of lives were changed, sometimes dramatically, for the better. Maynard James himself attributed the spiritual power to prayer. As well as 'the morning watch' with which every day began, there were half-days and even full days of prayer and fasting. It was not enough to view prayer as preparation for the spiritual battle which occurred when men and women were presented with the call of Christ. The phrase he often used was: 'Prayer IS the battle.'[4]

---

4 Paul James, *A Man on Fire*, 34ff.

Division

But in 1934, when the 'Forward Movement' of evangelism in the I.H.M, reached its height, it was marred by a tragic division, which was eventually followed by decline. There were various factors leading to the parting of the ways, but the heart of the matter was a division of opinion between Maynard James, supported by some of his contemporaries, and the older lay leadership of the I.H.M. It must not be thought that the older laymen were opposed to evangelism or antagonistic to this young fire-brand. Quite the opposite was true. David Thomas had rejoiced in the advances being made in the last years of his life, Leonard Wain's preaching had restored Maynard James to Christian commitment at the age of 17, and G.D. Holmes had supported him at Cliff College and was so enthusiastic about trekking that he was called 'the Chief Trekker'. What is more, they had promoted Maynard James to a place of leadership as pastor at the Manchester Tabernacle in succession to H.E. Jessop at the age of 27, and had given him Jessop's privilege of writing the 'Manchester Letter' in the *Holiness Mission Journal.* He had been given leave of absence from the Manchester Tabernacle for trekking and the tent campaigns. Finances had been made available. In fact 'by and large, he had had all he asked for.'[5] Nor should it be thought that Leonard Wain was clinging to power, for he handed over the editorship of the *Journal* to one of the young men, Jack Ford, and at one point he offered to resign as President of the I.H.M. council to let the presidency rotate.[6]

There seem to have been two points of tension. First, the young ministers saw that power was in the hands of the older laymen on the I.H.M council. It was not that they advocated some kind of democratic or Congregationalist polity, but rather that they wanted to be fully represented on the body which had the power! When trekking began, there were only six ministers in the I.H.M., but by 1934 there were sixteen. Quite reasonably they felt that some developments were needed in the I.H.M. constitution to take account of this evolution. But it is hard to see how that issue in itself could have caused such a

---

5 Paul James's comment, 47.

6 For the development of these points, see Colin H. Wood, 'Personalities and Powers', 31ff.

division (or justified it) unless there had been deadlock for years and the work was seen to be suffering as a result.

The second issue was whether the new developments were taking the I.H.M. too close to the new Pentecostalism, known among holiness people as the 'tongues movement'. Although trekking came from Methodism, the 'Revival and Healing Campaigns' were modelled on the work of the Jeffrey brothers, and there was a slight difference of opinion on the role of healing. G.D. Holmes maintained on the basis of James 5:14 that prayer for healing should be practised in the pastoral context, but Maynard James argued from Mark 6:13 that it could be done as part of evangelism.[7] Holmes disliked the fanatical and sensational, but James was by nature dramatic: 'Open-air antics, sensational sermon titles, controversial headlines and articles became James's stock in trade.'[8] There seems to have been some dispute over the word 'pilgrim' which was apparently significant for James. For some unknown reason it was rejected at a meeting of the I.H.M. council in April, 1934 much to his annoyance.[9] The council agreed readily to James's substantial proposals, to set him aside, along with Michael Keeley and Jack Ford, for revival work, but they changed James's proposed title, the 'Pilgrim Revival Party' to 'Revival Campaigners'. That scarcely seems a reason for causing a split.

But at the heart of the new Pentecostalism was its focus on 'tongues', and that was the issue at the meeting of the executive council on 9th and 10th October in Manchester. It was not the first time the matter had arisen, for it had been on the agenda the previous year as a result of the experience of Dan Philips, who had been a student at Cliff College and an assistant pastor at the Manchester Tabernacle. In 1933 Phillips had accepted the teaching of the new Pentecostalism that speaking in 'tongues' was the indispensable evidence of the baptism of the Spirit and had spoken in tongues himself. Leonard Wain had pointed out to Phillips how this denied the testimony of numerous members of the I.H.M. who testified to experiencing the baptism of the Spirit, purifying their hearts but not giving this gift. Phillips was asked

---

7 Paul James, *A Man on Fire*, 44

8 Colin H. Wood, 36.

9 Jack Ford, *In the Steps of John Wesley* (Kansas City: Nazarene Publishing House, 1968), 119; Paul James, 46; and Colin H. Wood, 34

to resign and given three months' stipend. Maynard James wrote an editorial for the *Journal* of July, 1933, which declared:

> We have no wish to depreciate the wonderful gifts and outward manifestations of the Holy Ghost, but we would strongly protest against that erroneous teaching which make one particular outward manifestation the infallible evidence of the Spirit's baptism.

This received Wain's seal of approval in these words which followed the article: 'The foregoing represents the official doctrine of the International Holiness Mission concerning the baptism with the Holy Ghost and Fire.'

But now a year later, in October, 1934, the council of the I.H.M. had reports that some Pentecostalists had spoken in tongues at the Keighley campaign, which had just ended. At the meeting on 9th October a motion was proposed that speaking in tongues should be forbidden at all I.H.M. meetings, and that posed a real problem for James. Although he agreed (as his editorial in the *Journal* had stated) that the gift of 'tongues' was *not* the indispensable evidence of the baptism of the Spirit (as many Pentecostalists taught), he had rejected his previous 'prejudice' (as he called it) against 'tongues' which had led him to declare (with other leaders of the holiness movement) that they were 'of Satan'. The turning point for him had come when he was astounded to be told in the midst of an argument with a Pentecostalist that Grace Langston (David Thomas's housemaid) spoke privately in tongues.[10] He was so impressed with Miss Langston and her quiet testimony that he accepted the validity of the gift, although not the idea that it was the necessary evidence for the baptism of the Spirit. On the basis of I Cor. 14:39, he now took the position that he could not agree to forbid 'tongues' in all I.H.M. meetings.

At this point in the council meeting, Jack Ford proposed a compromise resolution. Since leading the southern trek in the summer of 1930, he had been appointed to assist Leonard Wain at the I.H.M headquarters in Battersea and to edit the *Journal,* and had been pastor of the Addiscombe Holiness Mission in Croydon (south-east London) until

---

10 See Paul James, *A Man on Fire*, 145, and Colin H. Wood, 'Personalities and Powers', 37.

he was appointed to the revival party in May, 1934 with James and Keeley. As an associate of Leonard Wain, he had been appointed as a steadying influence on the passionate James,[11] and he now attempted to bring the two sides together. He formulated a compromise form of words in which tongues were to be forbidden unless the leader felt that he had come in contact with the genuine scriptural gift, in which case, he must inform the council. This was agreed. But when the council meeting resumed the next morning, James and Ford presented their resignations! Discussion with James overnight had changed Jack Ford's mind. He was persuaded that morning in the council meeting to consider the matter yet further, and later in the meeting, James withdrew his resignation. When the council meeting ended, the laymen all hurried back to their businesses, thinking the matter was resolved. But apparently James and Ford had a further discussion with two of the I.H.M. pastors, Leonard Ravenhill of Oldham and Clifford Filer of Salford, and the four agreed to resign together.

The *Journal* carried this notice in December, 1934:

> We regret to announce that Rev M.G. James, together with Pastors J. Ford, L. Ravenhill, and C. Filer have resigned from the International Holiness Movement. We remember their past services with thankfulness and regret the step they have taken.

Wain wrote a circular letter to the workers of the I.H.M. attributing the resignations to a disagreement on how to handle the issue of 'tongues', but followed it with another reporting that James and Ford had insisted that the issue was not 'tongues' but the constitution and administration of the I.H.M. He added however that that issue had not been raised at the recent council meeting.[12]

Why then did James, Ford, Ravenhill and Filer resign? There clearly was a divergence on the question of the 'gift' of tongues, for although they agreed that it was not the necessary evidence of the baptism of the Spirit, and although none of the four spoke in tongues themselves, they were no longer prepared to speak of it as 'diabolical' (as Leonard Wain did in these circular letters), and they were not prepared to forbid it

11 See Colin H. Wood, 'Personalities and Powers', 43.

12 See Colin H. Wood, 'Personalities and Powers', 41 and Appendix I.

provided they were convinced that it was genuinely 'of the Spirit'. But it was because that issue had become entangled with the issue of authority within the I.H.M. that they resigned. It had become quite clear in the October council meeting that the power was held by the council of older laymen, and there did not seem to be any prospect of that changing in the near future.

But behind all that, the underlying reason for the split may be seen to be the personality of Maynard James, a young man of undoubted charisma. Captivating and persuasive on the platform and in personal contact, highly regarded as a mentor and leader by his younger brethren, strongly committed to following what he individually believed to be the will of God and restless to be about the Lord's business of evangelism and revival, he did not intend to be held back by boards or committees who held the power. He had written in the *Journal* about a 'crisis' in the I.H.M. as early as February, 1933,[13] and it is possible to see the whole episode as typical of the tendency of revivalism and revivalists to live and thrive in an excited atmosphere of apocalyptic crisis and high drama. The regular routine of administration and committee meetings must not get in the way of confronting sin in the prophetic preaching of the Word. David Thomas too had had a dislike of organization. Like Reader Harris, John George Govan, Frank Crossley and J.D. Drysdale, he was an individualist who had struck out on his own. James was repeating a familiar pattern.

The I.H.M after 1934

The leaders of the I.H.M., who had left the council meeting believing that matters were settled at least for the moment, were no doubt shocked by the sudden resignations. They felt a real sense of betrayal. Throughout the I.H.M. many were 'hurt, confused and discouraged'.[14] Leonard Ravenhill's mission in Oldham and Clifford Filer's in Salford left the I.H.M., soon to be followed by the new mission in Queensbury and the older one in Bradford. But all the other missions, including those raised up by the trekkers and the revival and healing campaigns – Bolton, Atherton, Dewsbury and Keighley – stayed with the I.H.M. And none of the other ministers followed.

13 Wood, 33f. Compare the comments of Wood (45f.), who quotes Ford and Paul James to the same effect.

14 Wood, 47.

Arthur Fawcett, pastor of the Bolton church, now emerged as the leading figure among the I.H.M. ministers, but he was not given the position of 'superintendent minister'. He became editor of the *Journal* and a member of the Forward Work committee. Other able and leading ministers were Michael Keeley, the brothers William and Jock Henson, and Albert Lown. The tent campaigns continued, led by Fawcett, Maslen, Yeo and Food, but with less emphasis on faith healing. In the north-east of England a new mission was established in West Hartlepool in 1935, and many converts added to the Sunderland mission in 1936. In 1937 a tent campaign led by Albert Lown established a new mission in Batley in Yorkshire, but that was the last tent campaign and in 1940 the tent was sold. Three treks were arranged from Manchester in 1935-36 and a new mission established at Farnworth, but trekking then ceased till 1950 when it made a brief re-appearance.

On the I.H.M. executive council, Wain, Holmes, Dunning and Lucas remained the dominant members. The ministers led by Arthur Fawcett proposed a change to a quite democratic constitution. Final authority would lie with an annual conference composed of the council, the ministers and elected lay delegates from the missions. The executive council would still elect the president and treasurer, but the ministers would elect the secretary. This was considered, but then a committee of seven (including Wain, Dunning and Fawcett) recommended a structure much closer to the original. A council of ministers would sit with the executive council, but would not vote on matters of finance. An annual conference could pass resolutions by a two-thirds majority, but the final decision on any matter would lie with the executive council which could also withdraw the voting rights from the council of ministers! Nothing had really changed.

The Easter conventions continued in Battersea and Manchester. Sunday school work continued with an attempt to develop modern methods of teaching. The *Journal* published a series of articles by Sydney M'Caw, the superintendent of the Sunday school at the Manchester Tabernacle, on the psychology of teaching. But the great days of advance were over, and the aging leadership must have been aware of that, especially when they lost three of their leading preachers, Lown and Maslen in August, 1939, and Fawcett in 1940.

The outbreak of the Second World War did not promise to make things any easier.

The C.H.C.

Of the four founders of the Calvary Holiness Church, Maynard James was the only one over thirty and the only married man. Jack Ford was the youngest and the only one who had attended grammar school, his father being a Hull business man who had retired on his capital and so could afford to send his son to a fee-paying school. The other three (like those colleagues they left behind in the I.H.M.) were perfectly capable of benefiting from an academic education, but their parents had not been able to afford it. A grammar school education was really only accessible to the middle class, while a university education in England was still virtually impossible for working class young people.

Leonard Ravenhill was from Leeds. He had left school at thirteen and had become a 'cutter' in Montague Burton, the tailoring chain-store which made the business suit attainable for working men (along with lessons on polite manners!). He was always immaculately dressed. He had joined the southern trek led by Jack Ford in 1930, been a student at Cliff College, then assistant to Fawcett at Bolton and to James at Oldham, becoming pastor of the Oldham mission in 1934. He was a 'colourful personality' who could 'catch the imagination of the crowd', had 'a dynamic evangelistic ministry', and 'devoted himself to a ministry of preaching and prayer'.[15] Clifford Filer was a Welsh miner from Bedwas, near Bargoed. Influenced by Albert Maslen, he had joined the trekkers in 1931 and took part in the Bolton campaign. He too had been a student at Cliff College, was Assistant at the Manchester Tabernacle and participated in the Oldham and Salford campaigns. He remained Michael Keeley's assistant at Salford, becoming pastor of that mission when Keeley went with the revival party in 1934. Jack Ford later wrote: 'Filer was essentially a man's man. He gave the impression of strength and ruggedness, and he was no mean debater in a rather narrowly logical style.'[16]

15 Jack Ford, *In the Steps of John Wesley*, 141.

16 Ford, 142

In the first months after leaving the I.H.M., the four preachers conducted campaigns for the Nazarenes in Scotland, at Uddingston and Coatbridge in north Lanarkshire and in the Govan district of Glasgow. At the first Easter convention of the new movement in 1935, J.D. Lewis was the preacher and George Frame, J.B. Maclagan and James Macleod also participated as Dr Sharpe presided at the ordination of James, Ford, Ravenhill and Filer.[17]

By then, the four founders had formed themselves into an executive council on the model of the I.H.M., electing James as president and Ford as secretary. But now the power to make decisions rested with the pastors, not the laity. The request for ordination from the Nazarene ministers and the name 'Calvary Holiness Church' (a change from 'mission' to 'church') were also significant. The doctrine of the new movement was identical with that of the old with no mention of the gift of tongues. From their perspective, it was the council of the I.H.M. which had made that an issue. They recognized that 'gift' as biblical and would not forbid it when they were convinced that it was genuine, but they had no intention of propagating it or becoming a 'Pentecostal' church in the new meaning of the term.

At first, following their opposition to the I.H.M. constitution, the founders decided that they should remain in office on the council for only two years. Three laymen would be elected at Easter 1936 by delegates from the churches, and the entire council would stand for re-election in 1937, remaining in office then for three years. But as early as October, 1935, they changed their minds and decided that they, the four founders, would be life-members of the council. Two other ministers and four laymen would be elected for three years at a time.[18] After all, did they not have a right and a duty to ensure that the new movement they had founded continued on the right lines?

Maynard James wanted a 'red-hot' magazine and the first issue of *The Flame* appeared in April, 1935 with a masthead designed by a young commercial artist in the Bristol Holiness Mission, Len Shepherd. In his first editorial, James wrote:

---

17 Ford, 69
18 Ford, 148

> The need for pure, invigorating and spiritual reading is more pressing that ever before. We stand for aggressive evangelism. Our slogan is: 'Evangelize or perish!'

The back page concluded with an appeal:

> Our burning passion is to spread the glorious message of full salvation amongst the masses, and to set up live centres of holiness all over the land. Who will help us in this great adventure for the Lord?

Right from the beginning the bi-monthly magazine had a testimony page, 'In the Witness Box', and comments on current affairs. In the issue of September-October, 1937 Jack Ford wrote about Pastor Niemoller who was opposing the Nazis in Germany and there were several references to the persecution of the Jews there as well as the dangers of Communism and Romanism.

Revival Campaigns and the Oldham Easter Convention

They had already decided that pioneering work would be carried out by the 'Pilgrim Revival Party'. Following their ordination at the Easter convention of 1935 and a campaign at the Morley Church of the Nazarene, James and Ford held a 'revival and healing' campaign during June and July in Barnsley in Yorkshire, reaching many people outside the churches, and Ford stayed to minister to Sunday evening congregations of 250 or more. The rest of the team moved on to Bradford where a campaign lasting through August and September increased the attendance at the Bradford church from fifty to 250. In February, 1936, a campaign in the Yorkshire market town of Skipton led to the formation of a church with 200 in attendance. In Thornaby, Colne and Burnley churches were raised up with congregations of 150, 200 and 300, and finally a short campaign in Pudsey resulted in a smaller church of sixty. One notable healing occurred in Burnley when Harriet Roberts, who had been unable to speak for three years spoke again the morning after her anointing.[19] A small church was also started in Rochdale in 1936, formed by some who had attended the Oldham church. In 1936 two campaigns (in Barnoldswick and Haworth) failed to result in new churches, but a tent campaign in

---

19 See Paul James, *A Man on Fire*, 53f.

Eccles resulted in a congregation of a hundred. In 1938, tent campaigns resulted in a church in Sheffield with 180 members and in Hebden Bridge with a hundred. In 1939, tent campaigns led to a church of forty in Gillingham in Kent, a church of 170 at Middleton near Manchester, and an increase in the Grimsby church to about 130.

New pastors were obviously needed to care for the new churches, mostly composed of new Christians, and there was no shortage of men who heard the call. Three from their own ranks were enlisted in 1934 (John McMullen, George Thomas and H.E. Lewis). There were eight new preachers in 1935, seven in 1936, ten in 1937, four in 1938 and six in 1939. Twelve of these came from the I.H.M., three from the C.H.C., twelve from Methodism, six from the Pentecostal movement, two from the Baptists and one from the Church of England.[20] Probationary ministers were expected to pursue a set course of study for three years with annual examinations and to prove themselves in pastoral work. They were then ordained, would be addressed as 'reverend' and would wear the ministerial collar.[21]

Many of the churches declined quickly after the initial excitement of the founding campaign, but those who became members and remained formed a solid nucleus in each congregation, deeply committed and faithfully engaging in prayer meetings, holiness meetings, testimony meetings, Sunday school work, evangelistic open-air meetings and two Sunday services. Baptism was by immersion on profession of faith only, but it was on request and not a condition of membership, and the Lord's Supper was usually observed each Sunday morning seated around the table. Features here reflected James's Baptist background. The little denomination had a real sense of unity. It had a unified constitution and was not a loose affiliation of missions, and there was a distinctive lapel badge worn only by members.

Foreign missions were a concern of any lively group of evangelical Christians, and in 1935, the Calvary Holiness Church Missionary Society was organized. In October, 1936, Clifford Filer and his fiancée, Elenor Gregory, along with George Thomas and his fiancée, Edith Moore, were accepted as the first missionary candidates.

20 Ford, 145

21 But Maynard James himself never wore the clerical collar.

Norman P. Grubb, one of the initiators of the Intervarsity Fellowship, who had now succeeded his father-in-law, C.T. Studd, as the director of the Worldwide Evangelization Crusade, offered his help, and in April, 1937, Filer and Thomas sailed for Columbia, followed later by Elenor Gregory. After a time of preparation at the W.E.C. headquarters in Bogotá, they set out for Santa Marta in March 1938 to establish the first C.H.C. mission field. In 1939, Edith Moore and Annie Noble followed them.[22]

Since almost all of the churches were in the industrial north of England, most members could attend the annual Easter convention in Oldham. The convention meetings were chaired by Maynard James, who described the first Easter convention of 1935:

> Words fail to adequately describe the scenes of glory and power that marked the convention's gatherings... fervent singing, fiery testimonies, flaming messages, earnest seekers, record crowds, and wonderful offerings were the features of the meetings that nobody could help noticing. But best of all, far transcending all else, was the sense of God's presence that pervaded the atmosphere of all services.[23]

Norman Grubb was one of the preachers at the Easter convention of 1937. He recorded his impressions:[24]

> Holiness can be repellent. Here holiness was hilarity! In meeting after meeting ordinary members of the C.H.C. were called up to the platform without notice to testify, and out of the 25 or so I heard, there was not one weak one. Each told in the simplest fashion of the profoundest experiences of which human nature is capable, salvation from sin, its guilt and power; first sins forgiven, then full deliverance from enslaving appetite (such as drink in a number of cases), then the later need of heart cleansing to remove the roots of sin still remaining (such as love of the world, temper, impatience, etc.) and the experience of this second work of grace, accompanied by power to witness and live a Christian life.

---

22 Ford, 150

23 *The Flame*, June-July, 1935, 8 (quoted by Paul James, *A Man on Fire*, 57)

24 *The Flame*, May-June, 1937, 15 (quoted by Paul James, 57f.)

As I looked at the vast crowd thronging one of Oldham's largest halls, the majority were in their twenties. I saw the intensity of interest, the tremendous singing of full-salvation hymns to favourite old tunes, the outbursts of laughter, the evident enjoyment, hearty handshakes, and good fellowship… Whole countries such as Germany and Italy are in the hands of youth; and it is a sure sign of the Holy Ghost upon a movement when 'the dew of thy youth' and 'the oil of gladness' is upon such a vast number of its members. A full day's work lies ahead of, and not behind, the C.H.C. Its sun is only rising. The dew is still upon it. Thank God!

The Trekkers (c. 1932)
Seated l. to r.: A.J. Lown. M. James. W. Maslen. A. Fawcett

Putting up the tent: J. Ford, M. James and A.J. Lown and two other trekkers

Leonard Wain with the preachers who stayed with the I.H.M. at a convention on 'Jubilee Day', 1935 (a public holiday for the Silver Jubilee of King George V). Back, l. to r.: A. Fawcett, J.T. Henson, A.J. Lown, H. Waterson; front, l. to r.: H. Jessop, L. Wain, W. Maslen.

Ministers of the Calvary Holiness Church. Seated l. to r.: Randolph Murray, J. Ford, M.G. James, L. Ravenhill, C. Filer and H. Baldwin

Group at Beech Lawn Bible College: Ron Thomas (standing behind Mrs James), David Potts (standing behind M. James) and Glyn Thomas (behind J. Ford) served long-term in the Church of the Nazarene after the union.

Staff and students at Beech Lawn Bible College: Raymond Spence (who served long-term in the Church of the Nazarene after the union) is on the right in the back row.

Rev Clifford Filer and the deacons of the Calvary Holiness Church in Salford

Maynard James and Jack Ford ... as I remember them Raymond Spence

The two years at Beech Lawn Bible College were the most memorable of my life, setting the course for the next fifty years of ministry in this country and Canada. Apart from the academics, there was the example of holy living demonstrated by the principals, Maynard James and Jack Ford, whom I saw as a modern Moses and Joshua. Maynard James inspired a sort of reverential awe among the students with his uncompromising discipline, but also a great respect with his solid teaching and brilliant preaching. Even today I can't think of a better master of the pulpit. Never very approachable to students with problems, he was very different from his successor as principal, Jack Ford who was a man we could go to at any time. Periodically he would invite students into his office to discuss their progress and share their personal problems.

So impressed were the students with these giants of the Christian faith that many who were to listen to their sermons in future years would see James and Ford reflected in their deportation and sermon material. Even now, half a century later, their lives have an effect on me personally, and I continually thank the Lord that I was privileged to sit under their ministry. Their passing seemed to mark the end of a dispensation and sometimes I think their like will never be seen again.

Clifford Filer and Leonard Ravenhill... as I remember them Hugh Rae

Clifford Filer was a Welsh miner with enthusiasm and leadership qualities. He worked in Oldham before finally taking on the pastorate of the Llay church. He was a very friendly, down-to-earth kind of man who loved to work with his hands as well as minister to the spiritual needs of his congregation. His sudden home-call left us all the poorer as a result. Leonard Ravenhill was a radical rebel and it was not surprising that he joined Maynard James in breaking away from the IHM. He did not remain long with the Calvary Holiness Church and although he was pastor of a church, he was at heart an evangelist. On one occasion he led a group of young people into the open-air carrying a coffin. Laying it down in the street he immediately gathered a crowd by shouting, 'He's alive!' He then proceeded to take the Bible out of the coffin and preach about the risen Christ. He made his way to America where he spent his days as an evangelist. In the early days there he was in a hotel which caught fire. He jumped out of the window and broke his back. After months of convalescing he finally walked again, but always with a certain distinctive gait. He was a radical, roguish figure who, under the anointing of God, brought many to Christ. He was never a team player, which meant that he needed to be his own man.

Chapter Six

GEORGE FRAME, J.B. MACLAGAN AND UNION

The War and After

Britain declared war on Nazi Germany on 3rd September, 1939, but it was May, 1940 before the invasion of the Low Countries and France began and Winston Churchill became Prime Minister. At the Nazarene British Isles district assembly in Parkhead that same month, Robert Purvis resigned. He had served as district superintendent for nine years, and he seems to have been rather tired of the restlessness of two of his leading ministers who were very vocal in the district assembly, George Frame and J.B. Maclagan. It should be said that there was a strong tradition of plain speaking at both church business meetings and the district assembly. The egalitarian Congregationalist ethos prevailed! Mr Purvis was particularly criticized at that district assembly for his presumption in making arrangements to attend the forthcoming general assembly in America when he had not yet been elected a delegate.[1] It took nine ballots for anyone to receive the necessary two-thirds majority to succeed him as district superintendent, but eventually George Frame was elected.

Mr Frame had been minister of the Uddingston church since 1932. He had run a very successful boys' club there, had welcomed Maynard James and the trekkers for an effective evangelistic campaign, and had served on the district advisory board since 1936. An innovation long remembered in the Uddingston church was his production of a play, 'The Dawn', which recounted the missionary work of the Hynds in Swaziland. He had also succeeded Robert Collins as district treasurer and the Uddingston people had opened a branch church at Viewpark. In addition to all that, he had taken studies to gain mature university entrance qualifications and had completed a three-year course for the degree of MA at Glasgow, taking Russian for his required language course in addition to Philosophy and Psychology. He was highly regarded as a preacher. Speaking fluently without notes, he was at the

1 Decades later, district superintendents became *ex officio* members of the general assembly.

same time both thoughtful and dynamic. Mr Frame was succeeded at Uddingston by another excellent preacher, Arthur Fawcett, who came from the I.H.M. and who also entered studies at Glasgow, and he was succeeded as district treasurer by another member of the Uddingston church, Miss E.R.L. Baxter, who was a cousin of the Latta sisters and became a partner in Peacocks, a well-known Glasgow business which ran bakeries and tea rooms.

The membership statistics for the British Isles district showed a slight decline during the war, but rose again in 1945. During the war, three mobile canteens were bought to move into bombed areas of the cities in Scotland, Ireland and England. For safety, since the Parkhead church was close to Beardmore's forge and munitions factory, the district assemblies moved to Uddingston in 1942, Port Glasgow in 1943 and to the Central Halls in Bath Street in Glasgow's city centre for the next three years. Three new churches were started in Birmingham in 1942, 1944 and 1945, and the Rev Robert Deasley moved there from Dundee. Meanwhile, George Frame was remarkably successful in recruiting a whole generation of preachers, some of whom moved on, but some of whom would stay with the British Isles Church of the Nazarene for the next four decades.

George Brown as the first of these. He was from the Lambhill Mission Hall in Glasgow and came into contact with J.B. Maclagan while 'J.B.' was minister of the Parkhead church. Another Scot who entered the Nazarene ministry through contact with Mr Maclagan at Parkhead was T.C. Mitchell. Most of the others were English and had studied at Emmanuel Bible College, Birkenhead. W.S. Tranter, a former student of Emmanuel and pastor of the Emmanuel Church in Birmingham, went to the Gelderd Road church in Leeds in 1943, moving in 1945 to the Skegoneill Avenue church in Belfast. Ernest Eades had been brought up in the I.H.M. Tabernacle in Battersea and entered the Nazarene ministry in 1944 along with William Russell and Thomas Schofield. They were also Emmanuel students. Tom Schofield belonged to the Morley church and was the only one of this group who came from a Nazarene church. William Russell from Dublin graduated from Emmanuel Bible College and was granted a minister's licence along with Tom Schofield and Ernie Eades in 1944.

The next year, 1945, Mr Frame recruited Leslie Roberts and Sydney Martin. Leslie Roberts was the lay pastor of an independent Holiness Mission in Ilkeston in Derbyshire which united with the Church of the Nazarene that year. Sydney Martin had been brought up in Co. Durham in the Methodist Church and had been in the regular British Army. Since his conversion Sydney and Bessie Martin had run the Sandes Soldiers' Home near the army barracks in Catterick. He became minister of the church in Twechar, a mining village in Dunbartonshire, living with his family in the church hall until the men of the congregation built a new manse with bricks from a demolished factory chimney. David and Joy Tarrant, who had worked in the civil service in Llandudno during the war, moved to Ilkeston and joined the Holiness Mission there just after it had become a Nazarene church. David Tarrant became pastor of the new church in Carlisle while undertaking studies for ordination.

One very welcome recruit to the British Isles district was the Rev Fletcher Tink. In 1945, J.B. Maclagan had left Parkhead to accept the call to be superintendent minister of the I.H.M. based in Battersea. He had battled heroically to keep the Parkhead church open and active through the war. Young men had been called up into the forces, those at home were working long hours for the war effort, and children had been evacuated to the countryside because of the danger of bombing. Not surprisingly, membership had declined.

But even more heroic was the decision of Fletcher and Vernita Tink to come from Canada with their three children to share in the austerity and privations of post-war Britain. The country was suffering extreme austerity, having expended her considerable national wealth in the First World War and become a debtor nation in order to fight the Second World War. Cities had been bombed, trade had been dislocated, conditions were extremely difficult, and the winters at the end of the forties were particularly severe. Rationing severely limited diet and clothes were patched till they were old and sad. Glasgow in any case was a depressingly grey city in 1945, adding thick black winter fogs to its overcast skies, its once honey-coloured sandstone buildings turned black by decades of coal smoke.

The Tinks, a handsome young couple from the new world who were excellent musicians, came as a breath of fresh air. Vernita Tink played the cornet and her husband was a gospel pianist, fascinating his audience by his skill on the keyboard. Bright, positive and optimistic, they filled Parkhead church with 'Songfests' following the Sunday evening service and attended by people from miles around. The wide gallery would be filled with young people singing their hearts out and enjoying the latest gospel music from America.

The Hynds came home in 1946 for what was only their second furlough with their three children, Isabel, Samuel and Margaret. Since there had been no one to relieve the doctor at the hospital and with the war-time conditions, they had not been home since 1932. That was twice the normal seven-year period between furloughs. Mrs Hynd's mother, Mrs Sharpe, had died in 1943, and although her father was fit and active, this was to be the last time they were to be together. He was looked after at his house in Mount Vernon by his youngest daughter and son-in-law, Isabel and Victor Edwards. Samuel Hynd, having already graduated in science from Witswaterand University, stayed behind in Glasgow to start his medical studies.

In 1949, the international connections of the Church of the Nazarene produced another encouragement. Dr Samuel Young, whose family had been charter members of the Parkhead church in 1906 and had emigrated to the U.S.A. in 1916, returned in 1950 as a general superintendent to conduct the district assembly. It was a remarkable case of the old headline, 'Local boy makes good!' Sam Young had been converted under George Sharpe's ministry and had become a member of the Parkhead church in 1915. In the United States, he had entered the Nazarene ministry after graduating from Eastern Nazarene College and Boston University, and had been ordained in 1931. He had been head of the department of Theology at ENC (one of the six Nazarene liberal arts colleges at that time) and had been elected president of the College in 1945. At the general assembly in 1948, he had been elected one of the five general superintendents of the Church of the Nazarene. Many of the older members at Parkhead remembered the Young family, and one who was especially delighted to see him was his old Sunday school teacher, Robert Tanner.[2]

---

2 According to the author's father, this faithful old Sunday school teacher, the father of Dr Mary Tanner and Jean Tanner, was a keen supporter of the temperance movement. In the 1940s someone was alarmed to find a body in

Hurlet Nazarene College

By this time, Mr Frame had launched his most heroic venture - a theological college. In 1943 the British Isles district bought West Hurlet House for £4,000. A Georgian mansion built about 1830 with later Victorian additions; it was set in ten acres of land in the Renfrewshire countryside between the towns of Paisley and Barrhead and near the boundary of the city of Glasgow. Mr and Mrs Frame and their son Cyril moved into the mansion, giving up their home in Uddingston and paying rent to help meet the expenses. Mr Frame became principal of the new venture, Hurlet Nazarene College, although he only drew his salary as district superintendent. Here was a third attempt to found a College to prepare ministers to the highest standard.

Classes began in September, 1944, with two full-time students from the Morley church, Arthur Smith and Leslie Newton. Some of the newly licensed ministers had further studies to complete for ordination, including Ernest Eades, William Russell and Sydney Martin. When the war ended in the summer of 1945, Alfred Milliken and Hugh Rae, both from Troon, joined the full-time student body. In September, 1946, a further six students were enrolled, three from Ireland and three from England. Instruction was undertaken by Dr Sharpe (who became eighty in 1945, but was still very active), by George Frame, James Macleod and Arthur Fawcett (who were all university graduates), and by other visiting pastor-teachers such as J.D. Lewis, William Robertson and David Anderson. Two young M.A. graduates from Parkhead also taught classes, Jean Cameron (whose father, Alex Cameron, was long-serving church secretary and choir master), and Margaret Taylor, the sister of the late Rev William Taylor.

The cost of the College had to be borne at first by the British Isles district with fewer than a thousand members all suffering the post-war austerity. The possibility of asking the Calvary Holiness Church to join the project was considered, but in 1946, the General Board of the Church of the Nazarene recognized Hurlet as an official Nazarene

---

the roof-space of the Parkhead church, but it turned out to be a dummy which Bob Tanner had used to illustrate the ravages of drink! The Sunday school boys (including my father!) nick-named him 'One-and-sixpence', but the joke will only be understood by Scots over fifty.

College alongside the six colleges in the States and one in Canada and agreed that it would receive an annual grant of £300 to £400.

The large mansion was very sparsely furnished. Miss Baxter supplied old but good, hard-wearing carpeting which had already given twenty years' service in Peacocks' restaurants. This covered the lounge and the large central stair-case, but in most of the rest of the old building there were bare boards or linoleum. The building was heated with one coal fire and the winter drafts whistled through the doors and windows. Iron beds and bedding were purchased from army surplus. The College could not afford desks until 1950. The Rev Peter Clark assumed the responsibility of dean of students and business manager from 1948 until he retired in 1952, being paid £3 per week plus room and board for himself and his wife.

The Late Forties

By the time the Clarks came to Hurlet, Dr Sharpe had died. Active to the last, and planning a visit to Swaziland, he took ill and died suddenly during the district assembly of 1948. Dr G.B. Williamson was the presiding general superintendent at that assembly – a memorable one at which Williamson intervened to persuade the delegates to re-elect George Frame when it appeared that he was about to be voted out. But it was fitting that so many representatives were already at Parkhead to take part in a triumphant funeral on the day after the district assembly, when the life and ministry of George Sharpe was celebrated with thanksgiving.

Not everyone was sure that the Hurlet venture was wise. Some thought that it was foolhardy and that the building was a 'white elephant'. Others questioned the timing and whether the district had the necessary resources. Some thought that it was the wrong time when conditions were so difficult. Dr Sharpe's son-in-law, Victor Edwards, who served on the Board of Trustees, had particular worries about the soundness of West Hurlet House, believing it to be unsound owing to nearby underground workings and dry rot. He had already crossed swords with the district superintendent over finances, and wanted to sell the property and relocate the College at the coast. The debate continued for the first six months of 1949, but in the end the other trustees unanimously supported Mr Frame.

Victor Edwards was right about the dry rot. But in 1948, the general convention of the Nazarene Young People's Society, meeting in St Louis, had decided to make Hurlet Nazarene College their special project and to raise $10,000 dollars. The British Commonwealth representative on the general N.Y.P.S council, T.E. Martin, visited Hurlet in 1949 to present the cheque, and everyone was farther cheered by the fact that a recent devaluation of the pound made it even more valuable! The dry rot was repaired and many other necessary improvements made.

The year 1949 also saw the loss of Arthur Fawcett who resigned from the Uddingston church to undertake further studies at Glasgow University. Eventually completing a doctorate in church history,[3] he entered the ministry of the Church of Scotland, becoming minister of Johnstone High Parish Church for the rest of his ministry. This was a considerable loss. Fawcett was a man of intellectual ability, a stimulating teacher and powerful preacher, whose early experience in trekking and in his first pastorate at Bolton made him an engaging evangelist as well as a good pastor. The students were aware however that there was a certain tension between Fawcett and Frame, two strong characters who saw matters somewhat differently.

But in 1950, help arrived in the form of J. Kenneth Grider, a young American who had graduated from Olivet Nazarene College in Illinois and the newly-established Nazarene Theological Seminary in Kansas City. Joe Grider (as he was more commonly known at that time) was beginning PhD research in the Divinity Faculty at Glasgow, and he came with his wife Virginia to live at Hurlet and teach theology. That same year, Olivet Nazarene College recognized George Frame's courage and achievement by awarding him an honorary D.D., but those two happy developments were overshadowed by the increasing illness of Mrs Frame, who died early in 1951.

Despite George Frame's financial worries, his double load as College Principal and District Superintendent, and the crushing blow of the death of his wife, these years saw considerable growth in the churches

---

3 Published version: Arthur Fawcett, *The Cambuslang Revival* (Edinburgh: Banner of Truth, 1971)

of the British Isles district. Ten churches were added to the district in the years from 1945 to 1953, but only those in Chesterfield, Cosham in Portsmouth, Glenmore Street in the Ballymaccarett area of Belfast, and Battersea in London, had a sufficient nucleus of members to promise further growth. The churches in Chesterfield and Cosham had been independent missions, while the church in Ballymacarrett was started afresh by a home mission effort. But the addition in Battersea was none other than Speke Hall, Reader Harris's original mission which became the Clapham Junction Church of the Nazarene. By 1950, the great old days were a distant memory and its membership had declined to about 50. Under J.S. Logan and his assistant, William Claydon, Speke Hall decided to unite with the Church of the Nazarene. J.S. Logan became an evangelist, eventually moving to the States, and Fletcher Tink moved from Parkhead to Clapham Junction to guide the old mission hall as it adopted the Nazarene constitution and order. Overall, the membership of the British Isles district increased from 978 in 1945 to 1,407 in 1953. The enrolment of children and young people in Sunday school rose from 2,271 in 1945 to 3,293 in 1953, and in 1947 the Nazarene youth organizations, the 'Trailblazers' for boys and the 'Pathfinders' for girls were introduced to Britain. Membership of the Nazarene Young People's Society increased from 241 in 1945 to 488 in 1953.

Hugh Rae became president of the district N.Y.P.S. council in 1947. Having completed his studies at Hurlet Nazarene College, he went on in 1949, with the encouragement of Arthur Fawcett, to study at Glasgow University, graduating with the M.A. degree in 1952. Under his leadership, the district N.Y.P.S. council organized a summer youth conference in 1949 at Cormiston Towers, a large country house in the Scottish Borders adapted for use as a youth hostel. Adopting from the American N.Y.P.S. the curious name of 'Institute', these summer conferences, held in one of the many country houses which had been adapted as residential conference centres, enormously strengthened the Nazarene youth work. In contrast to campaigns and revivals which were generally strong in spiritual challenge, but could be weaker in content and teaching, these youth conferences challenged Nazarene youth intellectually. The Institute committee (at first Hugh Rae, Sydney Martin, Samuel Hynd and Christine Whitehurst) arranged a week's programme of events which included lectures and discussion groups in the morning, outings and sports in the afternoon and various games and amusements in the evening. Fawcett, Tink, Lown and Martin were favourite lecturers stimulating thought and debate. Cormiston Towers, Wiston Lodge near Biggar or Dene House near Alloa, resounded to the singing and laughter of an energetic and fun-loving group of sixty or seventy young people. The sense of camaraderie and group identity which this forged (not least as the time and place where relationships were formed leading to stable marriages!) gave a new unity to the British Isles district. Needless to say, with such a high-spirited group, pranks and practical jokes figured largely. One which went seriously wrong almost set one country house on fire! But after the fire engine had gone, such was the good impression the young people had made that the manageress refused payment (since insurance would cover the damage) and insisted that they come back the next year and as often as they wished.

For some years the trustees of Hurlet Nazarene College were aware of the need for a full-time principal, and at last, with Hugh Rae about to graduate, Dr Frame found the man he believed could fill that role. He was only thirty-one, but George Frame was always on the side of the youthful and vigorous. When Peter Clark retired as dean in 1952, he was appointed dean. Two years later in April, 1954, the trustees (Dr Frame, James Macleod, Sydney Martin, Walter Neil of Twechar and W.A. Noble of Parkhead) elected the Rev Hugh Rae, M.A. as principal.

The first twelve years of George Frame's superintendency thus showed considerable progress. But if the founding of the College was his most courageous achievement, recognized by the conferring of an honorary D.D. by Olivet Nazarene College in 1948, the union of two English holiness groups with the Church of the Nazarene was perhaps an even greater tribute to his vision and statesmanship.

Union with the I.H.M.

At the beginning of the Second World War, the leadership of the I.H.M. still lay with the laymen on the council, David Thomas's younger contemporaries, now rather elderly! A meeting with the leaders of the C.H.C. was arranged after Maynard James had approached Wain and Dunning in 1938, and on 30th October, 1939, not long after the outbreak of war, representatives of the two movements met in Bolton. Both groups participated in the forming of the National Holiness Association in 1942, and a reconciliation was effected when representatives met at the Battersea Tabernacle on 27th September, 1946. They met again on 4th March, 1948 to discuss reunion, but the I.H.M. decided to postpone the question.

By this time the ranks of the leadership were thinning. G.D. Holmes had died in 1942 and B.H. Dunning in 1945. Leonard Wain had a serious illness in 1949, and in 1951, since the I.H.M. had been incorporated as a company, a Board of Trade rule that executives must retire at age 70 removed him, along with Lucas, Lane, Evans and Seekings from the council. George Walker was elected president to succeed Wain at Easter, 1951, but died a few weeks later in May.

But the real leadership of the I.H.M. had passed by then to the new superintendent minister. The council may still have held the legal authority, but age had robbed them of any real ability to lead, and the real leadership of the movement had passed to the dynamic and warm-hearted Scotsman they had invited to join them in 1945, James Baxter Maclagan. The arrival of 'J.B.' in Battersea was a revolution. To his out-going optimistic character, he now added years of experience in the ministry, and he brought with him to the mission a sense of the dignity of worship which he saw as part of being a 'real church'. Things should be done 'decently and in order'. The rich tradition of British hymnody was part of his upbringing in the Parkhead church and so he introduced the Methodist hymnbook for Sunday morning worship. But that did not mean stiff formality. Far from it! 'J.B.' believed in 'aggressive evangelism' (in the popular phrase coined by Catherine Booth), and his concertina along with his clear Scottish accent with its characteristic, over-definite pronunciation brought a new attraction to the open-air services. One of his first moves was to visit Harry and Bessie Wood, who were attending a Baptist church, and invite them to come back to the I.H.M. A life-long friendship was formed and Mr Wood, who was with the Bank of England, embodied in one man a first-class treasurer and an excellent organist. Maclagan's warmth and sound doctrinal preaching was soon attracting new faces to the Battersea Tabernacle.

Although his friend George Frame may have been taken aback at Maclagan's departure to the I.H.M. (he always tended to see leaving the Church of the Nazarene as a 'betrayal'), 'J.B.' seems to have had in mind the possibility that accepting the invitation of the I.H.M. council might lead to union. From the time he went to Battersea, Nazarene terms and methods began to appear and, according to Jack Ford, there was an increasing desire there for a more democratic form of government.[4] Dr Frame was invited to the October convention in Bolton in 1951 and asked to see the council. Exploratory committees were appointed by both sides and favourably received by the I.H.M. council, who then in April, 1952 received Dr Frame and Dr Hardy C. Powers, the general superintendent presiding that year at the Nazarene district assembly. After they had given them some insight into the administration of the Church of the Nazarene, Powers and Frame withdrew and the council came to its decision. Jack Ford later wrote:

> Many factors must have been at work at that critical moment: the need of the South African field; the desire for a more democratic form of government; Maclagan's influence; the advantage of belonging to a larger denomination; the vacant presidential chair. The decision was almost unanimous.

On 29th October, 1952, in the Zion Methodist Church in Leeds, the International Holiness Mission formally united with the Church of the Nazarene. Twenty-four churches with a thousand members, nine ordained and nine licensed ministers and thirty-two missionaries with almost two thousand members in South Africa were added to the denomination.[5] The next day, 30th October, the joyful occasion was made yet more joyful by Dr Frame's marriage to Dr Mary Tanner.

In May, 1953, delegates from all the Nazarene churches in Britain met in the Morley Church of the Nazarene under the presiding general superintendent, Dr D.I. Vanderpool, and promptly formed two district assemblies. The British Isles North District included churches in Scotland, all of Ireland (although there were only churches in Northern

4 Ford, *In the Steps*, 129.

5 The ordained ministers were A.J. Lown, Wm Henson, John T. Henson, James R. Rigby, H. Baldwin, M. Carlile, J. Bell, J.B. Maclagan and A.L. Baxter: the licensed ministers were W.J.R. Wescott, John Townend, E.E. Dean, G. Palmer, N. Robinson, J. Moore, J.R. Weatherill, P. Mallender and Wm Lavery. For the thirty-two I.H.M. missionaries, see Chapter 7.

Ireland), and the four northern counties of England – Cumberland, Westmorland, Northumberland and Durham. George Frame was elected as superintendent of British Isles North District and his old friend and colleague, J.B. Maclagan, became superintendent of British Isles South, which included the churches in the rest of England and Wales. The two district advisory boards, elected by the district assemblies would meet as the British Isles executive council to transact business (such as the funds from the Pawson estate) affecting both districts.

The Problems of the C.H.C.

By 1952, problems were also mounting for the Calvary Holiness Church. The decade of the forties had brought some advances. The outbreak of war brought out a strain of pacifism, stronger in the C.H.C. than in the I.H.M. or the British Church of the Nazarene. Ravenhill was the strongest pacifist, Ford did not believe that a Christian could be a combatant but ought to undertake other work to help the war effort, and James, while he believed that a Christian minister ought not to fight (and perhaps not a layman), believed that there was a national duty to restrain an aggressor. Ford expressed his view in an editorial in *The Flame*, but it was balanced by a note from James.

Throughout the war, the Easter and autumn conventions and evangelistic campaigns continued. Thirteen tent campaigns were held, and seven small churches were established or joined the movement, including those in Sale, Llay, the Roath district of Cardiff, Bath, Bromley, Mossley near Ashton-under-Lyne and Walthamstow. The Cardiff and Grimsby missions previously affiliated with the I.H.M. transferred allegiance to the C.H.C. In Ashton-under-Lyne, the Old Cross Mission, begun in 1874 and affiliated with Star Hall from 1912 until Star Hall was given to the Salvation Army in 1918, joined the C.H.C. in 1942. Twenty-three new ministers were recruited during the war, but fifteen resigned. George Deakin and Cyril Pass, who both demonstrated administrative ability, were added to the executive council, and a genuine attempt was made to involve local church deacons and lay members of the council in decision-making. The Calvary Holiness Church Sunday School Union reported 109 teachers and 741 scholars at Easter 1941, and a youth organization, the Calvary Holiness Church Covenanters, was launched.

The Flame reached the highest circulation in its history in 1941, 25,000 copies, and the C.H.C. participated in the united prayer conference at Emmanuel Bible College in May, 1942 which led to the formation of the National Holiness Association. Two more missionaries sailed for Colombia at the end of 1940, Samuel E. Heap and Gwladys Jones.[6] In 1947 the seven missionaries abroad were joined by four others. Bessie Southall went to India in 1946, followed by Mr and Mrs R. Brown the next year, and Hilda Hartley in 1948. All of those developments were very encouraging. Moreover, Beech Lawn Bible College with seven students and James as principal was established in 1947 at Uppermill, a village close to the moors above Oldham, largely made possible by a gift from H.H. Hales. The following year the College moved to a larger house in Stalybridge some miles to the south. There were sixteen students by 1950.

However, other post-war trends were worrying. Out of five tent campaigns in the later forties, only one, at Rotherham, resulted in a permanent church. Further, financial strains became evident. Jack Ford later wrote, 'The giving of members was creditable and the sacrifice of the ministers and missionaries bordered on the heroic.' But despite that churches were defaulting on their payments to the central funds.

The income for overseas missions also decreased and the devaluation of the pound in 1949, which brought such joy at Hurlet Nazarene College, made the support of the C.H.C. missionaries in Colombia even more difficult. Clifford Filer advised the council in 1946 that the Heaps and the Thomases were almost at the end of their physical resources and it was decided that they should be brought home. But they had to return when the Filers' re-entry permits were held up. To make matters worse the very capable missionary secretary, George Deakin, adopted the Pentecostalist view that 'tongues' were the necessary evidence of the baptism of the Spirit and resigned. The leader of the youth work resigned in frustration at the lack of progress.

---

6 May Kneebone was also a C.H.C. missionary in Colombia.

At the heart of all this, Maynard James was unhappy with administration, grudged the time spent in committee meetings and had a fear of over-organization. Cyril Pass, a key administrator, resigned in 1948 to go to South Africa. Randolph Murray, a leading minister, left to become pastor of Zion Holiness Church in Birmingham. Leonard Ravenhill resigned in 1951 to become an itinerant evangelist and went to the United States. The problems of the mission field deepened in the early 1950s. In 1950 the Filers at last received their permission to return to Colombia after four years at home, but they soon came to the conclusion that there was not enough finance to sustain the work. They returned home at the end of 1952. The College saw a similar decline. Jack Ford became principal in 1950, but by 1954 the number of students had dropped to five, and he resigned.

But to cap all these problems, the issue of the gift of 'tongues' reared its head. Some of the recruits to the ministry placed more emphasis on the gifts than the founders had, and it became a concern to James and Ford that their 'holiness' denomination might turn into a Pentecostal one. As Ford later wrote: 'For the gifts to be permitted was one thing: for them to become paramount was another.' They realized that union with a larger body like the Church of the Nazarene would guard against that, and from 1952, they became aware that the union of the I.H.M. and the Church of the Nazarene was working well.

Towards Union

James and Ford arranged a meeting with Dr Frame in a Leeds hotel on 6th September, 1954, and invited him to meet the C.H.C. council in Ashton-under-Lyne the next day. This led to a consultation of C.H.C. ministers on 27th October, but of the thirty present, fewer than a dozen were definitely in favour of union. George Frame and J.B. Maclagan joined the consultation in the evening and answered questions on baptism, divorce, the gifts of the Spirit and pastors' stipends. The minutes of the meeting summed up the gist of Dr Frame's emphasis: 'Our job as the Church of the Nazarene is not to propagate or practise the gifts of the Spirit, but to emphasize the definite experience of full salvation.'

After they retired a vote was taken, twenty voting in favour of steps to union. It was agreed that members of the council would visit the

C.H.C. churches and if there was sufficient support would call a delegates conference to vote on setting up committees to consider union. There was considerable hesitation among some ministers however, and one sent out an open letter inviting those who preferred a reorganization of the Calvary Holiness Church to make their desire known. To avoid a split James immediately countered this with another open circular emphasizing that the C.H.C. would either unite as body with the Church of the Nazarene or remain independent.

Maynard James also wrote to Dr Frame setting out the position of the Calvary Holiness Church on the baptism of the Spirit and the gifts of the Spirit:

> We affirm as the Calvary Holiness Church that we are one with the Church of the Nazarene in the glorious doctrine of entire sanctification, wrought by the Baptism with the Holy Ghost and fire and receivable by faith…
>
> (1) We do *not* believe that speaking in other tongues is the initial evidence of the Baptism of the Holy Spirit.
> (2) We do not deny that there may be a genuine gift of 'tongues' in operation today, and so we dare not adopt the unscriptural attitude of forbidding to speak in another tongue *provided* we are *sure* it is really of the Holy Spirit…
> (3) We believe that 'speaking in tongues' is the least of the nine gifts… Time and again it has been found that its unwise use in the Church assemblies has led to strife, spiritual pride and division… Therefore … we feel, after painful experience, that we cannot encourage our people to speak in other tongues in Church gatherings…
> (4) We believe that the infallible proofs of a spirit-filled life are (a) purity of heart (Acts 15:8-9), (b) the fruit of the Spirit (Galatians 5:22-23), (c) perfect love to God and men (Romans 5:5; I Timothy 1:5), (d) power for effective service (Acts 1:8).
> (5) If freedom of conscience be given to us on the aforementioned matters, and confidence be reposed in us as ministers of Christ to do all in our power to further the interests of Scriptural Holiness through the agency of the Church of the Nazarene, then we would gladly welcome the

> fusion of the C.H.C. into the Church of the Nazarene and would count it a privilege to serve as ministers in its ranks.

As Jack Ford later commented, this was essentially the position of James, Ford, Ravenhill and Filer at the founding of the C.H.C. They still refused to forbid speaking in 'tongues', but 'after painful experience' of strife and spiritual pride, they were now more cautious about permitting it.

At a meeting of C.H.C. ministers in Oldham on 16th December, he read this, and declared that if the Nazarenes accepted it, 'there was no reason which he could give to the Lord for staying outside of fusion.' He also reported that sixteen out of nineteen churches had voted in favour of union, with a total vote of two hundred for union, ninety against, and fifty-five doubtful. In a vote at the end of the meeting, it was agreed to move ahead, provided the Church of the Nazarene agreed to James's statement in the issue of 'tongues'.

The Nazarene general superintendents brought the question of union with the C.H.C. to the general board of the denomination at their meeting in Kansas City in January, 1955, and the British executive council was given authority to negotiate the basis of union. The council met the C.H.C. council at Beech Lawn in February and agreement was reached on a number of issues. The C.H.C. missionaries not in favour of union would be brought home at C.H.C. expense, and *The Flame*, edited by Maynard James, would become the British Nazarene magazine in place of *The Way*. The final decision about the location of a joint college would be made in two years. The major point for discussion was whether the members of the C.H.C. would be free to hold their view on the gifts of the Spirit. James was particularly concerned to ensure this, but Ford put forward a resolution which secured the agreement of all present:

> That the statement drawn up by our President, Rev Maynard G. James, which has been laid before the general superintendents of the Church of the Nazarene expresses the convictions of those of the Calvary Holiness Church concerning the gifts of the Spirit.

> We understand that, in welcoming us into the Church of the Nazarene, the authorities give us freedom to hold these convictions although they may not express the official Nazarene attitude.
>
> We join the Church of the Nazarene loyally accepting the Manual and desiring to serve with freedom of conscience as loyal Nazarenes.

All the C.H.C. churches except Hebden Bridge and Bradford voted in favour of union, and after Frame and Maclagan had addressed the delegates conference and taken part in full discussion, James put the motion, seconded by Ford, that 'we fuse with the Church of the Nazarene.' It was approved by thirty-five votes to one. On 11th June, in the Houldsworth Hall in Manchester, the union was celebrated under the chairmanship of general superintendent Dr Samuel Young.

Dr George and Mrs Emily Frame with their son, Cyril

The $10,000 dollar cheque being presented to a beaming George Frame. Left to right: Peter Clark, George Frame, Fletcher Tink, Sydney Martin, Ted Martin, David Anderson.

Staff and students at Hurlet Nazarene College, 1948: Front l. to r.: T.C. Mitchell, H. Rae, J. Green, D. Anderson, S. Doctorian, T.W. Schofield; Second row: A. Loney, A. Milliken, G. Stewart, E. Dunn; Third row: G.L. Francis, J. Paterson, R. Noble

Dr G.B. Williamson and the British Isles district fraternal, 1951. Seated l. to r: J.K. Grider, S. Martin, P. Clark, Dr G.B. Williamson, Dr G. Frame, D. Anderson, J.S. Logan: Second row: H. Tattersall, L. Newton, H. Rae, T. Wilson, G. Brown, S. Doctorian, W.S. Tranter, T.C. Mitchell, G. Stewart, P. Ferguson, E. Dunn, A. Milliken, W. Robertson; Third row: D. Dixon, D.J. Tarrant, W. Claydon, R. Deasley, T.W. Schofield, M. Brown; Fourth row: J.E. Crouch, J. Macdonald, L. Roberts, A. Spence, A. Tatnall, R. Emslie, J. Macleod, J.D. Lewis

The Union of the International Holiness Mission with the Church of the Nazarene: J.B. Maclagan makes a presentation to Dr Hardy Powers

The united band of ministers and lay leaders at the union of the I.H.M. with the Church of the Nazarene. Front row: W.B. Kelly, T.C. Mitchell, E. Dunn, D. Anderson, G. Brown, H. Baldwin, G. Stewart, A. Jones; second row: not known, R. Rigby, Mrs Rigby, Mrs Schofield, T.W. Schofield, D. Dixon, W. Russell, A. Spence; third row: not known, H.E. Wood, J. Macleod, Mrs Macleod, Mrs Neil, W. Neil, Mrs Ferguson, P. Ferguson, W.S Tranter; fourth row: Mrs Roberts, L. Roberts, R. Emslie, Mrs Emslie, J. Baxter, Mrs Bell, J. Bell, J. Henson, not known; fifth row: L. Newton, J. Green, A. Milliken, J. Townend, E.E. Dean, not known, G. Palmer, not known, L. Hands; sixth row: P. Clark, W. Claydon, not known, not known, Nurse Agnes Willox, Mrs Robertson, W. Robertson, not known, R. Deasley.

The Wedding of Dr George Frame and Dr Mary Tanner:
l. to r.: Dr and Mrs Frame and Mr and Mrs Maclagan

Guests at the Frame-Tanner Wedding: l. to r. Mrs A. Robertson and her sister, Miss M.K. Latta, Mrs D. Hynd, Miss Sarah Bedford and her sister, Mrs Edgar Edginton. (Edgar Edginton was the brother of the first Mrs Frame)

Dr Samuel Young

Four Evangelists: Alex Jones, John Crouch, Hugh Rae & Cyril Frame Cosham 1950

Staff and students at Hurlet Nazarene College (1956-57)
Seated: W. Henson, D.J. Tarrant, S. Martin, H. Rae, Mrs Rae with Marjory, Miss M. Tumilson (later Mrs Reaney), J.T. Henson. Mrs Anderson (widow of D. Anderson) stands behind Mrs Rae, and J. Reaney and W.B. Kelly at the right. In the back row, Ian Robertson from Edinburgh (whose ministry has been in the USA) and Wm Stewart from Perth (life-long ministry in Canada) are 3rd and 4th from the left, and Eric Lucas of Bolton is 3rd from the right.

The British Isles south district fraternal, 1960.
Front row: G. Thomas, T.C. Mitchell, H. Rae, J. Ford, J.B. Maclagan, G. Ferguson, M. Carlile, T.W. Schofield, J. Jones. Second row: A. Spence, G.J. Green, J. Baxter, J. Bell, D. McCulloch, Snr, W. Robertson, W.S. Tranter, R. Rigby, J. Mason. Third row: W.B. Kelly, E. Gough, J. Baillie, M. Quick, E.E. Dean, G. Palmer, M. Winterburn, J. Brown, R. Quantz. Fourth row: D. Thirkell, N. Robinson, W. Lewis, R. Gillespie, D. Upton, F. Upton, F. Webster
Back row: J. Weatherill, W. Russell, G. Nunn, P. Gentry, L. Hands

George Sharpe...as I remember him
Sydney Martin

While at Hurlet I learned that Dr Sharpe was to be my tutor in Homiletics and for this I was to have good reason to be grateful. Both the man and his teaching impressed me. Those who knew him frequently saw him as an austere figure. He certainly was a demanding and exacting tutor, but his salutary discipline proved to be ideally suited to my needs. For instance, he convinced me that, beyond peradventure, preaching was a prime factor in the pastoral situation; that if this was to succeed, sermons must be prepared with consistent thoroughness and that the principles of homiletical structure would be diligently observed. Moreover, he strenuously refused to accept the notion that the time and effort spent in meeting such practical requirements would necessarily be to the detriment of routine pastoral care.

But his teaching methods were by no means limited to the classroom. As evidence of this I well remember being 'invited' to a certain holiness convention. The prospect was a daunting one yet, to my surprise – and relief! – I found him to be a sympathetic listener. However it was through my listening to him that I was to learn infinitely more. Nor can I forget the particular date when the most sensational lesson was given, in August 6th, 1945. On that fateful morning the headlines screamed the news that the atom bomb had been dropped on Hiroshima! How immense was my relief as I learned that I was not due to preach that day! Fifty years later and more have elapsed since then so that I cannot recollect the precise text Dr Sharpe used, but no one who heard it is likely to forget the impact of what was, virtually, his extempore discourse.

Returning to the more prosaic atmosphere of the classroom, one was to listen with still greater concentration to lectures on the subject of holiness as 'the many-splendoured thing' that it is. And by the time the course had ended I knew that I'd been sitting at the feet of one for whom the preaching of holiness was his *raison d'être*, the most demanding yet the most rewarding of all ministries.

Thus did Dr Sharpe by his total and passionate commitment to the call of God, become the human agency through whom my own call to live and labour towards the same end were confirmed. On March 27th, 1948 my erstwhile tutor and mentor passed to his reward. As I sat by his death-bed just shortly before his passing I thanked the God of all grace for having known one whom I had counted it a privilege to call a true father in God.

George Sharpe...as I remember him
R.F. Tink

The Rev Fletcher Tink wrote this recollection of Dr Sharpe for The Way of Holiness, *Vol. II, No. 9 (June-August, 1948).*

It was during a camp meeting in New York, under the inspired ministry of Dr George Sharpe that my father, a Methodist minister, re-dedicated his life to the preaching of holiness. Thus, the influence of Dr Sharpe had been felt in my parents' home long before my wife and I met him at the dock in Liverpool upon our arrival from Canada. Though we were strangers in a strange land, the kindness and consideration he showed to us in escorting us to Glasgow, provided us with many happy remembrances.

In the Parkhead church, of which he was the founder, Dr Sharpe was greatly loved by the congregation. It was an extraordinary experience to become the pastor of the one who had begun the church so many years ago, yet his co-operation and helpfulness were so marked that it was a pleasure to be associated with him. When the church decided to honour him with the title of *minister emeritus*, I was glad to join with the local church in conferring this honour upon him.

Rev George Sharpe *was a Christian gentleman.* Only a few days before his death, he raised himself in bed, shook my hand with the courtesy and graciousness that was so typical of him, and thanked me for conducting worship and praying with him.

Parkhead church, the British Isles district of the Church of the Nazarene, the ministers, and the cause of holiness in Britain had lost a true minister of the full gospel, and a leader of men, and Mrs Tink and I have lost a real friend.

Peter Clark...as I remember him
Hugh Rae

One of the earliest men to enter the ministry of the Pentecostal Church of Scotland was Peter Clark. He had been greatly influenced by the Pentecostal League of Prayer and in his early twenties he came in touch with George Sharpe and Parkhead Pentecostal Church. As one of the first students in the College of 1909 he was influenced in his ministry by the scholarship of Olive Winchester who, along with George and Jane Sharpe were formative in preparing the young Peter Clark for ministry. He was an excellent student. He had joined the Parkhead church and in 1911 was a delegate from that church to the district assembly. He tried to lay the foundation for a church in his native Forfar, but in 1916 the Clarks moved to Gildersome where work had been started under the direction of Rev J. E. Watson, pastor of the Morley congregation. After four years in Gildersome he and his family moved to the Uddingston Church of the Nazarene where he continued until his election in 1924 to the office of district superintendent. Peter Clark's delivery style was very slow and very much that of the older tradition but his sermons were remarkable for their content. It was remarked by one of his peers that the need was to speed Peter Clark up and slow J.D. Lewis down!

At the 1928 district assembly he was disappointed not to be re-elected as district superintendent and he accepted a call to Edmonton First Church in Alberta. Returning in 1937, he became minister at Port Glasgow, served as district secretary, and then moved in the 1940s to Perth. He served some years as dean of students at Hurlet Nazarene College before he and his wife retired to Forfar.

During the summer of 1953, after the death of Mrs. Clark, Peter spent time at the College. We were troubled with rabbits and Peter suggested that he would lay snares and have rabbit stew, but after about ten days there was no sign of a rabbit being caught. Suddenly outside the window of the kitchen I saw a stoat killing a rabbit. I suggested to Leslie Evans, who was working at the College for the summer, that we put the dead rabbit into one of the snares. Mr. Clark appeared in triumph! But of course we could not cook it and finally had to confess what we had done. I still feel ashamed when I think of the prank. Now that I am 'old' I feel even worse!

Arthur Fawcett... as I remember him

Hugh Rae

Arthur Fawcett was born in Doncaster and after a grammar school education worked in the offices of a mining company. He found Christ and began to serve the Lord. With a friend, Thomas Palmer, who later became a missionary in Argentina, he would go out into the country on Friday nights and preach in the open air or go to visit and clean house for the elderly. This sense of call to service found him as a student at Emmanuel Bible and Missionary Training College in Birkenhead. He was one of the I.H.M trekkers and when, after an amazing revival campaign in Bolton, they established a congregation, Arthur Fawcett became the first pastor and a legend in his own time. He suffered from poor eyesight, but was a widely read man and a preacher of considerable influence. He left Bolton with a thriving congregation, and indeed for them he was the preacher-pastor without peer. While many of his sympathies lay with the young men like James and Ford in the division of 1934, he was unwilling to join them in the break from the I.H.M. He became the editor of the *Holiness Journal* and a prolific writer.

In 1941 he came to succeed George Frame as pastor of the Uddingston Church of the Nazarene. Frame had studied for his MA while pastor at Uddingston and Fawcett proceeded to follow his example. He was a great favourite with young people and his teaching and preaching saw him a frequent guest at their functions and holidays. I was introduced to him in 1942 when he came to preach in Troon. He encouraged me to get university entrance and his encouragement was further heightened when I became a student at Hurlet College. He taught English Literature. There were many tensions between Frame and Fawcett, possibly because of their different church backgrounds. They used to sit at opposite ends of the dining room table at Hurlet with their supporters around them. Fawcett in my opinion would have made an excellent principal but the diverse views of these two made that difficult if not impossible. Fawcett proceeded to complete his BD at Glasgow, then resigned his church and worked on his PhD in church history. He became the parish minister at Johnstone High Church of Scotland where he remained past retirement age. He taught at the Bible Training Institute in Glasgow for many years and was a popular speaker on the 'Late Call' programme of Scottish Television.

J. Kenneth Grider… as I remember him
Hugh Rae

It was in the summer of 1950 that 'Joe' Grider arrived with his wife, Virginia, at Hurlet Nazarene College. He had been brought up in a Roman Catholic family out in the Ozarks and when he had an evangelical conversion he immersed himself in his new faith, studying at Olivet Nazarene College, Nazarene Theological Seminary and at Drew. He had come to work at Glasgow University for his PhD and George Frame enlisted him to teach at Hurlet. He and Virginia lived in a little room at the top of the building with little space and little furniture. By then I was also a student at Glasgow University and we used to meet from time to time. He also began a life-long friendship with Tom Mitchell.

He was the epitome of the absent-minded professor and many are the tales that are told. On one occasion, he demonstrated how he tried to remember arrangements. We agreed to meet at the university to play table tennis. 'Hugh,' he said, 'Let's meet at 3.58.' 'Why not four o'clock?' I asked. 'Because you might forget four o'clock,' he said, 'but you won't forget 3.58.' (That was right of course. I still remember it after fifty-five years!)

While they were in Scotland his wife gave birth to their first child, Jennifer, and on one occasion when Virginia asked him to watch the baby while she got ready to go shopping. The baby was in the pram and he stood rocking it gently while reading a book. He did not observe Virginia come in and lift the baby and hurry off to Paisley, and when she returned, he was still reading and gently rocking the empty pram! On another occasion, she developed a headache during the night and sent him off down to the kitchen to get her some aspirin. When he returned and lay down to sleep, she asked, 'What about the aspirin, dear?' 'Oh yes,' he replied, 'I took it!' Later in America, he went out to post some letters and Virginia asked him to collect some groceries. He returned with the mail, but had put the groceries in the mail box! Many other stories could be told.

The Griders left Scotland in 1952 and after teaching for a short time at Olivet, he became professor of theology at Nazarene Theological Seminary in Kansas City, a post he held for thirty-eight years. During general assemblies held there, the Griders would fill their house with British delegates. His two years at Hurlet made a significant contribution to the education of students who spent a life-time in ministry in the British Isles.

James Baxter Maclagan ... as I remember him
Hugh Rae

I was very familiar with the name of 'J.B.' many years before I met him. In the twenties and thirties he had given proof of his leadership and pastoral gifts. It was as a pastor that he was especially gifted. His work in Port Glasgow gave that church a firm foundation, and there are still people in Perth who remember the impact of that short, dynamic preacher. Many stories are told of those days, and several come to mind.

The first recalls the attitude of some early holiness people to worldly sports. An occasional game of football at the Sunday school trip was one thing (Dr Sharpe was known to play as goalkeeper): but playing in any kind of organized league (even a churches' league) was frowned upon. News reached his home church in Parkhead that he was to play in a ministers' football team against the police. It is said that one of the 'saints' prayed in the prayer meeting that the Lord would intervene and in the event J.B. broke his leg. I rather think that that was an unfortunate accident rather than divine intervention!

While he was minister at Parkhead, I recall an open air meeting at the corner of Burgher Street right at Parkhead cross. Mr Maclagan was in good form, leading the singing with his concertina. A member of his congregation rushed past, explaining that he was off to a meeting at the Tent Hall, a large mission hall in the centre of Glasgow. J.B. turned to me and remarked: 'There goes a spiritual gipsy!' On another occasion at the open air, a man asked for prayer and Mr Maclagan took off his frock coat, laid it on the wet pavement, and knelt with the seeker to lead him to Christ.

While J.B. was at Parkhead, Jock Troup, who had been a leader in the Peterhead revival, was superintendent of the Tent Hall. Several young people from the Tent Hall and the Bethany Hall (another inner-city mission) had been attending holiness meetings at Parkhead church. Among those from the Bethany Hall was Thomas C. Mitchell, who was to become a steadfast friend and colleague. Once a group from the Tent Hall asked J.B. if they could become members of Parkhead church, and, not wishing to be a 'sheep-stealer', J.B. asked if they had spoken to Mr Troup about this. The surprising reply was that they had, and that Mr Troup had advised them to join. The following Monday, J.B. met Jock Troup at the 'Noon Prayer Meeting', where all the evangelical leaders of Glasgow used to meet each week in the Christian Institute in Bothwell Street. He asked him why he had advised the group to become members at Parkhead. 'Well,' was the reply, 'I realized that they would attract other young people away from the Tent Hall to follow them to Parkhead, so I thought it was better to cut my losses!'

A decade or so after Mr Maclagan left Glasgow to accept the call to London and the I.H.M., he was back in the city, and I took him to the St Andrews Halls for the premiere viewing of the Billy Graham film, 'Fire in the Heather.' I stood in the queue in amazement as he went up and down talking to everyone - people he remembered and many he had never met. Of course the clerical collar which J.B. always wore was in itself an introduction.

This ability to strike up conversations with perfect strangers was demonstrated on another occasion. After a meeting of the Board of Governors at the College in Manchester, I drove him to Victoria Station to catch his train. We had time for a cup of tea at the station, but before I had even noticed the gentleman sitting opposite us, J.B. was already in conversation with him. The conversation went like this:

J.B.: 'I see that you are wearing a Glasgow University scarf. My daughter went to that university.
How do you come to be in this part of the country?'

Reply: 'I have just been appointed the medical officer based in Lancaster.'

J.B.: 'Isn't that interesting. I will be in Lancaster in two weeks to induct a new minister, the Rev William Robertson, into our church there. You will be more than welcome to attend.'

I was amazed at the speed with which he had turned the conversation and given the stranger an invitation.

Mr Maclagan worked very hard as a district superintendent, trying to weld three different groups with three different traditions into one, a task that surely shortened his life. His death at the age of sixty-five was an immense loss. In my mind's eye I can still see him standing on the steps of the Kansas City auditorium at the general assembly in 1952, small of stature, playing his concertina and leading a great crowd in an impromptu time of singing well-known Nazarene gospel songs.

Willie Robertson... as I remember him
Hugh Rae

One of the men who entered the ministry in the early thirties was William Robertson, eldest son of James Robertson, one of the founding members of the Perth Church. Willie Robertson was very much the 'canny Scot' but a man of quiet demeanour and a hard working pastor. He followed J.B. Maclagan as pastor in Port Glasgow, then only established some five years. He seldom moved from his own pulpit and outside his local congregations few heard him preach. Nevertheless when he moved to new ministries he left behind a church which was well established. He followed David Anderson in Ardrossan. Again he had a steady ministry where, despite the war, he maintained the membership at an average of 47. He spent thirteen years in Ardrossan and it was while there, that his first wife took ill and died. His second wife was Helen Blair, a consecrated deaconess from the Ardrossan congregation. After their wedding they moved to Twechar where he exercised a particularly good ministry amongst the young people. He moved from Twechar to Lancaster and then ended his ministry as pastor of the Heysham church before retiring to his native Perth.

When I was a student in 1947 Willie Robertson came in place of Dr Sharpe to teach Homiletics. He was remembered by us all as the teacher who would preface every second or third sentence with, 'Jot this down boys!' Quite unusually for a Nazarene minister in those days he owned a lovely Jowet Javelin car. On one occasion he and his wife were coming to a ministers' fraternal held in Lancaster and they arrived by bus from Heysham. It was a very wet morning and when they arrived they were soaked to the skin. I asked him what was wrong with the car. He replied, 'Oh, it's much too wet to bring the car out!' A canny Scot indeed! But both he and his wife were industrious workers for the kingdom.

David Anderson... as I remember him
Hugh Rae

The Parkhead congregation provided the major source for ministers in the early years. Some like David Anderson were to have a deeply spiritual impact on many lives. Others like Murdoch Luke were to move quickly to other ministries. David Anderson ministered in a number of churches. Perhaps it was in Ardrossan, where he succeeded Robert Purvis, that he had his greatest ministry.

In the 1930s as I was growing up we were frequently without a pastor. David Anderson would come week after week to take the holiness meeting and Bible studies. I recall the interest which that aroused, and although I was a very young Christian in both senses I was greatly helped in my Christian life by this man of God. He was a very quiet gentle Christian. He married one of the Ardrossan congregation and they moved to Leeds to minister in Gelderd Road, then returned to Ayr and finally served in the Nazarene Publishing House office at Hurlet Nazarene College. He died suddenly in 1954 and was greatly mourned by his many colleagues and friends. A former student at Hurlet recalling in a letter to me his impressions of College commented that David Anderson was one of the saintliest men he had ever known.

Hugh Rae... as I remember him
Sydney Martin

Dr Martin wrote this reminiscence for Dr Rae's 'This is Your Life' when he retired in 1986.

During Hugh Rae's days as a Hurlet student there were one or two occasions when his driving did not quite match up to his academic achievements. One of these occurred when he was the student in charge of the literature van and in the course of his book-selling ventures visited Kilsyth. Although this is a small town it has one or two very steep hills, one of which leads into the heart of a large housing estate. Since I was familiar with the geography of the town it was suggested that I should accompany him. In the course of climbing Balmalloch hill while attempting to change down, Hugh missed the gear and, subsequently, the local residents were given a remarkable display of driving technique. Either because of a defect in the driving or in the mechanics of the van, probably both, and in spite of an engine roar which even Concorde might envy, the vehicle slowly but surely increased its speed – backwards! By some means, now unrecalled, the van was halted in its backward career. To my shocked surprise (for my driving experience was virtually nil) I was asked to take over and, still to my astonishment, the vehicle began to labour up the hill. By the time we reached the summit neither bell nor horn were needed to announce our arrival at the sales pitch. I cannot remember how many books we sold, but at least the advertising method was effective.

On a second occasion, when again I had the dubious pleasure of being his passenger, Dr Rae subjected me to an experience which, while not so spectacular as the former, was no less soul-shaking. He had taken me on a demonstration spin in his newly acquired but somewhat ancient BSA three-wheeler. Having accelerated to a speed which no such vehicle was built to achieve, Dr Rae was suddenly confronted with a king-sized pot-hole. Not having yet become accustomed to driving a car with two wheels up front but only one at centre back, the driver applied the traditional method of avoiding the pot-hole by lining up with the middle of the front axle. The result was predictable. Fortunately the vehicle did not leave the road, but the passenger, in those days before seat belts were thought of, certainly did leave his seat!

Robert Deasley... as I remember him
Hugh Rae

In the late 1930's while J.B. Maclagan was in Perth, he made contact with a group in the Cherryfield Mission in Dundee led by Robert Deasley. Bob Deasley was a man of strong and forceful character whose ministry was to reach far beyond the confines of the city of 'jute, jam and journalism'. He and the congregation of the mission joined the Church of the Nazarene and Robert Deasley continued as pastor. In the early forties he suffered a great loss in the death of his wife, leaving him with two young children, Mary and Alex. During this period he made a visit to Troon to preach for Leonard Holmes and visited our home. That was my first contact with this family who were to make such a significant contribution to the church.

Bob Deasley had a brusque Scottish approach to life and called a spade a spade (or sometime a shovel). Once when preaching in Govan for George Brown at an open-air service at Govan Cross, a notorious communist speaker heckled him. Bob turned to this man and challenged him to a public debate the following night at the same place. The mistake the communist made was in assuming that this man had gone to college or university and never been in the work place, whereas Bob had worked for a long number of years in a jute factory. Needless to say they had no further trouble during the mission.

In the mid-forties Robert Deasley assumed the pastorate of the Smallheath church in Birmingham. There he met his second wife who became the mother of two children, Margaret and Stephen. His influence on the youth of Smallheath was considerable and resulted in several young men, Leslie and Don Evans, Brian Farmer and his own son, Alex, entering the ministry. He used to take them out in to the streets to hold open air services, but they would only know whether they had to preach when one of them was called forward.

Another incident comes to mind. While he was in Birmingham, a very well known Nazarene evangelist and academic from America came to preach. It was evident that he was not overly excited about being there for as they waited to start the service, the evangelist kept complaining: 'I didn't ask to come here!' Turning to him, Bob said (calling him by name), 'And we didn't ask to have you! Look, I have a full house of people out there waiting to hear the message. Make up your mind. Either go out and preach or get on the next train.' The visitor, suitably rebuked, opted to preach.

In 1954 he accepted a call to the Church of the Nazarene in Melfort, Saskatchewan. He also pastored in Rimbey and Lethbridge, Alberta.

On the last occasion of our meeting I saw behind the brusque manner a man who loved people. I was travelling with the choir from Canadian Nazarene College (not as a singer!). At that time revival had touched a number of Christian colleges in the States and Canada and had influenced CNC in a significant way. We had travelled all day from Abbotsford in British Columbia to Lethbridge. We left at 6.30 a.m., had a breakdown for several hours, reaching Lethbridge at close to midnight. An anxious pastor grabbed my arm and said, 'Leave it to these people to sort out the accommodation. What time of night is this to arrive?' What could I say? I hoped that the morning concert at the church would compensate. (No mobile phones in those days.) In the middle of the choir pieces next morning, one of the students, Larry

Spicer by name, stood up to testify to what God had been doing in his life. The presence of God was felt and at the close of the service the pastor opened the altar. Some twenty-five young people knelt and prayed and I witnessed this hardened old warrior, Bob Deasley, weep over those precious young people. As I recall that event today tears are not far from the surface. It was a moving moment, which I will never forget. Bob Deasley had just come to Lethbridge, where there had been some problem in the church. On Saturday night I had thought that he was the wrong man for such a situation, but by Sunday lunch-time I knew that he was God's man to bring healing to the congregation.

Samuel Young... as I remember him
Hugh Rae

Samuel Young was the son of Irish parents who had become charter members of Parkhead church in 1906. They emigrated as a family to Cleveland, Ohio in 1916 and after a brief business career; Samuel Young became a student at Eastern Nazarene College to answer the call to the ministry. He took a second degree at Boston University and served as pastor, district superintendent of the New England district, and president of Eastern Nazarene College. He was elected to the office of general superintendent at the 1948 General Assembly and returned to the British Isles to preside at the district assembly of 1950. He was the general superintendent who came to the Houldsworth Hall in Manchester to welcome the ministers and members of the Calvary Holiness Church into the Church of the Nazarene.

Samuel Young was very clearly an astute man, and he had a habit of peering at the world though half-shut eyes. On occasions when it seemed that he was not aware of what was happening he used to say, 'I see more through these slits than most people do with their eyes wide open!' He was renowned for his keen insight, as the denomination's general secretary, Dr B. Edgar Johnson put it, 'the ability to move through the chaff, the processes, and see the kernel, the important conclusion of the matter.' His financial acumen laid the groundwork for the sound financial basis of the denomination. He was 'analytical, direct and to the point' according to another colleague, and was renowned for his 'scholarly and practical' preaching with rich biblical content.

I did not find him an easy man in conversation and sometimes felt that he was more severe on the British than some of his brethren. Indeed another general superintendent said in passing that Samuel Young was the most difficult to convince that the British church needed help. Possibly the strong independence of the Irish made that more pronounced.

He was also well known for his Scots-Irish wit. At one general assembly he was invited to raise a special offering for a second time and began with the remark: 'It comes to it when they ask a Scot to take the offering a second time round!' The offerings were collected in large buckets and he put his request this way: 'I would like you each to take a quarter (25 cents) out of your pocket for the offering. Then wrap it in a dollar or five-dollar bill and we will have a silent offering.'

One wonders what would have developed had this man and his family remained in Glasgow and had he become part of the British church. But then 'what might have been' is never a very fruitful path to follow.

Stanley Tranter...as I remember him
Hugh Rae

Stanley Tranter was a minister with the Emmanuel Church in Birmingham and in 1943 he moved with his wife Edna and their family to Gelderd Road church in Leeds. He was what we would call a 'radical' holiness preacher and in 1945 he was called to pastor the church in Skegoneill Avenue, Belfast. His style of preaching enabled him to gather around him a strong band of men and women and they built the church in which the congregation still worships. His wife and children undoubtedly ably assisted him. He was ordained in 1948 and in 1951 moved with his family to Port Glasgow. Here again he had a challenging ministry and while there he used to come to Hurlet College to teach the class on the doctrine of Christian holiness. In 1953 my wife and I went through a difficult experience and I will never forget this man's arms around me and his tears and prayers for us both. God answered and gave us such comfort. He was a man of prayer and loved people.

He also served in Hull and Clapham Junction and was the first pastor of the new work in Woodside, Watford. From there he retired and spent his final years working with his second son, Warren, who was pastor when the present beautiful building was built. His wife Edna was a loyal loving wife, mother and friend to so many. Sixty years ago he came to us and for many his memory cast a fragrance which remains meaningful.

Walter Neil ... as I remember him
Hugh Rae

The Church of the Nazarene in the mining village of Twechar (Dunbartonshire) was founded through the commitment of Walter Neil. Walter had spent his early years as a miner in the Hamilton area of Lanarkshire and was brought to the Lord at an evangelistic meeting held in 1926. He was assoçiated with the Salvation Army in Hamilton, playing with his sons and nephews in the band. When he was asked to move to Twechar to salvage the mines there, he wanted to establish a Salvation Army corps there, but that did not take place. Mr Wilson, a long-standing member of the Church of the Nazarene in Uddingston, invited the Neils to the district camp meeting in Ardrossan and the district superintendent, Robert Purvis, encouraged Walter to establish a Church of the Nazarene in Twechar.

When one of Walter's brothers was killed along with his wife in an accident, Walter and Annie took the five orphaned children into their home and brought them up as their own. Another brother, Willie, and his family also came into the church and together they built the church building, first of all hacking their way into solid rock to provide a firm foundation. Later they demolished a tall chimney stack to provide bricks for the manse. Since so many of the congregation had Salvation Army training, the Twechar church soon had its own silver band. Walter was an ardent salesman for *The Way of Holiness* and *The Christian Home Calendar*. He was a member of the district advisory board for many years and also served on the board of College governors.

In 1948 Walter and the Rev Sydney Martin were delegates to the general assembly in the United States. The journey was made by boat and train in those days, and they travelled together for several weeks after the assembly and prior to returning home since Sydney Martin had a few preaching engagements. Once, when they were in the home of a banker and his sister (which I later visited), the hostess asked the two visitors if they had any laundry. Walter said that he had some, including his 'simmit'. The poor lady did not know what kind of a garment that was, and learned that it was an old Scottish term for an under-vest. Once when they were travelling by underground, Walter's expanding suitcase got jammed in the turnstile. It was rush hour and the queue that formed was less than patient - much to the embarrassment of the gentle Sydney Martin.

During the building of the church in Twechar, funds were getting low and Walter decided to sell his gold pocket watch, which had been a presentation to him some years before. He asked his friend Donald Orr, solicitor, to get the best price for him and sell it. He put the money in the building fund. Years later at a district assembly, Donald Orr was being honoured for his years of legal service as district solicitor. When he had finished his reply of thanks, he called Walter to the platform. Telling the story of the sold watch, he then proceeded to return the watch to Walter. He had been so moved by Walter's commitment that he had had the watch valued and had paid that amount to him for the church, but he had kept the watch in order to return it to him years later.

Neil Robertson ... as I remember him
Hugh Rae

In 1953 when the assembly was held in Morley following the union with the I.H.M. and the British Isles district was divided into North and South, the Rev Neil Robertson was accepted into the ministry of the denomination. He had been a Congregationalist minister for many years and had preached the message of Christian holiness. Changing circumstances in the church made it possible for him and his Albany Street congregation in Edinburgh to join the Church of the Nazarene. Amongst those who were members of that congregation were Arthur Coleman (who like his cousin, the Hurlet student Alvin Young, came from what was then British Honduras), Alex Downie, Miss Cherry-Garrard, Miss F.G.S. Munro and Major Frank Govan, son of the founder of Faith Mission.

Neil Robertson had studied for the ministry at New College, Edinburgh. He had gone blind while a student and while his sight returned for a brief period, he soon lost it completely. But with his mane of white hair and Highland accent, he was a powerful preacher. The Robertsons had a daughter and two sons, Ian and Colin, both of whom entered the ministry. The elder, Ian Robertson, graduated from Hurlet and Nazarene Theological Seminary, and not receiving any response to inquiries about returning to Britain, ministered effectively in America. Neil Robertson also went to minister in the U.S.A. and was appointed Dean of Vernard College. When his wife took ill and died, he returned to Edinburgh on retirement and there he married again and enjoyed some years in Britain. When his second wife died he returned to be near his family, all of whom were in the United States. He celebrated his hundredth birthday in 2004 and lives in Alaska with his daughter Sheila.

On one occasion I was travelling with him in Edinburgh, a city where I was a stranger. As we travelled, although he could not see, he would point out various sites and buildings accurately. As he did so he would give a chuckle, knowing how his visitor would be surprised!

Chapter Seven

JONES, HYND AND 'FOREIGN MISSIONS'

'Black Gold'

In 1906, when the Holiness Mission began in London and 'Sharpe's Kirk' was formed in Glasgow, the British missionary movement was at its height. A century before, 'foreign missions', the idea of sending Christian missionaries abroad, was still rather revolutionary and controversial, but the growing impact of the evangelical revival led to the formation of numerous independent missionary societies in addition to the denominational missions. The 'faith missions' which began later in the nineteenth century with Hudson Taylor's China Inland Missions had begun a new phase of missionary expansion, and Mary Slessor, the Dundee mill girl, having been refused by missionary societies, became a model of individual obedience to many Christians by simply going on her own at her own expense to Calabar in Nigeria. Whereas British missionaries had gone first to India, and Hudson Taylor had focused attention on China, David Livingstone and Mary Slessor had turned attention to Africa. But Africa was also in the British public eye for other reasons at the end of the nineteenth century.

When slavery had been abolished throughout the British Empire in 1833, the original Dutch or 'Boer' settlers in Cape Colony, now under British rule, had migrated north in the 'Great Trek', taking their slaves with them. There these god-fearing farmers, speaking the 'Afrikaans' language which had developed from Dutch, had set up two republics, the Transvaal and the Orange Free State. But the discovery of gold on the Witswatersrand (usually shortened to 'the Rand'), the high grassy veldt which was the watershed between the Vaal and Limpopo rivers, led to an influx of 'uitlanders', mainly British, to establish mines around the burgeoning city of Johannesburg. The resulting tensions led to the South African or 'Boer' War, in which by 1902 the British forces eventually conquered the Boer republics.

The settlement after the war eventually led in 1912 to the Union of South Africa, a self-governing Dominion within the British Empire alongside Canada, Australia and New Zealand. But only those of European descent in the new Union, British and Afrikaaners, had the vote. Outside the Union, three black African nations, Swaziland, Bechuanaland and Basutoland, were established as 'Protectorates', their own rulers retaining authority over their own people, lands and customs, but the British Resident Commissioner holding final authority subject to the High Commissioner, the Governor-General of South Africa.

The discovery of gold in the Transvaal, the 'Grab for Africa', the mood of Imperialism associated with Cecil Rhodes and Joseph Chamberlain, and the 'Boer' War had all focused British interest on South Africa.

David Jones

It was in 1908, only six years after the South African War had ended, and four years before the self-governing Union of South Africa was established, that David Jones and William Clements disembarked at Port Elizabeth.[1] Clements soon returned to Britain, but David Jones stayed. Jones had been converted through the influence of his fellow-workers while employed in David Thomas's drapery store. There too 'he began to fall under the spell of a pair of laughing blue eyes' belonging to Miss E.M. Harold ('Emily' to those who knew her!), also a shop assistant in David Thomas's firm. 'Friendship ripened into something deeper. No one knew of this delightful romance, not a single soul! At least, so they thought...'[2] When both sensed the missionary call, he set off for Africa with the savings which would have gone to set up their first home.

David Jones had no theological education, had not attended a Bible school, had no preparation whatever in 'missiology' or 'social anthropology', and he had not been sent by any missionary society. With his savings he rented a room, not among the white people, but among the Africans. Drinking, gambling and fighting were all around him, but he preached on the streets and visited every home in the area.

---

1 Much of the information in this chapter comes from J. Fred Parker, *Mission to the World: A History of Missions in the Church of the Nazarene through 1985* (Kansas City: Nazarene Publishing House, 1988) supplemented by a more primary work on the I.H.M, H.K. Bedwell, *Black Gold: The Story of the International Holiness Mission in South Africa, 1908-1936* (Cape Town: Cape Times, c.1936)

2 Bedwell, 4

While in Port Elizabeth he met Harmon Schmelzenbach and Herbert Shirley at the independent White Holiness Mission. Both of them were missionaries who were to work with the newly-forming American denomination, the Pentecostal Church of the Nazarene.

Moving to Johannesburg, David Jones volunteered to work with A.W. Baker of the South African Compounds and Interior Mission. Thousands of Africans came from all over southern Africa, leaving their families behind, in order to work for a time in the gold mines. There were Zulus, Basutos, Shangaans, Matabeles, Chopis, Pondos, Bacas, Swazis and many others in the 'compounds' which the mining companies provided for them, and Baker was experienced at working among them.

The Ferguson Compound and Gaza

Having gained experience, and discovering that there was no church in the Ferguson Compound (which with 5,000 men was the largest on the Rand), Jones applied to the manager for permission to start a mission. He sunk the last of his savings into a small church and cottage and was left penniless. No support was coming from home, so he took work with the mining company and paid off the debt on his little mission station.

In 1911, his fiancée, Miss Harold, arrived at Durban, and he travelled down to meet her. They drove by rickshaw straight to their wedding, and returned to their home in the Ferguson Compound as husband and wife. Again every room in the compound was visited and a regular Bible study became the means of conversion for many of the miners. Miners who moved to other compounds or went back home started Bible classes or held open air meetings. By 1920, largely through evangelism by Africans, there were sixteen schools in the compounds where miners were taught to read the Bible. Gradually through the teaching and the witness of the 'umpati' (the African teacher), a slow awakening would take place with conviction of sin, until the student came forward to the penitent form after the preaching of the gospel. Then after further teaching and preparation, he would be baptized and participate in the Lord's Supper for the first time.

Mrs Jones travelled back to Britain for a furlough after the war and recruited new workers. H.C. Best came in 1919, followed by Miss Latham and Miss Marsh in 1920. In 1922, Mr and Mrs C.H. Strickland[3] arrived with 'Dad' Groom (Mrs Strickland's father), Miss L. Davies and Miss M. Smith. The Stricklands had sold the family business to finance their way to Africa. By this time many newly converted Shangaans from Portuguese East Africa (now Mozambique) had returned home with the gospel. The pioneer here was Samuel Mlati, who had been restored to his Christian commitment at the Ferguson mission and had returned to establish the first I.H.M. mission at Moyeni in Gazaland. An appeal from him had reached Miss Latham in Yorkshire, and she had come to Africa to answer that call. She married Mr Best and the newly married couple ('Henry' and 'Lucy' to those who knew them well!) moved to establish a mission station at Chaimite in Gazaland in 1922, their new home being a small mud hut on the bank of the Limpopo River. She later told how the people accepted them:

> One woman brought us a large pot of thick porridge, and another of greens and pea-nuts made into gravy. She was ever so pleased when we ate and enjoyed it. 'Au,' she said, 'they are Mashangaan, just like us.' You see, we had picked up the porridge in our fingers and dipped into the gravy and popped it in our mouths.

Rehoboth

By that time there had been further developments on the Rand. A mission station was established at Modder Deep on the east Rand three miles from Benoni and a farm was bought at Kempton Park on the north Rand. It was named 'Rehoboth' and became the headquarters of the I.H.M. in Africa.[4] A Bible School was built there in 1923 and Mr & Mrs Jones took charge of it along with Miss Davies, the Stricklands taking over responsibility for the Ferguson work. H.J. White arrived from the Westhoughton Holiness Mission near Bolton and spent his first months at the Bible school. Miss Smith went to a mission among 'Europeans' at Regent's Park, which affiliated with the I.H.M.

---

3 C. Hapgood Strickland was known to his friends as 'Happy' Strickland.

4 'Rehoboth' means 'a broad place' in Hebrew (see Gen. 26:22)

The Rehoboth Bible School started with four students from Gazaland, one of whom, Jona Mahleyeye, went back there as an evangelist and was eventually ordained. Another was Enosi, who was supported as an evangelist by the Keighley Holiness Mission back in Yorkshire until his early death in 1929. By 1926 there were eighteen students. 'Dad' Groom went to live at the Bible School, and although he could not speak any of the African languages, he made a lasting impression on the students through participating in their prayer meetings. When 'the fire fell', they shouted and praised God together though they could not understand each other. Sometimes he would get the kitchen boy down on his knees amid the pots and pans and have 'a red-hot prayer meeting'! When he died in 1930 and was buried under the Mimosa trees where he so often went to pray, a little chapel was built in his memory at the College.

In 1926, Doris Brown from the Manchester Tabernacle arrived and the following year, the Stricklands moved to Gazaland to open a new station leaving the evangelist Daniel Ntibana in charge at Ferguson and Zakeu Muhlanga in charge at Modder Deep.

Cottondale and Tete

In Gazaland, Chaimite proved an unsuitable, often muddy, site. The Limpopo River flooded after the summer rains and malaria and blackwater fever were rife. In 1925 the station was moved from Chaimite to Magube and that same year, Mr and Mrs Harry White came to live at Chinavane. In 1927, the Stricklands went to live at Mangulane, halfway between Magube and the capital of Portuguese East Africa, then known as Lourenço Marques.[5] All of the missionaries in Portuguese territory had to spend some months in Lourenço Marques each year learning the Portuguese language.

Simone Ndhlova, a graduate of the Rehoboth Bible School, had established a mission at Livydale in a beautiful area called Mpisana across the border in the Eastern Transvaal. Henry Pope from the Manchester Tabernacle, who had arrived as a new missionary in 1928 (and had married the daughter of veteran missionaries, the McDougalls), was sent to investigate, and in 1930, the Stricklands, the

5 Now Maputo, the capital of independent Mozambique.

Whites, Doris Brown and Tabitha Evans (a school teacher who had arrived from Wales in 1929) made the sixty-mile trek to a five-hundred acre tract of land five miles from Livydale and close to a railway station at Cottondale. Doris Brown described the new mission station:

> The site the Lord has given us here is surrounded by glorious country. There is a magnificent mountain range in the distance with an ever-changing panorama of beauty. To see the mountain peaks in the light of the rising sun, their rich grey, mauve and purple in the glow of the setting sun, or the fiery trail of the grass fires gleaming through the darkness of the night, is an ever-present delight to our eyes, long accustomed to the flat uninteresting bush of the lower veldt.

At first the missionaries lived in traditional African huts, but then houses were built with steel-framed buildings to withstand the white ant. There were three stations on the five hundred acres: the Salem station for the Pedis, the Hebron station for the Shangaans, and the Ethel Lucas Memorial station. The last of these was named after the daughter of Frank Lucas of the Southampton Holiness Mission. Suffering from poor health, she had worked to bring in funds to build a hospital there before she died, but at first there was only a dispensary with six beds visited by two government doctors.

In 1930, Albert Walshaw from Yorkshire arrived. The short Mr Walshaw and the tall Mr Pope had been fellow students at Emmanuel Bible College in Birkenhead. In 1932, Albert Walshaw's fiancée, Miss Stephenson, arrived and worked first at the Ferguson Compound, then later at Cottondale. In 1931, Kenneth Bedwell came from England, taking responsibility for the mission at Modder Deep, and then for wider evangelism on the Rand. That same year, the Bests pioneered in new territory in Portuguese East Africa, north of the Zambesi River in the province of Macanga where the climate was hotter and wetter. They crossed the Zambezi at Tete, the provincial capital and drove about a hundred miles further north, establishing a new mission station twelve miles from the administrative outpost of Furancungo. They later recalled:

> Arriving in Tete just at the beginning of the rainy season, we had to erect buildings with mackintoshes not swords in our hands! Living in a bell tent while temporary huts were being

> built, imagine our feelings one morning, after a whole day and night of tropical torrential rain, when we found the half-finished hut had taken a decided bend earthwards.'

No missionaries had ever been in the area before, so this was really pioneering work. The local people had never heard the gospel, did not know what a service was, were not used to sitting listening for any time, had never known what it was to close their eyes for prayer, and no one at all could read or write. Unexpected help came to overcome the language barrier. Elia, born in Nyasaland (now Malawi) and converted when he came in contact with the I.H.M. Bible School in Johannesburg, spoke the same language as the local people, and came with his wife to help. The Stricklands came with their son, David, to help build a permanent house and stayed to carry on the work when Mr Best took seriously ill and had to drive himself first to Blantyre in Nyasaland and then on to Salisbury, the capital of Rhodesia (now Harare in Zimbabwe). In 1935, the Popes arrived and began some simple medical work.

Acornhoek

Meanwhile the disadvantages of the Cottondale land had become evident. In the rainy season, the valley between the dispensary and the other two stations became a raging river and the two ladies at the dispensary were isolated for weeks. The question was also raised whether a hospital should not be nearer to a railway station. Reginald Jones, the older son of the pioneer missionaries, was appointed an I.H.M. missionary in 1932 and took the lead in transferring the clinic building to a ten-acre site at Acornhoek, the next station up the railway line from Cottondale. By the end of 1936 a new dispensary, school and church had been built there. In 1939, the Rehoboth Bible School was closed and the mission headquarters were moved to Cottondale. In 1940, the government gave the mission land at Islington, seven miles from Cottondale, and after their marriage Reginald and Nurse Lilian Jones were placed there, transferring to Acornhoek in 1942. Meanwhile, Reginald's younger brother, Harold, who had been head of the Bible School in Rehoboth till it closed, began medical studies at Witwatersrand University in Johannesburg.

By 1939, the Ethel Lucas hospital at Acornhoek had sixty-six beds, and expansion was to continue until it had three hundred. At the end of the Second World War, the Rev and Mrs I.E. Dayhoff of the Hepzibah Faith Mission became I.H.M. missionaries and opened work at Lorraine, seventy miles north of Acornhoek. A dispensary was established there by Hazel Pass. In 1946 a farm was donated to the mission at Carolina, 150 miles south-east of Johannesburg and the C.H. Stricklands established the work there. In 1947 the Rehoboth Bible School was re-opened under Kenneth Bedwell, and a dispensary established near Lorraine by Doris Brown. Miriam Evans, a science graduate and schoolteacher from the Battersea Tabernacle, established a high school at Cottondale. The Courtney-Smiths arrived in 1947 and worked at Islington. C.V. Blaney joined the mission and worked at The Downs north of Lorraine, followed there by the Rex Emslies. Finally, having completed his medical training, Dr T. Harold Jones took charge of the Ethel Lucas Memorial Hospital at Acornhoek in 1949 supported by a staff of missionary nurses – Minnie Hope, Joan Bradshaw, Abigail Hewson and Hazel Pass.

In forty years, the pioneers, David and Emily Jones, had seen the International Holiness Mission grow till there were thirty-five missionaries and well over a thousand African members, with many more adherents.

The Hynds at Manzini

Unlike the I.H.M., the Pentecostal Church of Scotland had no missionaries during its brief life. But the missionary interest was there, stimulated by Olive Winchester, to support Nazarene missions even before the union of 1915. But the response of David and Nema Hynd to the advert in *The Other Sheep*, and George Sharpe's appointment as missionary superintendent in 1923 launched a deep and lasting concern with missions, particularly in Swaziland.[6]

When the Sharpes left their daughter and son-in-law and their two children at Bremersdorp in 1925, their house on the grassy hillside was

6 See pages [58-60] for this and the other events leading up to the arrival in Swaziland.

barely finished.[7] Unlike David Jones in Port Elizabeth and Johannesburg, they were starting out in a remote area with no modern amenities, but at least the pioneer Nazarene missionaries had been in the country for fifteen years. On Sunday 30th August, they banged an empty paraffin tin on their veranda and gathered a congregation of two boys who were working on the building and a man whose eye had been punctured during a drinking session. The congregation grew slowly week by week till, on Sunday, 25th October, the doctor's thirtieth birthday, three Swazis at the service indicated that they wanted to become Christians. These were his first converts.

Work on the new hospital began immediately. Dr Hynd planned it and built it largely with his own hands, assisted by local workers. He bought bricks at first, but then, guided by a book, he found the right kind of clay and made them. He taught himself how to lay bricks, Mrs Hynd acting as the bricklayer's mate. He found out from a book how to lay drains. All the material had to be hauled to the site by oxen, and when the oxen escaped overnight and wandered into a quarantine area, he was fined by the local British magistrate and had to go to Sobhuza, the Paramount Chief, for other oxen to replace them. Unfortunately these oxen were untrained, so he had to learn on the job how to train them and on one occasion was almost gored when an ox's horn took a button off his waistcoat. Having hardly driven a car until he drove to Swaziland from Johannesburg, he now learned how to ride a horse simply by riding it! He performed his first operation in Africa, amputating a leg on the table in his store-room. Mrs Hynd administered the chloroform under his direction and the girl working in their vegetable garden, Kelina, held the leg!

The Raleigh Fitkin Memorial Hospital was opened by the resident commissioner, Mr Honey, on 16th July, 1927, two years after they arrived.[8] It was rather an ambitious building for that time in Swaziland, built not of corrugated iron, but of brick, with a series of stately arches along the front veranda. Sobhuza was present for the opening, as was the Rev Susan Fitkin of New York, the president of

7 Bremersdorp is now 'Manzini', but we shall use the name familiar to English-speaking people at the time.

8 As a 'protectorate', not a 'colony', Swaziland had a 'resident commissioner' instead of a 'governor'.

the Nazarene Women's Missionary Society, and Mrs Ada Bresee. Mrs Fitkin and her husband, a New York financier, had given most of the money in memory of their son, Raleigh, after whom the hospital was named. He had sensed a call to be a missionary, but had died in his teens. In addition to the hospital, a stone church had been built, and Harmon Schmelzenbach, the Nazarene pioneer in Swaziland, dedicated it the next day.

The new mission station was rather larger and more ambitious than those already established at Pigg's Peak, Endzingeni and Siteki, and since it was much more strategically placed in the centre of Swaziland, it was to grow much larger. Also, whereas the other Nazarene missionaries were American, as a British doctor employed by the British administration to look after their policemen and other government workers, David Hynd had a special status in the protectorate and a close relationship with the civil authorities. He also had a special status among the missionaries as their doctor and so their confidant. He provided the medical care for Schmelzenbach in his last four years, when he was gradually succumbing to malaria, and he also conducted his funeral.

Beyond the Nazarene mission, Dr Hynd was the one who was invited to join the Board of Advice for Native Education set up by the resident commissioner in 1929. That same year, he was the one who took the initiative in inviting the missionaries from all the missionary societies to form the Swaziland Missionary Conference. An elderly Methodist missionary was the first president, but Dr Hynd then succeeded him and was president for forty-two years.

But Dr Hynd's primary concern was the R.F.M. Hospital and the Bremerdorp mission station. One Scot, Sarah Munro from Perth, came to join the American missionary nurses for a few years until she had a breakdown in health. Mrs Hynd began a school in her home in addition to serving as pastor of the new church, and in 1931, education took a major step forward with the arrival of Margaret K. Latta. 'Miss Peggy' (as she was known at home) was one of the Latta sisters in the Uddingston church and an experienced teacher. She was already over forty years of age, and as district missionary treasurer, had been praying that God would send someone to Swaziland to start schools.

The problem was that with the depression, the church could not afford to send anyone. Then it occurred to her that she had some money, compensation from a bus accident, which would pay her boat fare to Africa. Her sisters and several laymen in the Scottish churches covenanted to pay her salary, and so she resigned her teaching post and set out for far-distant Swaziland.

Another arrival earlier in 1931, also from home, was Dr Mary Tanner from the Parkhead church. Newly qualified as a doctor, she had to learn the ropes of running the hospital quickly so that she could take charge while the Hynds returned home in 1932 for their first furlough. On that furlough, Mrs Hynd took a course in radiography in Glasgow. Her husband had planned to take his examination to be admitted as a Fellow of the Royal College of Surgeons, but the furlough was too busy. Visiting the States for the Nazarene general assembly of 1932, he interviewed Evelyn Fox, who was to become the long-serving matron of the R.F.M.

The Threefold Ministry

Upon their return in October, 1932, David and Nema Hynd began their longest term of service. Missionaries were supposed to have a furlough every seven years, but because of shortage of staff and the Second World War, they were not to return home for fourteen years. In many ways, these were the golden years, with a small, dedicated and united team at the mission station.

Dr Hynd summed up his philosophy of mission in the phrase 'the threefold ministry', a theme taken from his key text, Matthew 4:23: 'And he [Jesus] went about all Galilee, teaching in their synagogues and preaching the gospel of the kingdom and healing every disease and every infirmity among the people.' This was the basis for what (in later language) was 'holistic' ministry to the whole person. The three ministries of teaching, preaching and healing reinforced each other and missionary doctors, nurses and teachers were therefore the best evangelists.

The twenties and thirties were the very decades when 'fundamentalism' developed in America, partly in reaction to the 'social gospel' of Walter Rauschenbusch which had reduced

Christianity to the here and now. Shaped by premillennialism, fundamentalism reacted by demoting the works of charity and mercy which had always been part of evangelical Christianity. All Christian missions could do was save souls from a doomed world: it was a waste of precious time to engage in any kind of social or educational reform. In Western countries where secular government and private agencies had taken over health services and education, it was all too easy to accept this split between the 'spiritual' and the physical and practical, and an otherworldly 'spirituality' came to dominate. But in Africa, it was evident how unbiblical and impractical that was. Christian missions had to minister to the whole person.

On the mission station, the healing ministry was evident first of all in the R.F.M. Hospital. After the Hynds' return a radiography unit was installed and the young people in the British Isles district, led enthusiastically by Joe Irvine, collected money for an ambulance. Evelyn Fox arrived to be matron and Elizabeth Cole from Montana strengthened the nursing staff. Dr Tanner's health was affected by the strain of her term of service, and she did not return after her first furlough, and no other Nazarene doctors were available. A South African, Dr Minnie du Toit, served for a number of years. During the Second World War some refugee Jewish doctors helped. In the first year of the war there were some 1,234 in-patients and 17,721 out-patients and Dr Hynd developed the ability to work round the clock. By then there were eleven Swazi student nurses. That same year, the sixth missionary came from Scotland, Nurse Jessie Rennie of the Paisley church.[9]

But the healing ministry was not restricted to the hospital and its outlying clinics. The doctor also had the care of all government employees in the middle of Swaziland and had to perform post-mortems for the police. Further, during his furlough in 1932, he had made contact with the British Red Cross and began a Swaziland branch in 1933. He had come to the conclusion that primary health care (as it is now called) was vital to cut the infant mortality rate. The resident commissioner of Swaziland became the president and Dr Hynd the territorial director. A British Baptist nurse who had been working at

9 This is counting Dr and Mrs Hynd, Sarah Munro, Dr Tanner and Miss Latta as the previous five.

the R.F.M., Ruby Sipple, was transferred to work with the Red Cross in maternity care and child welfare.

The teaching ministry was furthered by Dr Hynd's service on the Board for Native Education, which oversaw the development of the Swaziland education system in all the mission schools. Just as the government salary paid to Dr Hynd for looking after its own civil servants enabled Nazarene missions to run a hospital, so the government grant enabled them along with other missions to finance Christian schools. Dr Hynd's service on this board was crucial for that development.

The development of education was furthered by the arrival of Bertha Parker, a teacher from Canada who arrived to help Miss Latta.[10] They started a hostel for girls who attended the school, often giving shelter to Christian girls who had run away from home to avoid a forced marriage to some old chief. On one or two occasions, Dr Hynd even withstood the agents of Sobhuza, the Paramount Chief or king of the Swazis, who had the right to choose one new wife each year. In 1936, Miss Latta and Miss Parker started a Teacher Training College, soon being joined on the staff by an African teacher, Miss Mary Coleman (later Mrs Kamanga). Training of nurses also began at the hospital.

As for the preaching ministry, Mrs Hynd served as joint pastor of the church on the mission station jointly with a Swazi preacher. Right from the beginning, unlike many other missionaries, the Hynds aimed at self-governing, self-supporting churches. Over difficult cultural questions (like the issue of polygamy) the Swazi Christians were encouraged to develop their own discrimination as to what was acceptable in the culture and what was contrary to the law of Christ. Traditional healers, whom the missionaries called 'witch-doctors', were linked with the placating of ancestral spirits, and hence with ritual murders. But Sobhuza claimed to be both Christian and an observer of the ancient Swazi customs such as polygamy, and respect for him could easily blur the lines. Preachers had to know where they stood and Harmon Schmelzenbach had raised up a core of Swazi evangelists the first four of whom were ordained in 1939.

---

10 Miss Parker was a sister of J. Fred Parker, the author of *Mission to the World.*

Also connected with the ministry of preaching was the initiative to found the Holiness Association of Africa in 1935. The Hynd family had connections with the International Holiness Mission from their days in Perth, and David Hynd had visited the Holiness Mission headquarters in Battersea as a schoolboy before the First World War. The Holiness Association helped to increase fellowship between Nazarene and I.H.M. missionaries, undoubtedly helping to prepare the way towards union.

Margaret Hynd, born after her parents returned to Swaziland from their first furlough, later reflected on her father's life at this time during her childhood:

> I marvelled that he was able to keep on working day after day with only two to six hours sleep and quite often none at all, and yet never be grumpy or incapable of getting through mounds of work. He dealt with each individual as if that person were the most important one, tasks galore awaiting him or not. No matter when he went to bed he was up by 4.00 a.m. each morning to have a quiet time and to read before going to his office to type with two fingers all the letters awaiting a reply.

Post-war Developments

In 1944, Dr Hynd drew up a paper for the African Nazarene Mission Council: 'Memorandum on Post-war Advance for the Church of the Nazarene in Africa.' This displayed a strategic vision for the opportunities which the end of the war would bring for Christian missions, and became the basis for Nazarene expansion.

The war ended two years later, and with some medical help at the hospital, the Hynds were able to go home for a long-overdue furlough. On their return they had to face the problem posed by a group of keen, brash, young missionaries sent out at the end of the war. Miss Latta, who had been head of the station during the Hynds' furlough, had just managed to contain their impatience, but with the doctor's return the storm broke. Whatever the cultural and personal differences which led to the tensions, David Hynd rode out the storm with skill and patience until most of the young missionaries were integrated into the work.

There were also more recruits from Britain who came to join the Hynds. Eileen Flitcroft from Carlisle came to teach at the Bible College in Siteki for a while. The sisters Agnes and Betty Clark from the Perth church, both nurses, arrived to work at the hospital. The Rev Jim Graham from Northern Ireland came to do evangelism. Mary McKinley came from the Ayr church to undertake administrative responsibilities, particularly accounts, in 1947. Nurse Jessie Rennie from the Paisley church who had served at the Raleigh Fitkin Memorial since 1939 became matron of the Acornhoek hospital after the union with the I.H.M. Then much to their joy, their son Samuel, newly graduated from the Medical Faculty at Glasgow, returned with his charming young English wife, Rosemarie. Marjory Burne, a South African, was already serving as Dr Hynd's very efficient secretary, and Mabel Skinner, an English missionary, came to take charge of the kitchens and domestic services at the hospital. But on the other hand there was also the loss of Miss Latta when she retired in 1954. Her strong, outgoing personality and utter loyalty were sadly missed, but her remarkable work in the schools and the teacher training college had been recognized when she was given the award of MBE (Member of the Order of the British Empire).

In 1950, David Jones of the I.H.M. died and two years later the I.H.M. in Britain and Africa united with the Church of the Nazarene. This brought over thirty British missionaries and almost two thousand full members in Africa into the denomination, as well as thousands of adherents. Among the missionaries, Kenneth Bedwell was to play a particular role in the education of preachers, becoming principal when the I.H.M. Bible College was united with the Nazarene Bible College at Siteki.

New developments in Swaziland after the war included the Thembelihle Leper Colony, set up in 1948 in the beautiful valley of the Mbuluzi River in the hills above Mbabane, the administrative capital, and the development of outstations from the Bremersdorp station. By 1952 there were five outstations, all giving physical reality to the 'threefold ministry' with a church, a school and a clinic. A high school was opened on the mission station in 1954, and the same year, a large church was opened as a memorial to Mrs Hynd's parents, Dr and Mrs

Sharpe, who had given a considerable portion of the cost. A physiotherapy department was opened at the hospital in 1961.

Beyond the Nazarene missionary work, David Hynd took the initiative in calling for the setting up of the Nursing Council for the three British High Commission Territories, Swaziland, Bechuanaland and Basutoland.[11] He served as vice-chairman, and it was a nurse from the Nazarene College of Nursing, Eva Mthethwa, who was the first nurse to be registered. He also took the initiative in establishing the Swaziland Medical Association and served four years as its first president.

'Retirement' came in 1961, but David Hynd still had almost thirty years of service to Swaziland. For five years, he and Mrs Hynd lived and worked at the leper colony and he travelled down to the hospital each week to help Dr Samuel, the new medical superintendent and head of station, with surgical operations. He took over again as director of the Red Cross branch. In 1963, he was invited to take part in the constitutional conference in London, chaired by the British Commonwealth Secretary, Duncan Sandys, to hammer out a constitution for Swaziland before independence. He continued to be president of the Swaziland Missionary Conference, now known as the Swaziland Conference of Churches, till 1974. Through this, he initiated religious broadcasting and often spoke himself on the 'thought for the day' which was broadcast each morning. Through the Conference of Churches, he also invited the British and Foreign Bible Society to come to Swaziland, and opened a youth centre for the urban young people of the capital, Mbabane, administering this till not long before he died. He was a member of ACAT, the Africa Co-operative Action Trust, which served rural communities in agriculture and health, and of COSAD, the National Council on Smoking, Alcohol and Drug Dependency. And for the last twenty-five years of his life, he became virtually a one-man refugee agency, managing the funds to provide for the refugees who came across Swaziland's borders because of the resistance to the apartheid regime in South Africa and the civil war and unrest in Mozambique.

---

11 Later at independence Bechuanaland became Lesotho and Basutoland became Botswana.

When David Hynd died in 1991 at the age of ninety-five, he had given sixty-five years of missionary service to Swaziland. His Herculean labours during the first twenty years had been recognized by the British government when he was made a C.B.E. (Commander of the Order of the British Empire), an award made personally by King George VI in Swaziland during the royal family's tour of South Africa in 1947. But equally treasured was the award given to him when he was ninety by the young University of Swaziland, the honorary degree of Doctor of Laws, recognizing his long service to the nation and government of Swaziland.

'The Time Would Fail Me to Tell...'

After the Second World War, a whole new generation of Nazarene missionaries went out from the United Kingdom. The Rev Jim Graham, the Irish evangelist, married Nurse Agnes Clark from Perth in Manzini and they moved to Malawi in 1956, a new field which soon saw growth and the establishing of a Bible school. Nurse Agnes Willox from the Parkhead church (the sister of Mrs J.B. Maclagan) was appointed to India in 1946 and later gave service in British Honduras (now Belize).

When Dr Samuel Hynd succeeded his father as medical superintendent of the Raleigh Fitkin and head of station in the early 1960s, it became apparent that a major re-building programme was necessary, and since the denomination did not think it could finance this, he raised the money from church agencies in West Germany and the Netherlands. The re-building was hardly started however when Rosemarie Hynd was fatally injured in a freak car accident beside their home. Bereft of the support of his wife, Samuel Hynd worked tirelessly to keep up with his medical and administrative work while guiding the hospital through a complete re-building. The result was one of the finest and most modern hospitals in the third world, but the church now struggled to finance its running, and the additional demands of the expansion, together with the chronic shortage of suitable staff, compounded by cultural and personal differences, led to severe tensions. The director of the denomination's world mission division, Dr Jerald D. Johnson, had to resolve the situation.

With a heavy heart, Samuel Hynd, having married nursing tutor Phyllis McNeil, set up in private medical practice in Manzini. His call was still to serve the Swazis among whom he had grown up and whose language and culture he knew so intimately. Sobhuza was now King of an independent Swaziland, and Dr Samuel was asked to serve in the government as Minister of Health. He moved his membership from one Sharpe Memorial Church (in Glasgow) where he was a missionary member to the other (in Manzini), and continued his work as a missionary in Swaziland through various agencies. Working into his eighties combating the scourge of HIV-AIDS in his clinic and through agencies such as the Swaziland Conference of Churches, he was recognized like his father with the high honours of D.Sc. (Doctor of Science) by the University of Swaziland and C.B.E.

In 1947, the Rev and Mrs William Russell were sent to the British mandated territory of Palestine to help Samuel Krikorian establish work in the Kingdom of Jordan. They were in Jerusalem undertaking language study when Britain decided to withdraw and civil war was breaking out between Jews and Arabs. In 1949 they moved to Jordan and worked in Zerka, fifteen miles north of the capital, Amman. But during the Suez crisis of 1956, they had to leave when Jordan broke off diplomatic relations with Britain.

The Rev Clifford Gay was the first British missionary appointed to the Cape Verde Islands, arriving there in 1939. Nazarene missions had been established in the Cape Verde Island in the Atlantic by an islander, John Diaz, who had worked alone until the Rev and Mrs Everett Howard arrived in 1936. The Rev and Mrs Ernest Eades were appointed in 1948 and served sacrificially for twelve years, being joined by Mrs Eades' sister, Charlotte Munn, who married Clifford Gay. Ernest Eades had been brought up in the Battersea Tabernacle of the I.H.M. and had been a student at Emmanuel Bible College, while the sisters Jessie and Lottie Munn had been active in the Skegoneill Avenue church in Belfast.

The Rev Thomas Ainscough, a Yorkshireman who had been with Emmanuel Missions in Argentina since 1930, joined the Church of the Nazarene in 1936 and officially became a Nazarene missionary along with his Argentinian wife, Romana, in 1947. Their son, Dr Alberto

Ainscough and daughter-in-law, Dr Rosa Ainscough, later went to serve in the Reynolds Memorial Hospital in India. The CHC missionaries also served in South America and India.[12] Some years later in 1969, Victor and Beryl Edwards, who had also been Emmanuel missionaries in Argentina, became Nazarene missionaries and served till 1982.

The Rev Frank and Heather Howie were appointed to Mozambique just as the country gained independence from Portugal and was taken over by Marxists. Two American Nazarene missionaries, Armand Doll and Hugh Friberg, were imprisoned and Frank Howie had to act as mission director from South Africa, supporting and advising the five district superintendents. Peggy Trumble from the Sheffield church was in charge of the medical laboratory and trained lab-technicians at the Raleigh Fitkin Memorial, also chairing the hospital evangelism committee, before she was forced to return home after a serious car accident. Kenneth and Minnie Singleton served in South Africa, as did Philip Bedwell, the son of Kenneth and Margaret, who was principal of the Zulu Bible College before all the Nazarene colleges in the Republic of South Africa were united. Tom and Mary Robinson from Carrickfergus worked for a term in Swaziland.

Next to Africa, the largest number of British Nazarene missionaries served in Papua New Guinea. The Rev Clive and Grace Burrows served there mainly at the Bible College in Ningei where Mr Burrows was principal during their second term. The Burrows later served under missionary appointment at European Nazarene Bible College. Joyce Skea and Ellen Syvret, members of the Perth church, also served in Papua New Guinea being joined for a time by Irene Skea (later the Rev Irene Wallace). Nurse Joyce Skea married the New Zealand missionary, Neville Bartle, and they served their final term of service in Fiji. Eleanor Brocklebank from the Troon church also served for a time in PNG.

The Rev Harry and Grace Stevenson served in Bolivia and Spain and then returned to their native Ireland to re-establish the church in Greystones, south of Dublin, completing their missionary service in the

---

12 An account of these is given in Chapter 5 (see pages 121-122) and Chapter 6 (p. 143)

Hashemite Kingdom of the Jordan. The Rev David and Elizabeth McCulloch served in Guatemala for ten years, Mr McCulloch becoming principal of the Bible College there. The Rev Ernie and Anne Stafford served in Colombia, and the Rev Brian and Beryl Adams, members of the Perth church, served in Brazil. The Rev Robert McMurdock served first with the Oriental Missionary Society and then with Nazarene missions in Taiwan.

Included in the missionary band are Robert and Grace Brown (Barbados), Edward and Margaret Cairns (British Honduras), Norman and Joan Salmons (Portuguese East Africa), Lois Pass and Nellie Storey (South Africa), Trevor and Mary Johnstone (Haiti and France), Gwyn and Klawdia Downing from Llay (Panama), Dr Dwight and Kathy Swanson (at European Nazarene Bible College and the Nazarene seminary in Manila), Douglas and Jennifer Mann recently appointed to Peru,[13] David and Rhoda Restrick, serving in Mozambique, Audrey Simpson from Thetford (Romania), Hilary Evans from Woodside church, Watford (Albania), and Colin and Tanya McConkey (Poland).

There have also been unofficial missionaries: Carolyn White served at EuNC and in Poland, while some years earlier the Rev Tom Findlay from Ardrossan, graduate of BINC and Nazarene Theological Seminary in Kansas City, served long-term on the academic staff of European Nazarene Bible College. His stimulating lectures and robust approach fired many students with a love of learning and his scholarship also laid the foundations of a good theological library. More recently Norman and Linda Patterson have served in a much needed work, including the care of orphans in Romania.

Others have served with other missionary societies. These include Ina McLachlan of Paisley who served with the China Inland Mission and was a prisoner of war, Maureen Smith and Roger Williams of Sharpe Memorial who served with the JEB in Japan, Lilian Hamer of the Daubhill church in Bolton who served in Thailand, Sue Trenier of Sharpe Memorial who served with RBMU, later with UFM, in Irian Jaya (now West Papua), Indonesia. From the Victoria Street church in

---

[13] Jennifer Mann is the daughter of Dr Philip Weatherill, the south district missionary president, and the granddaughter of the Rev John Weatherill.

Sheffield, Joe and Betty Liveridge served with the JEB, Ian and Sheila Currie in Spain, and Doris Woodward in Pakistan.

Several have also served short-term or in other capacities with Nazarene missions, such as Gordon and Betty-May Thomas in Swaziland and Christine, Dorothy and Dr Paul Tarrant. Altogether well over a hundred missionaries have gone from the British churches, I.H.M., C.H.C. and Nazarene, in the hundred years from 1906 to today.

Dr and Mrs David Hynd: a photograph on a post card sent back from on board ship on the way to Africa in 1925.

Mr and Mrs David Jones & Luti Melati

Dr David Hynd receives his C.B.E. from King George VI during the royal tour of South Africa in 1947

Miss M.K. Latta

Miriam Evans

Rev & Mrs Henry Pope

David Hynd kraaling in 1929

King Sobhuza II with Dr Hynd at his official retirement in 1961

Dr & Mrs Samuel and Dr & Mrs David Hynd

David Jones... as I remember him
R. E. Jones, Dr T.H. Jones and Doris Brown

These excerpts are from the articles in the memorial edition of Africa Calling *(Vol. 3, No.2, April-June, 1950). The first was written by David Jones' elder son, Reginald Jones.*

My father was essentially a man for the Africans – a missionary of the first order. The black people were his people. They were his concern. They were his life's work. In them he saw the treasures of darkness. Thousands have come to this land of sunshine and spiritual darkness: they saw and have dug out for themselves the gold, silver, diamonds, and other precious metals, out of its soil. My father saw the black gold, the rough diamonds, the jewels of the Lord, when they were sunk in the mire of superstition, witchcraft and sin. It was his sole aim that these might be brought out into the light, refined, polished, and prepared for the heavenly Jerusalem and to stud the diadem of the King of kings. His one purpose was that they should know Christ, whom to know is life eternal. Other missionaries might teach education, civilization, social culture: my father's concern was to preach to them Christ and him crucified...

My father was retiring among white people, but he was untiring among the black peoples. He never wearied of them nor lost faith in them. Long hours he spent pouring over the word of God explaining it in his unique and jovial manner; working by their sides in the fields; in building operations; down in the rough and hard and undeveloped gold mines as they were then; sitting long hours in debate over some knotty problem, whether spiritual difficulty or some difference of opinion among the brethren; trudging day after day though Africa's bush and swamps in scorching sun and perils of night, once travelling in a native train a day and night, and for years living in a native village.

Dr T.H. Jones, the younger son, recalled this of his father:
Amidst all his humility, which was profound, he had a prevailing consciousness that in humility was greatness and in love was leadership. It was from God...that he sought strength for the discharge of duty... The effect was to impart habitual tranquillity and composure of spirit... This uniform self-possession was manifest in everything he did, even in a matter so minute as his handwriting. His

most hurried notes show no symptoms of haste or bustle, but ended in the same neat regular style in which they began. So this quietness of spirit accompanied him into the most arduous labours and critical emergencies. Popularity he shunned, sin he hated, and insincerity he despised, but his godly life attracted many to the Saviour.

Doris Brown wrote:
He maintained a simple faith in the grand old gospel of the grace of God. 'Jesus keep me near the cross... In the cross, in the cross be my glory ever,' was a favourite hymn of his. Prayer and reading of the Word were the mainsprings of his life. Ever an early riser, the dawn found him seeking God for the new day and its untrodden ways. He was a happy Christian. Problems and cares of a growing work might crowd in but he had learned to take his burdens to the Lord and leave them there, and I wonder how many thousands of African miles have been covered with a *singing* superintendent at the wheel!

D.B. Jones was very appreciative of the work of others... Any little improvement about the mission property was quickly noted and praised – nothing escaped his eye. For himself he set the standard of perfection – nothing shoddy was good enough, so that some of the mission's buildings are a standing monument to his painstaking work. He was a humble man, self-effacing and always pushing others to the fore. He was our leader but actually he seemed to lead from behind! – holding loosely all the steering reins.

David Hynd ....as I remember him
Hugh Rae

As a boy of eleven years the name of David Hynd was one with which I was familiar. Unfortunately I did not get to hear him when he was on his first furlough in 1932. I learned a great deal about him when Joseph Irvine became my pastor. As Joe Irvine was undoubtedly an early mentor of mine, so David Hynd was for Joe Irvine. He was in regular correspondence with Dr Hynd and expressed to him some of the frustrations which he felt about his lack of preparation for the ministry. In 1934 for some reason I decided to write to Dr Hynd expressing my desire to be a missionary. How delighted I was to receive a hand written reply from this all too busy man encouraging me to keep open to God's will. Along with encouragement from Joe Irvine, that gave my life its focus on service.

I recall the enthusiasm of the crowd at Parkhead on the return of the Hynd family in 1946. I was then a student at Hurlet and met Dr & Mrs Hynd when they came to speak at the summer convention. Two things impressed me about this man of God. One was his deep commitment to God and his work in Africa: even by the 1940's he was already a legend among us. When his son Samuel came to Glasgow to study medicine and quickly joined in the youth work of the district, my sense of the influence of these godly parents was heightened. I recall an event in Bath Street Central Halls at the district assembly. Tensions were running high over several developments. We had not had a general superintendent since 1939 and George Frame was in the chair as the district superintendent. These had not been easy years through the war. There was still strong feeling about the loss of Robert Purvis and, more recently, that of J. B. Maclagan, plus undercurrents of opposition to the purchase of West Hurlet House for the College. In the midst of this situation David Hynd stood up in the assembly discussion and in his quiet but skilful way seemed to bring a quiet assurance of the presence of God. Here was a man whom I felt I would like to emulate, one who could see beyond the human frailties of us all to the greater call of God on our lives.

Agnes Kanema Hynd... as I remember her
Hugh Rae

Mrs Hynd was the second daughter of Dr and Mrs Sharpe: her older sister, Ina, married Bob Robertson, one of the sons of Andrew Robertson, Snr., and her younger sister, Isabel, became Mrs Victor Edwards. She was always known by her unusual middle name, Kanema, shortened to 'Nema'. Apparently Mrs Sharpe heard a mother call her child by that name on board ship while crossing the Atlantic. When she asked its origin, the mother explained that she was of 'Red Indian' descent and that that was where the name came from. (We now say 'native American'.)

Nema was born in upper New York State in 1893 and returned with her parents to Scotland in 1901. She was thirteen when her father was evicted from his church and the new church was founded. She attended Whitehill School in Dennistoun and studied for several years at the Glasgow School of Art before going on to take her M.A. at the University of Glasgow in order to teach in her father's new theological college. She was a strong supporter of the suffragette movement. At university she became friendly with her fellow-student, David Hynd, who attended her father's church. They were married at New Year, 1918, and decided together that he would return to university to take his medical qualification to go to Swaziland.

In 1924, she became only the third woman to be ordained in Scotland, following her mentor, Olive Winchester, and her own mother, Mrs Sharpe. The Hynds left for Swaziland in 1925. Nema looked after their two small children, Isabel and Samuel (later joined by Margaret), and in addition filled the roles of nurse, teacher, radiographer, brick-layer's mate, book-keeper, perpetual hostess and pastor. She was highly respected by all as a firm disciplinarian of the old school!

One anecdote about her tells of some criticism of the African missionaries for extravagant living, for each of the women returning to Britain on furlough wore a fur coat. I believe it was Mrs Hynd who revealed that it was always the same (second-hand) fur coat! The simple explanation was that, living in the heat of Swaziland, they felt keenly the chill of the British climate. But like her father, Dr Sharpe, she always took the view that sacrifices should be equally shared in the church, and that missionaries and pastors should not be expected to have a lower standard of living than any other committed Christian.

The Latta Sisters… as I remember them
Marion Doherty

Mrs Marion Doherty, the daughter of Andrew and Rina Robertson o f Uddingston, recalls two of her aunts, Lizzie and Peggy Latta.

I remember being with my mother on Uddingston Main Street when she was asked, 'How is your missionary sister?' To this my mother replied, 'Which sister? They are all missionaries!' And the lady had to say, 'The one in Africa.' I have never forgotten that. And they were indeed all missionaries: Lizzie principally in Uddingston, Peggy in Africa, Jenny in Tannochside and Viewpark, and Helen to her neighbours and the wider family. Mary, who never attended the Church of the Nazarene, was supportive of the rest of the family in it, and was an enthusiastic member of Chalmers Church, keen member of the Women's Guild and leader of the girls' auxiliary which met on a Sunday evening for those who had left the girls' Bible Class.

I was closest to Aunt Lizzie and remember her best. She was the leader of the junior Sunday school when I was in it. I knew she had an evening for preparation when she chose the hymns and prepared her own lesson. Everything seemed to run smoothly. I can still hear hymns like, 'Mighty army of the young', 'The world looks very beautiful', 'Dare to be a Daniel', and I can see her leading at the front.

Aunt Lizzie also had a missionary sewing class for girls. We met straight out of school so we took a sandwich with us and she made tea for us. She read missionary stories to us and we prayed for the missionaries we knew. I think we sewed hankies which would be gifts in the huge missionary box which went out to Swaziland from our church and Sunday school once a year. Before the annual Bible exam she would have special coaching classes on the chosen passages and had us all in top form for the big day. She was also involved with the women's meeting at the church every Monday evening. She attended every meeting of the church and on Sundays that involved walking over a mile from their home three times there and back.

When I was younger, Aunt Lizzie would come off a train from Newton where she taught and meet me at the gate of my primary school each Friday. I would go with her on her rounds delivering *The Way of Holiness*. She would knock on the door and always seemed to have a word to say, recommending an article in the magazine or some word for a family problem. Occasionally we would meet a certain lady in the street and she would stop to chat. She would plead with her to think about the mess she was making of her life; of the sadness she was bringing to her family, and how much better life would be if she became a Christian. It was several years later that I discovered that this lady was a prostitute. (Do we still seek out prostitutes these days or do we pass by on the other side?)

Calendars! Remember those? Aunt Lizzie had a huge order every year and as she sold them always prayed that some verse for the day might be read and bring a blessing. I learned later that because of her extensive knowledge of Uddingston families, shopkeepers would ask her to recommend school leavers for employment.

Before my time, Aunt Lizzie and Aunt Peggy taught night school classes to give more to the church building fund. The family was renting quite a large house in Uddingston and when the first council houses were built at Viewpark, the Latta family was delighted to qualify for a five-apartment house at such an economical rent because it meant more money for the church. (This was much to Aunt Mary's sorrow as she would much have preferred to stay in the village.)

Aunt Lizzie was *in* every service from beginning to end. She followed the preacher very carefully and her reaction would show on her face. That was fine for the preacher when all was going well, but not so good when her head would shake vigorously in disagreement! As she followed the minister's prayer she would very quietly be saying, 'Yes…yes…yes, Lord.' People nearby could hear only, 'S…s…s.' This was a wee bit of an embarrassment to me when we were on holiday in a Church of Scotland, which, in those days, was very sedate! She loved to pray (just as now I may say to someone, 'I've enjoyed talking to you'), and if she woke up in the middle of the night, she would have a short prayer for somebody or something.

It was Aunt Peggy (Margaret K. Latta) who went to be the missionary in Africa. I remember being told that she had been the district missionary secretary and that when the Hynds went to Africa, Mrs Hynd was teacher and minister. They asked the church for another teacher, but no funds were available, so they asked Aunt Peggy if she could find a young teacher who would come out to teach without a salary and live as one of the family until the general church could support her. Aunt Peggy prayed to be led to someone.

But some time previously she had been in a bus involved in a collision and had a slight injury to a leg. In due time some compensation arrived and the idea struck her that, since she hadn't found a young teacher to go to Swaziland, this unexpected money could pay for her to go. The more she considered the idea, the more she was convinced that she should be the volunteer. Some others also volunteered to support her till the church could do it. (Mrs Brand washing stairs is one of the stories.) I understand that she was Sunday school superintendent before she went to Africa and the late Sadie Murphy of the Uddingston church had strong memories of an excellent Sunday school at that time.

I always thought she was 40 when she went out in 1931, but I realize now that she must have been older than that. There were two sons in the family between Peggy and my mother, and since my mother was 42 in 1932, Aunt Peggy must have been 45 or 46. (John died just after

Mum was born and Tom and a younger brother, George, were both killed in France in the First World War.)

Gordon Thomas told me that when he was in Swaziland working with teachers who had been trained by Aunt Peggy, he was most impressed with the very high regard in which they held her. Most of all she taught them from the Bible and by example how to live their daily lives as Christians. She was a very conscientious and industrious person. Everything she did she had to do to the best of her ability. She didn't just read her Bible, but studied it and drew strength from it. It was part of her daily food, especially in Africa. One Bible I remember was well worn, not from a life-time, but from a few years!

My strongest memory of her first furlough was actually when she was having her farewell to go back to the field. It was during the Second World War and it was known that it would be a dangerous voyage. No one knew when she would be able to come back home again. I remember the church singing, 'Blest be the ties that bind' and a circle standing at the front holding hands as we sang. I feel the emotion as I type. We learned later that her ship had to change course and took a longer route to avoid a meeting with (I think) the Graf Spee. It was on her next furlough that I appreciated her most. In addition to her reports of the mission field, I was also impressed with her preaching.

Aunt Peggy was one of four teachers in the family who took an active interest in the E.I.S. [the Educational Institute of Scotland, the teachers' professional association], fighting for better pay and conditions. She tackled issues and didn't just sit back and hope for change. She had to make it happen. And this also showed in her life in the church. As I remember her, she had penetrating eyes and it was as if she could see into your soul and you could have no secrets from her. Excellent for a teacher! And probably excellent for Swaziland. She also had the loveliest smile that lit up her face.
She was awarded an MBE by the British government and the school on the Manzini Mission Station was named the Margaret Latta Memorial High school. Her MBE medal was given to the school after she died and was displayed there. But after it was stolen and recovered it was sent back and is now in my possession.

M.K. Latta ... Goes to Her Reward
David Hynd

An article by Dr David Hynd which was published in The Flame *(XXVIII, No. 5, September-October, 1962)*

It was July 5th, 1962, at Manzini (Bremersdorp), Swaziland, that a cablegram was received from Scotland saying that Miss M.K. Latta had passed away the previous day. It arrived on the first day of the annual camp meeting, when all the Swazi Nazarenes and their families had come in from the surrounding churches. When the announcement was made in the crowded Sharpe Memorial Church a hush, followed by an audible groan, swept over the congregation. Pangs of sorrow and a deep sense of loss flashed through the minds of missionaries and Swazi Christians alike, together with a feeling of deep thankfulness to God as many recalled the train of blessings that had flowed from the life of this servant of God who had given the best part of her life (1931 to 1954) in sacrificial service amongst them.

There were preachers present who knew that they had her to thank for the Christian wives whom she had trained and educated for them in their work. Behind the preachers on the platform was a choir formed by uniformed nurses, many of whom would never have qualified for entrance to the nursing school had they not passed through her boarding school. There were teachers present from all the surrounding Nazarene mission schools who are fulfilling her vision of trained Christian teachers giving a Christian education to the rising generation of Swazi children, and who would never have been teachers had she not left a teaching career in her native Scotland and started the Nazarene Teacher Training College which, since its inception, has sent out into the country 550 trained teachers.

At the dedication service for babies born to our Nazarene laity during the past year, one could see many couples presenting their plump, healthy babies into the arms of the dedicating ministers (there were 60 of them in 5 rows of 12 each), couples who had passed through her school and hostels and had set up Christian homes in the country around our Nazarene churches. At the adult baptismal service which is held every year at the camp meeting, one could recognize teenagers who had first learned to love the Lord while children in her day school and were now publicly confessing their faith and being accepted at the following communion service into the full membership of the church. At the Sunday school rally and the rally for the missionary societies which are operating in each local church, one saw the fruits of the years of pioneering effort which she had contributed to the establishing of these organisations among them.

What a rich influence has flowed out for her Master in a foreign land. When she retired and said goodbye to them in 1954, she said, 'I will be waiting for you all on the other side.' Many remembered her words, and now that she is on the 'other side' they are pledged to meet her there.

Jessie Rennie, Agnes Clark, Agnes Willox and Mary McKinley ...as I remember them
Hugh Rae

One of the most loved of our missionaries was Jessie Rennie. When she was born, her mother had said, 'Lord, here is your missionary!' Coming to faith early in life Jessie felt the call of God to overseas missions, trained as a nurse and, encouraged by her mother, went to Swaziland in the late 1930s. Small of stature, she served in the Raleigh Fitkin Memorial Hospital, and after the union with the I.H.M. became matron of the Ethel Lucas Memorial Hospital at Acornhoek. She often felt tempted to return home to her widowed mother but her mother encouraged her to stay. When she came home to retire she served for the remainder of her days as district president of the NWMS in the north district.

Agnes Clark was the second daughter of Hugh Clark and his wife of Perth. She was brought up in a home in which godly parents demonstrated in their daily living the doctrine of Christian holiness. Agnes left home to be a nurse and was appointed to Swaziland. There she met missionary James Graham, an Irishman with a thunderous voice and a magic smile. They were married and became pioneers for Nazarene missions in Malawi.

Agnes Willox was the youngest sister in her family. Her eldest sister, Jean (who later married J.B. Maclagan) had been taken by their mother at the age of six to the first Sunday service to be held by the Parkhead church in the Great Eastern Road Halls. Agnes trained as a nurse and midwife in preparation for overseas missions, but had to wait until after the Second World War for appointment to India. Agnes was then appointed to British Honduras (now Belize). During the years when appointment was delayed, the text she held on to was: 'For the vision is yet for an appointed time, but at the end it shall speak, and not lie. Though it tarry, wait for it, because it will surely come: it will not tarry' (Hab. 2:3). The third sister, Bessie (younger than Jean, older than Agnes) remained at home and was a faithful member of the church, keeping the home that Agnes returned to on her retirement.

Mary McKinley belonged to the church pioneered in Ayr from 1936 by William Taylor. A great group of young people were brought into the church and amongst these were Mary and her brother Harry. The war came in 1939 and many of the young people were scattered in the services, Mary in the army. In 1946 when Dr & Mrs Hynd were home on furlough, they enlisted her as an accountant for the business office of the mission station and hospital. Mary was also a very fine speaker and pioneered a church there. Many of the young people did not return to the Ayr church at the end of the war and Mary's departure for Africa was a severe loss to the dwindling congregation. In retirement she was a member of the Troon church and became one of Samuel Hynd's staunchest supporters when difficulties hit the Manzini mission station. She spoke at the district assembly with direct experience of the situation and could be quite fearless in the face of what she deemed injustice.

H.K. Bedwell ... as I remember him
Philip Bedwell

My father, Kenneth Bedwell, was born into the home of the Rev James Bedwell, an I.H.M. preacher. The influences of a godly home led him to accept Christ at an early age, and he came into the experience of entire sanctification under the preaching of Dr Harry Jessop. Called to be a missionary, he attended Emmanuel Bible College in Birkenhead and on graduating, joined the trekkers, walking 800 miles across England evangelizing. It was on one of these campaigns in Sunderland, Co. Durham, that he met Margaret Hewson and they fell in love. They kept in contact when he went to Africa as an I.H.M. missionary and remained loyal during the five years they were apart.

The proposal of marriage came through the mail, and they were married two days after she arrived in Africa. Someone suggested that Ken made sure the marriage took place quickly just in case she changed her mind!

On his arrival in Africa in 1931, he was stationed at the headquarters of the I.H.M. at Rehoboth near Johannesburg and buried himself in the study of Zulu. He would spend hours each day learning the grammar and then go and try it out on the Bible College students. Within six months he was proficient in Zulu and went on to master the Shangaan language.

Later he was stationed at Cottondale in the Eastern Transvaal and spent three years evangelizing in the rural areas. Such was his enthusiasm that the African people in Mozambique named him 'Yahuhuma' which means 'Running over'. He and the Rev Harry White crossed over into Mozambique on bicycles to evangelize and slept many nights in African huts. The story is told that one night as they slept, a lion climbed on the roof of the hut and began scratching at the thatch to get at the sleeping missionaries. Somehow they managed to persuade it to leave.

My father was a gifted leader and efficient administrator, but these were not his first love. He was passionate about three things. First, he was passionate about preaching. He was well-read, but, like John Wesley, essentially 'a man of one book'. His powerful expository messages, studded with gems of humour, arrested the attention of his congregation and probed to the quick of their hearts. After a massive heart attack in 1974, the doctor told him that he would never preach again. He did! When my mother warned him not to get too excited when he preached, he replied, 'How can I help but get excited with a gospel like we have?'

Secondly, he was passionate about teaching. The main assignment of his missionary career was the training of preachers and evangelists. He became principal of the I.H.M. Bible College at Rehoboth and then after the union of 1952, principal of the Nazarene Bible College at Siteki. He remained there seventeen years.

Thirdly he was passionate about literature and saw his work as an author as a vital and effective part of his ministry. His book, *Black Gold* was a history of the beginning of the I.H.M. work in Africa, a number of Bible study books were translated into three languages, and he edited the Zulu preachers' magazine for many years. He died in 1983, testifying in his last words: 'I have had a good life and I am ready to go.'

Miriam Evans ... as I remember her
Vernon Rayner

Dr Vernon Rayner recalls his aunt, Miriam Evans

Miriam Evans was born on 12th July, 1906, in Shepherds Bush, the second child of Benjamin and Laura Evans. Ben Evans was a younger son of a farming family and I think had served his apprenticeship as a draper in Wales before coming to London to seek his fortune. He ended up working in David Thomas's department store in Falcon Road, Battersea, as well as worshipping at 'The Tab', the headquarters of the International Holiness Mission. Church and store were inextricably linked. The church was organized along business lines, and commercial travellers said that you had to attend the prayer meeting to secure an order! Miriam's mother, Laura Brigden was a Londoner, a real cockney, born within the sound of Bow Bells, but judging from the sketchy details of her education, she came from a relatively wealthy London family. She worked in the accounts department of David Thomas's business before her marriage.

Life for the Evans family was very hard. They lived for many years in a small house alongside 'the shop' (as David Thomas's store was known) and Ben Evans doubled, working both as the caretaker and in the shop. Despite the lack of money their oldest boy, Will, qualified as a chartered accountant and Miriam went to London University where she obtained a first class honours in Chemistry. She was offered a position as a research student, but decided to pursue a teaching career in part because of the need to contribute to the family budget, but probably also because she wanted to work with people. All this has to be put in the context of the 1920s when opportunities for most people were limited and this success of the older two children was exceptional. The two boys that followed, David and Leslie, became drapers, while my mother, Vera, became a teacher of domestic science. While a student my mother did administrative work for Leonard Wain. Miriam was by this time teaching in Rotherham, but she then moved back home, possibly because of the chronic ill health of my grandmother and my grandfather's lack of domestic skills. She obtained a teaching position at Shepherd's Bush. Family fortunes had improved just before the Second World War and they purchased a house in Chatto Road. Ben Evans was involved in the IHM missionary work and his home was used for hospitality for visiting missionaries and speakers. Perhaps that is how Miriam was called to serve as a missionary for the IHM in South Africa.

Aunty Miriam was a very strong and determined lady in the best possible way. She had a considerable ministry among young women prior to her going to South Africa. She ran a Girl Guide unit and a girls' Bible study group when teaching in Rotherham. I guess that she was the instigator of the trips to Cliff College at Easter and Whitsun that folk from Rotherham and Battersea attended prior to the Second World War. One of the couples featured were Mr and Mrs Lambert who founded Lebanon Bible College at Berwick-on-Tweed to preach the holiness message. She used to visit Lebanon Bible College each time when on furlough and I guess lectured to the students there.

In the Thomas Memorial Church, two of the long-term members who were closely associated with Miriam were Alice Thorpe (later Colwell), whom Miriam brought from Rotherham to look after my grandmother, and Ada Rickards, who was part of Miriam's Bible study group. Mrs Bessie Wood was also closely associated with her.

Miriam left for South Africa in 1947, serving for her first term at Cottondale where she developed secondary education for young men and women. A striking feature of photographs of this time is the lack of any indication of barriers between the races. This work became difficult to continue because of the development of apartheid after the Nationalists gained power in South Africa. However, students went on to be teachers and I believe active politically in the anti-apartheid struggle. There was a measure of disappointment that some students had opted to serve a secular rather than a spiritual kingdom, but judging from her retiral testimonials, many still asked after her.

The rest of Miriam's career was spent teaching at the Bible College at Siteki in Swaziland. Again from photographs and the testimonials given at her retirement, she was greatly loved and no doubt contributed greatly to the growth of the Church in Swaziland. I sense that she understood the aspirations and concerns of the Swazis with whom she worked, and Juliet Ndzimandze, to whom she left her estate, was particularly close to her. By the time she retired, I think she sensed that her work in Siteki was done, and she was looking forward to a new field of ministry in Britain.

People who change things are not always the easiest to live with. My mother told of having to refuse to go with Miriam on her various ploys rather than being with her own family. My father despaired when teaching her to drive on her second furlough. She drove through a red traffic light in her brand new Austin A40 coming from Epsom to Battersea one Sunday morning, hit another car and escaped prosecution provided she did not drive again in the UK. I am sure that had no legal force, but she never did drive in Britain again. She had problems on the trains too and was known to get lost between Battersea and Epsom.

As a child I had no problems with her. She delivered the booty from mysterious Africa, wooden crocodiles for my windowsill and propelling pencils from the Union Castle shipping line. On her first assignment she arranged that one of her school students write to me, no doubt to improve his writing skills in what to him was a foreign language. But it was great as a very small boy to receive these airmails. It was also exciting saying farewell to her and meeting her when she was on furlough. I vaguely remember seeing her off from Southampton the first time in 1948. I think the whole church went. My father drove one of Mr Francis' Rolls Royce hearses. At the end of her first furlough she was needed back urgently. I think the Bible school principal was ill, and unusually, she was sent back to Africa by air. It seemed to take several days and we got postcards from stops along the way.

By her second furlough I was about 16, and it was just after my grandfather's death. We met her at Gatwick along with Mr Maclagan who was the district superintendent at the time. He had a black Austin A50 like my father. This would be the furlough where she learned to drive. I don't think I met her after that. Her final furlough would have been while I was in Uganda. We had intended to visit her on our way back to the UK, but in the rush to finish my Ph.D., and with the antics of Idi Amin, that did not work out.

Sue and I were looking forward to getting to know her as adults on her retiral, but that was not to be. She rushed to come home after a very busy schedule at Siteki and did not take advice to have a break in

South Africa prior to flying home. On the aeroplane she had a heart attack (I wonder now whether it was deep vein thrombosis leading to a heart attack). They wanted to put her off the plane at Frankfurt, but she prevailed on the crew to let her fly on to Heathrow. My father was confronted with a very sick sister-in-law at the airport and no one (by his account) was very interested in doing anything about it. He got her in the car and home, called the doctor and had her admitted to Epsom District Hospital. She did well at first and was out of intensive care, but unfortunately later died in hospital. One of my parents' regrets was that they were instructed by the hospital not to allow visitors other than relatives. Miriam was therefore unable to say goodbye to her friends as she would have wished. However, with the terminal illness of a loved one it is easy to know in retrospect what you should have done. She is buried in Epsom cemetery in a corner where there are many travelling people and jockeys. Do missionaries come in the same category of unusual people?

Did my Aunty Miriam affect my life? Well, yes. Africa was not an unknown frightening place, and I went there - not to South Africa, but to Uganda where the ideals embraced by Miriam Evans were well-advanced by 1966. It was a special time soon after independence when the barriers of the colonial period had broken down and I studied for a Ph.D. in the University in Kampala. I was a small part of a community of Ugandan, expatriate, and missionary friends of differing backgrounds and ages, working and learning and praying together to show that being a Christian is not just something for the poorly educated. One of the Ugandan members of our community, John Sentanu, has just become the Archbishop of York. See how God uses us both as individuals but collectively to work together for his kingdom? I then can trace a link from the IHM in Battersea via my parents (the first couple married in the Tab), through Miriam Evans, my going to Uganda to the first black archbishop in the Church of England!

There will be many thousands all over the world who have been touched directly or indirectly by Miriam Evans' life and witness in Cottondale and Siteki and as she undertook deputation work in Britain and the United States. We need more like her.

Miriam Evans … as I remember her
Charles E. Gailey

After the IHM union with the Church of the Nazarene, Dr Charles (Chuck) Gailey, now Emeritus Professor of Missions at Nazarene Theological Seminary, Kansas City, was a colleague of Miriam Evans at the Nazarene Bible College in Siteki in Swaziland.

When I think of Miriam Evans, the word that comes to mind is 'single-minded'. She was single-minded in her devotion to the Lord, to her friends, and to her work. One example comes at the level of the mundane. Whenever it was necessary for the missionary ladies to prepare a big meal, they would meet and each one would volunteer to bring a portion of the food for the feast. One would offer to bring the roast, another the Yorkshire pudding, another salad, and so on. But Miriam did not like to cook, and she had discovered that she could buy three or four tins of peas and heat them up. As soon as the discussion would open Miriam's hand would shoot up: 'I'll bring peas!' Not once or twice, but every time: 'I'll bring peas!' This became something of a joke among the ladies. They knew that they could always count on Miriam for peas!

But Miriam was single-minded in her devotion to young people. Even as she aged, she kept involved with NaYoYo (NYI). She encouraged the Rev Juliet Ndzimandze to become a great evangelist, and arranged for her to do preaching missions in Great Britain. Even after her death she continued to help. Juliet was in desperate need of housing (as I record in my book, *Daughter of Africa*, NPH, 1998, pp. 37-39):

> One day Juliet received a letter from a bank manager. It read: 'Please sign the enclosed forms and bring them to the bank. Someone in Britain has sent you R10,000 (approximately £7,000).' Miriam Evans had left a legacy to Juliet. It was almost the exact amount needed to buy the house – and just in the nick of time! The 'miracle house' was purchased.'

Juliet told the 'miracle house' story as she preached through Africa. In 1996, ten years after he heard the story, a district superintendent in Central Africa repeated it to me almost word for word.

Miriam's single-mindedness was evident in her work at the Bible College in Swaziland. She worked hard, long hours. She was so devoted to her labours that she asked to stay on beyond the normal retirement age, and was allowed to do so. When she finally retired on 2nd January, 1974, she suffered a heart attack on the plane *en route* to England. She passed away shortly thereafter. Her sister sent us a letter to say that as she was dying, she was praying for me and for the College. She was single-minded – to the end.

Minnie Singleton ... as I remember her
Arthur Fawcett

Dr Fawcett appeared in a series of programmes on Scottish Television in the 1970s ('Late Call', a five-minute religious programme), recalling people he had known in his days in the IHM in Lancashire. This is a transcript of his talk on Minnie Singleton.

I first met Minnie some fifty years ago. Her father had moved up from the Cotswolds to find work. The air of the Lancashire town was quite different from that of the Cotswolds and, working in the mills, he finally was riddled with consumption, and unable to work. Minnie was the eldest of three girls and they were hard times. She got a job as soon as she left school at fourteen, working in the cotton mills there as a 'winder' – up and down the slippery floor polished with grease, vapour and heat, in her bare feet, twisting with nimble fingers. All the time she was dreaming of something else. She became a Christian when she was about fourteen. Minnie was a *real* Christian, dedicated to the task of serving others. She desperately wanted to go overseas, but the door wasn't open for her. She had to provide for father, mother, and two younger sisters.

I can see her now going out to work, her white, long face, and those long sausage curls, three on either side of her cheeks, made by a hot poker. Minnie went to work at the mill dreaming of Africa, China or some distant part. Year after year she waited. Her hope deferred must have made her heartsick. Eventually she got her chance and when her two sisters were old enough to take up the burden of caring for the home, providing for father and mother, Minnie made her way to train. After doing her general training and midwifery training, away she went to Africa, and for the last thirty-odd years she has been nursing in the eastern Transvaal, a matron caring for babies. She might have been factory fodder. She might have had a chip on her shoulder because life had been unrewarding. She might have resented the economic necessities that bound her to machine-minding. But she did her duty while she could and as soon as she was set free she was away to serve. She with her husband Ken found that the way of saving others was the way of serving.

Minnie Singleton ... as I remember her
Olwyn Edge

The funeral tribute to Mrs Singleton, who died in 2005, was based largely on the memories of her life-long friend, Mrs Olwyn Edge

Minnie was born on 24th September, 1917, one of the three daughters of John and Annie Hope. She came to the tent campaign held by Maynard James at Daubhill crossing when a thousand decisions were registered and which led to the founding of a new church and she was introduced to me by Pastor Fawcett. My husband, Norman, who was also converted in the campaign, met Ken Singleton when he served in the R.A.F. medical corps and invited him to the church.

Minnie had received her call to be a missionary in Africa when she was fourteen years old, and although nursing was the last thing she wanted to do (she couldn't stand the smell of hospitals or the sight of blood!), she trained as a nurse in Bolton during the war. Although advised to go to St James' in Leeds or St Luke's in Bradford, where there were Christian matrons, she believed that she was directed to a local hospital which had a dreadful reputation for overworking nurses. It was known as 'the slave house'. She then went to London during the Blitz to do her midwifery training, and on returning to Bolton she was promoted to be a sister. One day in the dining room, a battle-axe of a senior sister, who had given her the hardest time during her training, confessed why: 'Other sisters were always talking about you, saying what a good nurse and a good Christian you were, and I was determined to shake the Christianity out of you! But I couldn't.' Minnie's reply was that God had given her the grace to stick it out even though she came home in tears every day.

Before Minnie left for Africa, she had led the matron and deputy matron back to faith in Christ. They set up a Nurses Christian Fellowship in the hospital, with dozens of nurses meeting for prayer and Bible study. Ninety-six of them came to her farewell service when she left for Africa. She used to say: 'Missionary service begins at home.'

Albert Lown was minister in the Bolton church when she left for Africa. She sailed from Southampton on 6th June, 1946 on the *Edinburgh Castle*. On the quayside her family sang, 'God be with you till we meet again.' Her father had said to her, 'If I don't see you again, I'll see you in heaven.' He died before her first furlough.

She arrived in Africa at a time of great hardship and privation, for the missionary work of the I.H.M. had far outstripped the ability of the home church to support it. She wrote home that they had no furniture, but had made some from wooden boxes and crates. Abigail Hewson from Sunderland, also a highly qualified nurse, arrived the next year, and the two were to serve for over thirty years. Minnie sent many photographs of the babies she delivered back to her mother, with an inscription on the back: 'Another little treasure.' She once had to perform an emergency operation on a man who had been mauled by an ox and had his intestines hanging out, following directions on the phone from a doctor sixty-seven miles away. On her first attempt at dentistry, she eventually extracted a tooth whole after three attempts and much prayer!

Ken Singleton studied at Emmanuel Bible College and followed her to Africa. They were married there on 10th May, 1952, with two little African girls as bridesmaids, and served in South Africa and Mozambique till they retired in 1983.

Ernie Eades... as I think of him
Hugh Rae

Ernest (or Ernie as he is always called) was born in London and had his early contacts with the Christian faith at the Holiness Tabernacle, now Thomas Memorial Church. Interested in all manner of things when young, it was a great day for him when he responded to the call of the preacher and went forward to give his life to God. Ever the effervescent youth, he has carried that spirit through the years in every area of life and even today in his eighties when he greets you in person or on the telephone you can see the smile break over his face and the joy of the Lord is revealed.

This Battersea lad felt the call of God to be a missionary and enrolled in Emmanuel College at Birkenhead. There the discipline shaped his life for what was to be an effective ministry. While at College he met a kindred spirit in the person of Jessie Munn who hailed from a family in Belfast, all of whom had missions at heart.

In the 1940s Ernie and Jessie came to the Church of the Nazarene in Motherwell and he took further studies at Hurlet Nazarene College. After his ordination he and Jessie were appointed to be missionaries to the Cape Verde Islands. The first time I heard Ernie testify was at a district rally and his testimony has stuck with me through the years: 'I'm glad, the devil's mad, he lost a lad he thought he had.' That summed up the total commitment of this couple as they left for their missionary assignment. One daughter, Margaret Anne, was born to them and for many years they served faithfully alongside such missionaries as Earl Mostellor and Clifford Gay. Clifford was to become Ernie's brother-in-law when he married Lottie Munn.

In the late sixties Jessie Eades took ill and the family were forced to come home. The church at Skegoneill Avenue, Belfast, called him to be their minister and during the final years of Jessie's life he both cared for her and for the congregation there. He also carried on a programme of 'aggressive evangelism', reaching out to the young people of the area through café evangelism. But his heart was all the time on the mission field. Finally Jessie died and was laid to rest in the Nazarene church yard at the country church in Desertmartin. Ernie eventually married Kay, his second wife, and served for several years in Keighley (Yorkshire) before retiring back to Ireland. Even in retirement he served for a time in Greenisland church, and has been a source of encouragement to many. His spirit of optimism still overflows. His contagious faith has encouraged many a discouraged heart and brought many a stricken soul to a place of peace.

Chapter Eight

MID-CENTURY

The North District in the Fifties

Although not reaching the peak of the Edwardian era, church attendance nationally showed some recovery in the 1950s. Billy Graham's London 'Crusade' at Harringay in 1954 and 'All-Scotland Crusade' at the Kelvin Hall in Glasgow in 1955 won national headlines and resulted in thousands of conversions. British Nazarenes participated in the advances and were encouraged by the growth of their tiny denomination through the two unions and through church extension.

In the British Isles north district another congregation which united with the Church of the Nazarene in 1954 gave them at last a church in the Scottish capital. This was Albany Street Congregational Church in the centre of Edinburgh, under the leadership of the blind Highland preacher, the Rev Neil Robertson. The stately old church was on the edge of Edinburgh's historic eighteenth-century 'New Town' with its notable Georgian architecture. Among the leading members were Major Frank Govan, the son of J.G. Govan of the Faith Mission, and Miss Cherry-Garrard, a redoubtable 'holiness' warrior whose brother had been photographer on the famous and ill-fated expedition of Captain Scott to the South pole in 1912.[1] When Neil Robertson went to the United States in 1960, the Rev Cyril Frame succeeded him. He had studied first in the College his father founded at Hurlet and had just graduated with the B.D. degree from Nazarene Theological Seminary in Kansas City. In 1956, the possibility of establishing a church in a third of the four capital cities of the British Isles opened up when Dr Frame received a letter from a Dublin business man, James Hogan.

---

1 In the flat in Spottiswood Street, Marchmont which she shared with Miss F.G.S. Munro, large prints of Antartica photographed by Apsley Cherry-Garrard hung in the drawing room. 'Cherry' herself was no mean explorer, having been one of the first women (if not the first) to climb the Matterhorn. She had been a strong supporter of Lebanon Bible College founded by David Lambert.

One of the most encouraging developments in the 1950s was the growth of the church at Irvine on the Clyde coast under its young minister, Rev James Doherty, another of the graduates of the new Hurlet Nazarene College. The redevelopment of Irvine by the town council brought compensation for the hall they had been meeting in, and they built one of the first bright 'modern' post-war buildings which the denomination had in the whole of Britain, opened in July 1956. Mrs Marion Doherty was a school teacher, the daughter of Andrew and Rina Robertson of Uddingston, and her work in building up a large Sunday school gave the congregation an effective means of outreach into the community. The Irvine Sunday school won the district Sunday school shield year after year.

In 1957 the Perth church, where the Rev Leslie Hands was minister, also moved into a modern brick-building in Milne Street after decades in temporary accommodation. A new brick building also went up in Ballymacarrett in Belfast, where the dynamic ministry of the Rev Raymond Spence gathered a congregation of committed young people. Skegoneill Avenue Church in Belfast already had a new brick-built building, and the church in Dromore, Co. Down, also moved into a permanent building under the leadership of the Rev James Macleod. His aquiline nose, clerical collar, and black army beret made him a well-known figure in that rural area for many years as he turned up in market places with his concertina to preach in the open-air in his clear Fife accent.

Meanwhile, having been surprisingly voted out at the Daubhill Church in Bolton, Albert Lown planted a vigorous new church in Lisburn, a growing town in Co. Down, just south of Belfast. Here too a modern brick building was built. The Uddingston church called an American minister, the Rev Don Zimmerli, who had a fruitful ministry in which his wife's musicianship was an enormous help. Sydney Martin was followed in Twechar by William Robertson, Jock Henson and then the Rev David McCulloch, Snr, the gracious and gifted preacher who had been a leading layman in the Paisley church.

Sydney Martin followed Fletcher Tink at Parkhead church in 1950. The church was renamed 'Sharpe Memorial Church of the Nazarene' in 1953 and an electronic organ installed in memory of Dr and Mrs

Sharpe. In 1956, the congregation celebrated their golden jubilee. Writing forty years later, Sydney Martin gave a fascinating insight into the challenge of following faithfully Dr Sharpe's example in the pulpit of the Parkhead church:

> In the main, the problem I was now encountering derived from the increasing difficulty involved in seeking to justify his staunch defence of what – for want of a better term – may be described as traditional holiness terminology. In the course of my ministry (still in Twechar), my growing preference was for the use of strictly Bible terms but then I awoke to the fact that this demanded expository skills which I had yet to develop. This, in turn, rendered it imperative that I pursue a more assiduous study in the field of biblical exegesis, besides giving much more serious attention to the theology of holiness.[2]

Clearly, although he strongly adhered to the holiness tradition, Sydney Martin was becoming aware that some of the biblical exegesis which supported the doctrine and the somewhat stereotypical theological terminology and categories were inadequate. But as one brought up in the Methodist Church, he could not but be aware that behind the inadequacies of the nineteenth-century holiness movement, there was the more profound and scholarly teaching of the Wesleys. When he moved from Twechar to Parkhead he was also aware of the 'Instituters' in the congregation, a questioning, thinking group of young people with educational advantages not known to their parents and grandparents who challenged him to think through his preaching of the doctrine of Christian holiness more rigorously. The consequence was the development of a preaching ministry which was shaped by some of the outstanding preachers of the mid-twentieth century. He read and learned from the clarity and challenge of the Kirk's greatest preacher, James S. Stewart, the warm pastoral appeal of the leading Methodist, W.E. Sangster, and the expository approach being modelled by the great Calvinist preacher, Dr Martin Lloyd-Jones and by the young rector of All Souls, Langham Place, John Stott. Sydney Martin maintained the tradition of the Sunday evening 'altar call', but his preaching was in no way the superficial or legalistic preaching which

---

2 Sharpe Memorial Church of the Nazarene, 1906-1996: Ninety Years at Parkhead – A Celebration (Glasgow: Sharpe Memorial, 1996), 33.

could sometimes precede that. His congregation never left without some new insight – something to think about and apply to their lives – so that even though many families began to move out to the suburbs, they gladly travelled back to the warm fellowship, the hearty singing and the spiritual food available, morning and evening, at Sharpe Memorial.

The hymnody of the congregation continued to combine classical hymnody and anthems and Scottish metrical psalms in morning worship with the gospel song tradition in the evening, creatively developed by the choral music of the Lillenas Publishing Company. 'Glory marches' had passed into history, but a little band led by the irrepressible Mrs Brough sat in the 'Amen corner' and continued to encourage the preacher with their 'Amens'. On one occasion, blessed by the choir's rendering of the 'Hallelujah Chorus', she broke into Handel's final dramatic silence with her own heartfelt 'Hallelujah!'

The city of Glasgow was building new housing estates on the periphery in the 1950s, principally to demolish some of the older housing, particularly in slum areas. The Sharpe Memorial Church answered this challenge by opening a branch church in the new housing area of Barlanark, and built a temporary hall church. The initial work of forming a congregation was undertaken by Leslie Evans, who had recently completed his studies at Hurlet, and when the church was organized, his friend Brian Farmer was called to be the first minister of the newly organized church.

In 1958, the denomination world-wide celebrated the fiftieth anniversary of the uniting assembly at Pilot Point which had brought the three American groups together. Dr Frame hired the Lyric Theatre in the Y.M.C.A. building in the centre of Glasgow for a campaign with Dr Edward Lawlor, one of the Nazarene district superintendents from Canada. June Zimmerli from Uddingston, Arthur Noble from Parkhead and Tom Pollock from Paisley jointly trained a united choir from the churches in the North district, and the congregation learned the gospel song written by the Nazarene song-writer, Haldor Lillenas, for the occasion, and based on words of Phineas Bresee, 'The sun never sets in the morning.' The mood was one of optimism and advance. At the end of the decade, the Rev Leslie Roberts moved to plant a new church in Dublin.

The South District in the Fifties

The British Isles south district was originally designed to be approximately equal in size to British Isles north, but when the Calvary Holiness Church united with the Church of the Nazarene in 1955, it became significantly larger. Yet its churches were scattered more widely in a country with a very much larger population, and many of them, begun in revival, were now mainly older congregations in unattractive old buildings in depressed areas. The old I.H.M. Battersea Tabernacle was re-named the Thomas Memorial Church of the Nazarene and J.B. Maclagan was succeeded as minister by the Rev Maurice Winterburn. J.B. brought T.C. Mitchell to Bolton in succession to Albert Lown, and later, in the sixties, to Battersea. In both churches, this widely read Scottish preacher with his love of the Wesleys, his sharp critique of everything superficial and trivial, and his incisive and witty turn of phrase, attracted good congregations of regular attenders.

The Maclagan family and the Morley congregation were long-established Nazarenes, and Speke Hall (now the Clapham Junction church) and the missions in Ilkeston and Cosham had united with the Nazarenes before the unions with the I.H.M. and the C.H.C. There had also been Nazarene churches established in Birmingham and Leeds. But the rest of the churches in England had been part of the I.H.M. or the C.H.C., and to all of those, the annual district assembly, presided over by an American general superintendent and with annual reports and opportunities for wide-ranging discussion, was a new experience. The five general superintendents in office together for about twenty years in the fifties and sixties were authority figures and dynamic pulpiteers – Hardy C. Powers, G.B. Williamson, D.I. Vanderpool, Samuel Young, and Hugh C. Benner. Americans were popular in the fifties and American influence on British popular culture was strong. The 'Western' with its 'cowboys and Indians' was a familiar genre, even in Nazarene homes, where televisions were making their appearance.[3] The Billy Graham crusades, popularizing American 'gospel' music, made the Nazarene gospel songs seem fashionable and 'modern', and the general superintendents brought a new breadth of perspective and the sense of belonging to a much larger international church with a world vision.

J.B. Maclagan was also adept at putting the church in the public eye. He invited local dignitaries to bring civic greetings – the Mayor of Bolton to the district assembly there in 1954, the Mayor of Battersea in 1955, and Sir Harry Hardy, the county alderman of the West Riding of Yorkshire, to the assembly at Morley in 1956. The union had also brought together some very able people. Among the leading lay people in the south district were several members of Thomas Memorial Church. These included Harry Wood, who became district treasurer, Mrs Maclagan, who served as district president of the N.F.M.S.,[4] S.F. Francis, who served as chairman of the district Church School Board, and two children of W.S. Milbank who were school teachers. Douglas Milbank (who was to marry Jean Maclagan) and his sister, Ruth, organized the annual boys' and girls' camps. Large Sunday schools in the district included the branch Sunday school started by the church in Balmoral Road, Watford, in the new Woodside housing estate. It had 250 children by 1957. Sunday school enrolment in the British Isles South District rose to 4,391 by the end of the decade.

But although the unions brought increased strength and wider perspective and were very encouraging, there were some underlying problems which the Church of the Nazarene in England and Wales

---

3 Among older and stricter members there was some opposition to television which 'brought the world into your home'. Dr Sydney Martin chose not to have one till the older generation in Sharpe Memorial had passed on to their reward. Once, when Mr and Mrs Maclagan came to the author's home for a meal in the early sixties, J.B. was highly amused at the cabinet doors on our television set. 'So that's how you hide it when the minister comes to call!' The Billy Graham films of the fifties helped some to see that the technique of cinematography was not intrinsically evil.

4 What was originally the Women's Foreign Missionary Society had become the N.F.M.S. (Nazarene Foreign Missionary Society) in 1952, but women still took the leadership roles. In 1964 the name was changed again to N.W.M.S. (Nazarene World Missionary Society, changed again in 1976 to 'Mission' Society). It is now NMI, Nazarene Missions International.

needed to face. First, there was the question whether the district was too spread out geographically. No longer 'superintendent minister' with only his own congregation, but now a 'district superintendent' feeling responsibility for all the congregations, J.B. took to road and rail. Although Britain's system of motorways had not yet been constructed, he covered between 35,000 and 50,000 miles a year, much of this because he was based in the old I.H.M headquarters in London and most of the congregations were in Yorkshire and Lancashire. A second critical problem was the shortage of ministers. He reported to the district assembly in 1957 that fourteen of the C.H.C. churches had no pastor after the union of 1955. That year, he reported, he had visited all of the churches except two, had conducted thirty annual business meetings and preached virtually every Sunday as well as at mid-week meetings, conventions, and anniversaries. He had chaired district boards and fraternals and had met town clerks, city engineers, solicitors and the director of the BBC. His conscientious service in attempting to be a senior pastor to his far-flung churches and especially those without ministers had led however to an ominous warning sign:

> Unfortunately the travelling by day and night over the past years, and the care of so many vacant churches took toll of my strength, and for the first time in my life I was compelled to give in because of a heart condition. After three weeks' rest in bed I felt quite a bit stronger and resumed my duties.

A commission was set up in 1957 to study the question whether the district should be divided, but when it reported three years later, it was inconclusive. The north of England could form a fairly strong and closely-knit district, but the south would hardly be able to do more than pay its district superintendent's salary. The commission recommended that no further steps be taken till the work in the south had been strengthened, so Mr Maclagan continued to travel.

BINC

The union with the Calvary Holiness Church raised the question of what to do with the two colleges, Hurlet and Beech Lawn. Hurlet had twenty students, Beach Lawn had four: there was more space for expansion in Hurlet's ten acres, but Stalybridge was more central for the newly united church. Naturally there were emotional attachments to both. After prolonged debate, the matter was referred to the board of general superintendents who came up with the judgment worthy of Solomon that both properties should be put on the market and a new property purchased. West Hurlet House sold first and the staff and students moved to Beech Lawn College in Stalybridge. When that property was sold, they were accommodated in Ashton-under-Lyne in the church building and in the homes of members until a suitable property, The White House, was found in Didsbury in south Manchester. It was bought for £9,500 and staff and students moved in during April, 1959. Now re-named 'British Isles Nazarene College' and situated right at the geographical centre of the British Isles, the new College symbolized the newly united British Church of the Nazarene.

At the same time there was an intangible loss for the north district and for the College itself which did not show up on any balance sheet. Hurlet Nazarene College had become a centre for the young people of the district with vibrant Friday night gatherings which had developed an irreplaceable sense of identity and belonging. Its strategic location within travelling distance of major Nazarene churches also allowed students to experience the ministries of T.C. Mitchell at Paisley or Sydney Martin at Parkhead and to enjoy the warm hospitality of other well-established churches at Port Glasgow, Govan or Uddingston. Preparation for ministry at Hurlet was in this way an enculturation into a whole living tradition. The welcome was equally warm of course in Ashton or Salford, at the Manchester church or in Bolton where T.C. Mitchell was now preaching, soon followed by T.W. Schofield. But there were fewer young people, distances to Bolton or Ashton were greater, and the Manchester congregation had shrunk. Their large Manchester Tabernacle in Brunswick Street had fallen to redevelopment, and a remnant was now meeting in an unprepossessing hall in Carmoor Road.

The White House was built in the Tudor half-timber style popular in the Edwardian era, with solid oak timbers and a most authentic-looking roof of Yorkshire stone. But with only seven bedrooms and three public rooms, it was difficult to accommodate twenty students, a resident cook and the principal with his family. By 1961 however, the two districts had raised the money (with help from the general funds of the denomination) to build a new residence with twenty-one study-bedrooms, a lecture room and a common room. This was named 'Hurlet Hall' and opened by Dr G.B. Williamson. It cost £18,000 and the rooms were named after churches which had particularly contributed to the building fund. The garage wing of the White House was also converted into several study-bedrooms and named 'Beech Wing'. Space was still short, however, since the Rev and Mrs Alex Deasley and their young family moved in when he became a resident lecturer, and a little later, the Rev and Mrs Jack Ford and their daughter Pauline also moved into the White House.

For six years (1959 to 1965) these 'three wise men' formed the academic staff of BINC. Alex Deasley, the son of the Rev Robert Deasley of Dundee and then Birmingham, was a graduate of Cambridge, having specialized there in New Testament studies. His meticulous scholarship and incisive expository preaching provided an excellent model for a new generation of students.[5] Jack Ford had achieved the feat of serving in active ministry in the Victoria Street church in Sheffield[6] while also undertaking a B.D. degree from London University, a very rigorous academic preparation in which the university supplies only syllabuses and final examinations and the student must provide his own tuition. He lectured in Old Testament and Church History and pursued PhD studies, writing a thesis on the history of the three groups now forming the Church of the Nazarene in Britain.[7] The Principal, Hugh Rae, who had managed the long-drawn move from Paisley via Stalybridge and Ashton to Didsbury, lectured in philosophy and systematic theology, balanced the books, maintained the property, counselled and disciplined the students, oversaw the domestic life of the institution, took his turn in preaching both in college and out in the churches, and miraculously even found time for an occasional game of golf! His notable service to theological

---

5 His musical abilities are not so often noted but the district NYPS report in 1960 commented on the visit of the general NYPS secretary, Ponder Gilliland, and added the tribute: 'The ministry of Mr Paul Skiles on the trombone accompanied by Rev Alex Deasley on the piano was thrilling.'

6 The Victoria Street building had been built by the Irvingites, the Catholic Apostolic Church, who tried to revive the architecture of the Middle Ages. It was the only Church of the Nazarene anywhere in the world with authentic gargoyles!

7 Jack Ford, *In the Steps of John Wesley: The Church of the Nazarene in Britain* (Kansas City: Nazarene Publishing House, 1968).

education was recognized by a doctorate from Olivet Nazarene College.

The Swinging Sixties

The united college was established at the beginning of a decade which was to prove a turning point in the mood and culture of Britain. The decade of the fifties has been called the last 'Victorian' decade, and at the time, the maintenance of long-established norms and customs did not appear at all remarkable. But it was evident at the beginning of the nineteen-sixties, and has become increasingly evident since, that there was a profound change in the national mood early in the new decade. At the level of public affairs, Harold Macmillan, the Prime Minister who had won the 1959 general election as 'Wondermac' with his slogan, 'You've never had it so good!', very quickly was made to appear remote and old-fashioned by a daring new fashion for satire on stage and television. The Profumo scandal, when a minister of the Crown lied to Parliament about his extra-marital affair, shook public confidence in 'the establishment', the governing upper class who still dominated national life. 'Rock 'n' roll' signalled the appearance of 'pop' culture and a new cultural figure, the 'teenager', appeared for the first time, with money to spend on records and dress styles distinctly different from parents. Hugh Carlton-Greene, the first humanist to hold the influential position of director-general of the BBC, promoted the new mood of questioning and even mocking authority figures who had previously been treated with respect. Deference was out!

While the questioning of authority and of the snobbery which attached to social class may have been healthy, there was inextricably connected with that a questioning of the Christian 'establishment' and the Christian consensus which had been dominant for over a century. The liberalizing of the laws on gambling, censorship, the licensing of pubs, and Sabbath observance, together with the introduction of 'Premium Bonds', were significant enough, but perhaps even more momentous for moral standards was the legislation which made divorce easier, de-criminalized homosexual relations between 'consenting adults in private', and legalized abortion. The introduction of what was called 'the permissive society' in the 'swinging sixties' marked a decisive turning point for the influence of the Christian church in Britain. Statistical graphs of church attendance, church membership, infant baptisms, and Sunday school enrolment all show that drastic decline began in that decade.[8]

It is clear from committee reports to the Nazarene district assemblies that the change of national mood was evident at the time. Reporting to the south district assembly in 1964, the committee on the 'State of the Church and Public Morals', chaired by A.R.G. Deasley, commented on 'the steady drift from standards of Christian morality' and the 'flippant spurning of values which made Britain great'. They criticized 'eminent clerics' who spoke on behalf of the so-called 'new morality' which was neither new nor moral, and they noted particularly the decline in temperance, the increase in the profaning of the Lord's Day and in swearing, and the 'violence and sensuality on television'. They also noted that a 'colour problem' could arise from the influx of Commonwealth citizens and urged that those who believed in 'perfect love' ought to give a lead in promoting inter-racial harmony. Even stronger was the 'Church and Nation' committee report at the north district assembly the following year, which was disturbed by the 'rapid decline in moral standards in the nation.' They specified 'the increasing flood of filthy literature in bookstalls, the licentious plays on radio and television and the coarse suggestive talk heard everywhere.' They warned that 'Sodom's sins will bring Sodom's judgment,' they denounced a recent bill introduced into the House of Lords to legalize homosexuality, and declared, 'We are shocked and angered at the press's exploiting of moral failure and its every attempt to glamourize divorce and undermine the sacredness of marriage.'

The change in the national mood seemed to be reflected too by a change in the church, even among the 'holiness people'. J.B. Maclagan issued a warning against materialism in his assembly report of 1960:

> There must be hundreds of Christian homes where the deposit and payments on the television set take priority over giving to the Lord's work. There must be many hearts where the tenth commandment is put on one side and every energy is

---

8 For the argument that secularization was not so much a gradual development of two centuries as a sudden collapse of the Christian consensus in the 1960s, see Callum G. Brown, *The Death of Christian Britain* (London and New York: Routledge, 2001).

expended in keeping abreast of the world's standards of comfort and entertainment.

The same south district committee report of 1964 referred to a 'spirit of stagnation', 'the creeping progress of Sunday Christianity', and was disturbed at the defeatism which sees only difficulties and not opportunities for the denomination. The same north district committee report the next year added criticism of the growing unwillingness of members to be delegates at the district assembly: 'Many of our people regard it as of little importance.'

Both districts were also concerned that there was not more growth in membership. The north district established new churches in Dublin, where the Rev Leslie Roberts was the pioneer, in Clermiston, a new housing estate in Edinburgh where the Tarrant family and other helpers formed a team, in Camelon near Falkirk, and in Greenisland on the Antrim shore of Belfast Lough. Dr Frame published a district bulletin when David Tarrant left the solid church in Port Glasgow to pioneer a home mission church in Clermiston with a typically journalistic headline: 'Is Tarrant mad?' However, ably assisted by his family and their friends, David Tarrant built up a large Sunday school and established a good congregation in a modern brick-built hall-church suitable for youth activities.[9] Also during the decade a mission hall in Kilmarnock in Ayrshire became a Nazarene church, and a Mr Farmer, who *was* a farmer in Desertmartin, a small country town in Co. Londonderry, gave land to establish a new congregation, possibly the first truly rural Nazarene church in the United Kingdom. The Rev Bert Kelly established a good foundation there. J.B. Maclagan returned to preach at the dedication of a large new church in Port Glasgow, when the congregation at last left their old 'iron kirk' on the railway land at the end of a cul-de-sac, and moved to a beautiful new church on the hill above the town.

In the south district, the Rev Frank Webster moved to Bargoed and launched a new work in the city of Cardiff ably assisted by Mrs Mary Webster and two nurses, Anne Stead and Diane Robinson, along with

---

9 Sharpe Memorial Church had been given the communion table from Parkhead Methodist Church further down Burgher Street when that church closed, and so gave its original communion table to Clermiston.

Nova Gill and the Rice family from Ilkeston. There were now Nazarene churches in all four capitals of the British Isles.[10] In 1963-64, a church in Longton, Stoke-on-Trent, affiliated with the denomination and a church was begun in Brooklands, a new housing estate in Manchester a few miles from the College.

Severe Losses and Slow Gains

Slow but steady growth was the picture in both districts when the British Church of the Nazarene was hit by the severe loss of two dynamic Scotsmen in its leadership, Hugh Rae and J.B. Maclagan.

The resignation of Hugh Rae as Principal of the College came unexpectedly in 1965. He has given an account of the circumstances:

> In 1964 a decision was taken by the General Church of the Nazarene – without any consultation with the College authorities in Britain – to establish a Bible College in Europe to prepare young people on the continent for ministry in the church. Although there was no obligation to consult British Nazarenes, the fact that this College, situated in Büsingen, Germany, was to carry out its instruction in English made the lack of communication very evident. This event made me very unsettled. Here in Britain, a College established some 20 years, labouring under staggering financial demands but well situated to teach students from the continent, was left to struggle on while the church spent thousands of dollars (millions, in the longer run) to establish an English-speaking college where students were surrounded by a German-speaking population.[11]

It is clear that this development was the last straw after years of sacrificial service and unceasing pressure. But after wrestling with the issue month after month until he was weary and frustrated, Hugh Rae decided that it was best to resign. The board of trustees were shocked, but there can be little doubt that for his own health and long-term service, this was the right decision. Jack Ford was just completing the long and painstaking task of primary research for his doctoral thesis,

---

10 That was the way it was expressed – surprisingly, since Ulstermen would claim Belfast as the fifth!

11 Hugh Rae, *Scholarship on Fire*, 86f.

collecting minute books and letters and other material scattered over the country and writing the first scholarly history of the British Nazarenes. He was appointed principal, and the Rae family moved back to Troon for a few years and then on to serve at Canadian Nazarene College in Winnipeg.

One of Dr Rae's last engagements before he left for Canada was to be the speaker at the Parkhead NYPS weekend conference in the lovely old guest house of Piersland in his home town of Troon. He was given the topic of 'The Church of the Nazarene in the British Isles', and among his comments picked out the crying need to tackle the low remuneration of ministers. The NYPS president, George Irvine (the son of Hugh Rae's beloved pastor, Joseph Irvine), who was (in a phrase typical of George Frame) 'a young executive', believed that actions spoke louder than words, and galvanized the group of young people to draw up a scheme utilizing the return of tax now available to those who signed a 'covenant' to give to a charity over seven years. The group met with the district advisory board who supported a scheme presented to the district assembly in 1969 to set up a 'Maintenance of the Ministry' Fund administered by a board of lay people. David Henson of Uddingston chaired this board for most of the next thirty years.

Jack Ford succeeded Hugh Rae as principal of BINC, having just completed his University of London PhD on the history of the three movements which were united as the Church of the Nazarene in the British Isles. It was published by the Nazarene Publishing House in Kansas City.[12]

The second loss was more final. J.B. Maclagan, two months before the district assembly of 1967 at which he would have retired, suffered a heart attack and died. Two years earlier he had reported: 'Through the providence of God I have been blessed this year with the best health I have known for some years, and have been able to carry a heavy load of work. It would seem that there are several years of good service in me yet…' But at the 1967 assembly, the advisory board had to append to their report 'a brief outline of the sacrificial labours of our late

---

[12] Ford, Jack, In the Steps of John Wesley: The Church of the Nazarene in Britain (Kansas City: Nazarene Publishing House, 1968).

district superintendent during the ten months in which he served the district prior to his home-call.'

The memorial service after the assembly began with the Scottish metrical paraphrase of Genesis 28: 20-22, 'O God of Bethel' which includes the stanza:

O spread Thy covering wings around,
Till all our strivings cease,
And at our Father's loved abode
Our souls arrive in peace.

T.C. Mitchell and Jack Ford led in prayer, George Frame gave a warm tribute to his old comrade-in-arms, and G.B. Williamson preached on the text, 'A prince and a great man has fallen in Israel.'

At the north district assembly, which met first, a debate on whether the two districts should unite was allowed and then, when it became rather excited and divisive, was badly mishandled by the general superintendent. But at the south district assembly, T.W. Schofield, the district secretary, was elected district superintendent on the third ballot. He was a Yorkshireman, had been converted and discipled in the Morley church, had studied at Emmanuel Bible College when there was no Nazarene College, and after ministries in Govan (Glasgow), Ardrossan and Dewsbury, had come to the Daubhill church in Bolton. There a large modern church had been constructed, complete with a three-manual pipe organ built as a sacrificial labour of love by Frank Barnes, who sadly died before it was finally complete.[13]

There were other major changes of leadership. The Rev Peter Gentry became district secretary, and Mrs Maclagan retired as president of the NWMS (as she had intended to do) to be succeeded by a doctor's wife from the Bolton church, Mrs Elizabeth Grace. Douglas Milbank, the Maclagans' son-in-law, resigned as chairman of the district Church School Board, receiving a standing ovation (unusual in Britain!) for his

13 See the pamphlet by his son, David Barnes, 'A Pipe Dream: The History of the Organ of the Bolton First Church of the Nazarene.'

long and effective service.[14] The Rev Frank Morley was now district NYPS president. T.W. Schofield sold the district manse in London and stayed in the north: the main centre of district leadership had passed from Battersea to Bolton.

Further changes came in 1968. T.C. Mitchell left the district to lecture at the new European Nazarene Bible College in Büsingen on the Swiss-German border, and was succeeded at Thomas Memorial by Albert Lown. E.E. Dean resigned because of ill-health after a long and effective ministry in Totterdown in Bristol.

That same year Maynard James, who had a wide ministry outside the denomination, resigned as district evangelist. Throughout the late sixties, the Clapham Junction church struggled with the deteriorating state of the old Speke Hall and the area around it, with the accompanying problem of vandalism. But under the Rev Ron Thomas they persevered till they won compensation as part of urban redevelopment and opened a strikingly modern building on 23rd May, 1970

Maynard James still edited *The Flame*, which had been accepted at the union of 1955 as in effect the British Nazarene magazine in place of *The Way*. However, there was continuing dissatisfaction with it, expressed at both north and south district assemblies. In 1964, the south district assembly committee on publishing interests had expressed concern 'that sometimes the emphases of *The Flame* are not necessarily those of the church.' Four years later, the same committee expressed interest in a British edition of the general church magazine, *The Herald of Holiness*. The suggestion of a *British* edition clearly implies that the strongly American flavour of *The Herald* was now seen as a disadvantage. The committee commended the staff of *The Flame*, but they recommended that 'articles expressing a personal or extreme doctrinal viewpoint not in harmony with the *Manual* or teaching of the Church of the Nazarene should be accompanied by a footnote to this effect.'

---

14 Douglas Milbank eventually became principal of Southlands College (a Methodist institution). His son, the theologian, Professor John Milbank, is one of the leading exponents of 'Radical Orthodoxy'.

In truth, *The Flame*, while it declared itself to be 'a bi-monthly for the spread of full salvation', reflected the opinions of its editor, particularly his pre-millennial (even British Israelite) interest in the state of Israel, his tendency to interpret the struggle against Russian Communism in the light of 'biblical prophecy', his views on how women should dress, and most offensive to many, his apparent sympathy for the apartheid regime in South Africa. The space he gave to articles by his long-standing South African friend, the Salvation Army major, Alister Smith, provoked a notable riposte in a letter published in *The Flame* from the College lecturer, A.R.G. Deasley, whose contempt for the South African regime was trenchantly expressed in the suggestion that Major Smith should go and 'stick his head in a bucket'!

Meanwhile in the north district as the decade ended, Dr Frame took the risk of inviting another charismatic itinerant preacher to conduct two 'crusades' in Ireland. The Rev Samuel Doctorian, an Armenian Christian whose testimony tells of his conversion right at the geographical site of Calvary, and who had been one of George Frame's students in the earliest years of Hurlet, had left the Church of the Nazarene to found his own mission and ran an orphanage in Beirut. Dr Frame invited Doctorian to be the preacher at the 'Ulster Hall Crusade' in Belfast in the September, 1967. A powerful orator and revivalist with a magnetic personality and a fund of remarkable stories about God's providential leadings in his life, Doctorian returned the next summer to preach at a second crusade held in the Y.M.C.A. in Dublin. The blind Welsh preacher, the Rev Glyn Thomas, also something of a charismatic personality, was by now minister of the Dublin church. This crusade produced such scenes of revival that the meetings were extended for several further weeks in the Presbyterian Church across the street, and many testified to the life-changing effect. Sadly rumours later reached Ireland about Doctorian which damaged the effect of his ministry.

Sydney Martin

T.C. Mitchell

The Rev and Mrs J.B. Maclagan

The 'Three Wise Men'
The academic staff of BINC in 1961: l. to r.: Jack Ford, Hugh Rae and Alex Deasley

Seated l. to r.: George Frame, Hugh Rae, J.B. Maclagan.
Standing l. to r.: H.E. Wood, J. Ford, S. Martin, W. Henson, and L.C. Shepherd

The opening of Hurlet Hall at BINC in 1961:
l. to r.: Hugh Rae, Jack Ford, George Frame, A.R.G. Deasley, J.B. Maclagan and G.B. Williamson

The opening of the new church in Lisburn.
On the left, A.J. Lown, in the centre, Dr Frame, on the right, James Macleod; behind Dr Frame, Peter Ferguson (in dark suit).

George Frame...as I remember him
Hugh Rae

I first met George Frame in 1935 at the dedication of the Irvine Church. A friend, Nancy Burgess, had accompanied my mother and my brother and me. Suddenly the friend collapsed and my mother helped her out, leaving us two boys a bit anxious. This minister on the platform leaned forward and said kindly, 'Your mum will be back.' Over the years I came to appreciate greatly his deep concern for children and young people. At the 1939 district assembly, which was my first as a delegate, I noticed that he and his friend J.B. were somewhat intent on putting the then district superintendent under pressure. One of the criticisms was that he had been arranging a preaching tour in America for 1940 and thus assumed that he would be elected as a delegate to the 1940 General Assembly. To the mind of this teenager all that seemed to be inconsequential to the business of the assembly.

With the resignation of Robert Purvis, in 1940, Frame was elected district superintendent, an office that he held for thirty-two years. He soon was instrumental in establishing three churches in Birmingham and in finding new recruits for the ministry, including George Brown, W. S. Tranter, Ernest Eades, William Russell, Leslie Roberts, T. W. Schofield, Sydney Martin and David Tarrant.

Not always an easy man to converse with, probably because he was basically shy, his mind was ever active about the work of the Church, for Frame was a passionate Nazarene. Such was his loyalty that he seemed to feel that those who left the denomination were guilty of some kind of betrayal. This was evident by his feelings about such men as Robert Purvis, his friend J. B. Maclagan when he went to the I.H.M., and also Arthur Fawcett. This made his relations with those men difficult. Robert Purvis was a great favourite in the Troon church and they invited him to be the anniversary speaker and George Frame to chair the evening. Frame had great hesitation in coming since he saw Purvis, now a United Free Church minister, as one who had betrayed the cause.

Of the many qualities of his leadership, his courage, seen in the founding of Hurlet Nazarene College in the midst of war, must rank high. I remember him as Principal when I was a student at the College and particularly appreciated his ability to laugh at himself. He very much wanted to drive, but his poor eyesight made that difficult. He went out with David Anderson as the qualified driver in the Morris car they had bought, but we as students only knew about this when we discovered skid marks on the driveway and the large five-foot by 18 inches gatepost lying on the ground! Greeted by a jocular buzz of conversation when he arrived back at the College, he called out, 'If you want to know about the gatepost, I will tell you!' Finally, he did pass his test, but he would only drive out in the countryside.

I remember him later as the chairman of the board of trustees who had the courage to invite me to be principal. It was in 1952, while attending the general assembly in Kansas City that Dr Frame, J.S. Logan and I were talking of the day's events in the Katz Drug Store. Suddenly, out of the blue, Dr Frame looked across the table and said, 'Hugh, how old are you?' I answered that I was thirty-one. That was the end of that part of the conversation. We continued with the meal and then went to our respective hotel rooms. I was sharing with J.S., who later in the evening asked me what George Frame's question was about. I put him off with some answer, but in my mind I had already figured out the import of the question.

Over the years from 1952 till his death in 1979 George Frame was a constant source of encouragement and strength. He was an ill man when he visited us in Winnipeg in 1972 and persuaded me to give the invitation back to Manchester serious thought. His diplomatic skills were seen at their best in the discussions which brought both the International Holiness Mission and the Calvary Holiness Church into union with the Church of the Nazarene.

His later years saw declining health due to Parkinson's but never a complaint. One of his last preaching engagements was as speaker at the College graduation banquet in 1977 when those of us present can never forget this frail and failing man speaking as always fluently without a note on the text, 'Though the outer man perisheth, the inner man is renewed from day to day.' George Frame's impact on the church in Britain is still with us.

Maynard G. James … as I remember him
Hugh Rae

The anointing of the Spirit was upon Maynard James and in the depression days of the 1930s many hundreds found salvation through his preaching. He was indeed a charismatic figure with that characteristic Welsh winsomeness. However in assessing the strength of his leadership, I think it would be fair to say that he had little time or inclination for the minute detail that is so essential to establishing a firm foundation. Others made up in some measure for this, but his was the hand at the helm of the Calvary Holiness Church and therefore his lack of administrative technique meant that when the pressures came in the post-war world, the edifice built under the dynamic and charismatic leadership of James was seen to be less substantial than it appeared. Perhaps that was best seen in the running of Beech Lawn where evidently no records of student examinations or term papers were kept. But for vision and accepting challenge he could not be faulted, as his founding of the Southport Convention for Revival indicates.

His spirit was magnanimous and he was a great encourager to those of us who were involved in ministry of different kinds. In his travels and in his preaching he endeared himself to thousands around the world, but in his editing of *The Flame* he encouraged controversy, particularly over the regime in South Africa.

After the union of the C.H.C. with the Church of the Nazarene, the discussion about the uniting of the colleges, Hurlet and Beech Lawn, went on for hours, even days, and an impasse was reached. One former trustee of Beech Lawn saw Hurlet as a dull, oppressive grey-stone building while those of us who had come to love that Georgian building saw Beech Lawn as plain red brick, not to be compared with the dignity of grey sandstone. As principal of Hurlet, I suggested that we place both properties on the market. One would obviously be sold first, and we would simply keep the other. It was a mischievous suggestion, since I wanted to remain at Hurlet, but I recall with some amusement the look and tone of amazement in the eyes and voice of dear Brother James, for whom this was a particularly sensitive issue. He said with no small amount of Welsh fervour, 'Is that a serious suggestion, my dear brother? Everybody knows which building will sell first.' He of course meant that it would be an unfair contest, since

Beech Lawn would sell immediately, while no one would want to purchase West Hurlet. The matter was finally referred to the board of general superintendents for their combined judgment. When that came, it was that we should sell both properties and move to a neutral location, probably further south. Both Beech Lawn and Hurlet were placed on the market in the same month, and, ironically, Hurlet was sold eighteen months before Beech Lawn!

In the latter years of his life after his dear wife Lois died Maynard James was a very lonely man. She had cared for him in every area of life and he was not in the least able to do that for himself. To all of us who knew him, he brought challenge and encouragement, and in the history of the holiness movement in Britain he stands large in so many ways.

Jack Ford... as I remember him
Hugh Rae

Born in Hull and given a good education, Jack Ford became associated with the I.H.M in Coltman Street, Hull. He spent a year in Cliff College and was invited to pastor the I.H.M. mission in Gillingham. He was twenty-six when he joined Maynard in the founding of the Calvary Holiness Church. It would be difficult to imagine him as a present day charismatic, but his admiration for Maynard made him go along with the other three. He was very clearly a man of great ability, was very able as a public speaker and debater, and was very much the scholar and theologian of the four founders. His ministry in Sheffield was remarkable in terms of the growth of the church but also in terms of his own academic achievements. It was there that he studied for a University of London B.D.

Our paths crossed several times over the years before the Calvary Holiness Church united with the Church of the Nazarene in 1955. When the College moved to Stalybridge in 1958 we were for several months under his splendid ministry. Then in 1961 he joined the academic staff and he and Alex Deasley were my colleagues until 1966. His contribution to any discussion was always lively. He was a founding member of E.C.M.A., the Evangelical Council for the Manchester Area.

At Didsbury, a golf course extends beyond the College lawn, and we spent some happy hours *trying* to play golf. On one of the first occasions we took the general superintendent, Dr G. B. Williamson. At the end of the round Dr Williamson said that he could easily assure the assembly that we did not spend all our time on the golf course! (It must have been pretty bad.) Jack was not fond of administration. On one occasion I mentioned in a letter from Canadian Nazarene College in Winnipeg that I was enjoying teaching but missed administration. The reply that came included the sentence: 'I cannot understand how anyone could miss administration.'

Jack was always interested in people but he related to them in a kind of Edwardian way. Respect came by recognising your place and role. He became Principal of the College at a difficult time when around the student world there was a growing sense of rebellion to authority and even Christian colleges were not immune. It was difficult for a disciplinarian like Jack Ford to understand that.

I have a reputation as a driver (undeserved of course!) and on one occasion when our children were small, Dr & Mrs Ford were taking my wife and children back from church. Jack joked with the children: 'Your dad doesn't drive like this?' to which came the reply, 'No! My dad's a good driver.' This was much to the amusement of Mrs Ford!

My last visit to him was to his home two days prior to his unexpected death. His first question was about Marjory and Peter. This touched me and reminded me that here was a man of God, a man of prayer and a man concerned with others, a deeply spiritual man, with academic ability which was always at the disposal of the Kingdom. He was fiercely loyal to his leaders and, above all, a superb communicator of the gospel. The church owes him a considerable debt and his place in the growth of the holiness movement internationally is assured.

Bill and Jock Henson... as I remember them
Hugh Rae

The Henson brothers, William and John, were the product of Cliff College and the I.H.M. They were both trekkers and then prepared for ministry. They were quite different in their approach to life. Bill always appeared to be pessimistic about things while brother Jock was a great optimist. This assessment was made to me by Jock as we walked along Renfield Street in Glasgow. They were the sons of a quite outstanding Scottish cricketer and at fraternals they would show their prowess (at least Jock would) at the bat. His brilliant smile and hearty handshake were proverbial. He travelled from Twechar when he was pastor there to teach at Hurlet. On one occasion when he arrived I could tell as he stood in my office that something was bothering him. Finally he said, 'Hugh my wife is pregnant!' Their son David was seventeen and he was in some turmoil as to how they would cope. 'If this had happened fourteen years ago it would have been fine.' I encouraged him and his daughter was to prove to be such a blessing to them all. On another occasion he was quite wet having walked through the rain from the bus. Standing with his back to the Courtier stove in my office he suddenly caught fire. Well, that was a laugh as far as he was concerned, and a new coat from the insurance was the result! A wonderful pastor and friend, in retirement after the death of his wife, Kathleen, he was always happy to receive a visit and produce some 'Jock-made' scones.

Bill Henson was minister in Ardrossan and a member of the board of college governors when the decision to move south to England was made. Bill, Sydney Martin and I had travelled to Leeds to view property. I was driving with my usual care, and on the way back we decided to travel to Ardrossan via Dumfries. There were no motorways then. The Henson brothers had spent their youth in Dumfries and I can tell you that Bill knew every bend and bump on the road! The conversation went as follows: 'This is a bad bend. There is a large wall round this corner. Several people have died at this point.' When we finally arrived at Ardrossan and Bill left us, Sydney gave a huge sigh and asked, 'How did you manage to be so patient?' That episode however was an indicator of the attention to detail which Bill Henson gave to his work.

Albert Lown... as I remember him
Hugh Rae

Born in Grimsby and a joiner to trade, Albert Lown spent a year in Cliff College and joined the Trekkers. My association with him goes back to 1953 when he was in Bolton. No effort was too demanding if it enabled him to serve his people. He was also a servant to the community in which he ministered. People outside his church would be served where necessary. When I was minister in the Dundee church, which met in a temporary building, we had to move from our site. The Keighley church, which needed a building like that, bought the Dundee one. Albert came with the Rev Herbert Baldwin (who makes me feel tall!) to dismantle it. While we were inside working on the roof, Herbert was working outside. He suddenly pulled out a bolt, and the roof came swinging in. A few more inches and Bolton would have lost their minister and I would never have made it to university! Albert laughed and remarked that we must still have work to do.

The Bolton congregation loved their pastor but at a recall meeting he did not receive the necessary two-thirds vote. Naturally that was a great disappointment to him. Why did it happen? I am not sure that I have the answer, but this congregation had never been able to vote on pastoral arrangements. The London executive of the I.H.M. had done that. Thus when they had the opportunity under the Nazarene constitution, some may well have thought a change would be nice.

George Frame invited Albert to pioneer the work in Lisburn, Co. Down, and that was a divinely guided choice. The foundation was laid for both congregation and building, and a strong church emerged. Moving to Paisley, Albert Lown found the congregation meeting in a small building in Marshall's Lane and led them in building a new church in Orchard Street with a large hall under the sanctuary. He was, I think, still smarting from the Bolton vote and possibly became oversensitive to situations which otherwise would not have troubled him. Always an interesting preacher and an excellent leader, at home with young and old, his last church prior to his retirement, Thomas Memorial, probably gave him less satisfaction. His latter years were spent travelling to the USA to preach. There he had many friends and influenced many lives.

As it turned out, he never had the opportunity to lead one or other of the districts as superintendent, but he certainly had many of the qualities needed for such a task. Young people always enjoyed his energy and sense of fun, and he was a great favourite at NYPS 'Institutes'. At one Institute in the Lake District the proprietor was rather mean with the food (the roast beef was cut in extremely thin slices with a ham machine) and a bit of a straight-laced kill-joy. On the last night one young man (Bert Rae) was discovered joining in a midnight bean-feast with twelve girls. The proprietor was scandalised and called Sydney Martin, Albert Lown and myself, to report this gross immorality. Albert laughed: 'Why! Don't you know, Mr X, that there is safety in numbers!'

The story is also told (and he confirmed it) that at a certain convention meeting where he was the preacher, someone gave a testimony which lasted longer than a sermon. The chairman then announced that Dr Lown would now bring his address. Albert stepped to the sacred desk. 'My address,' he said, 'is 12 Hillier Road, Battersea, London, and if you will now please stand, I will pronounce the benediction!'

One of my last memories of Albert was when he participated in a re-union of old 'Institutors' at Wiston Lodge in the Scottish borders. On the Saturday morning at breakfast, there was an ear-splitting bang as the heavy old plaster of the Victorian ceiling suddenly crashed down on the dining room. We all jumped up in alarm, but after the dust had settled, Albert was to be seen at his table calmly eating his bacon and eggs. With all the British spirit of the Blitz, he was determined not to miss his breakfast! His last months, as he battled with cancer, revealed a strong faith and great courage. His service to the Kingdom will only be truly known when we all stand to give our account.

Andrew Spence, William Claydon and Leslie Hands… as I remember them – Hugh Rae

Andrew Spence was a rough diamond with a heart of gold. Irish to the backbone and an inch further, he was an indefatigable worker. His pastorates included Workington, Salford, Batley and Morley. He was pastor of the Morley church when the roof blew off in a freak storm and he was responsible for getting the insurance through to build the new building. He and his wife Edith were students at Emmanuel College in the days when male and female students were not allowed to meet. Somehow they did!

William Claydon, known as 'BBC' (Big Bill Claydon), was over six feet tall. He gave service for a number of years particularly with the bookstore in Ireland. He served in Blantyre and Lurgan before working for the Beacon Hill Press. A big warm-hearted man, he was always ready to give support to others.

The small Smallheath church in Birmingham was to produce outstanding ministers in the 1940s and 1950s. The first of that splendid group was Leslie Hands. Beginning ministry in Motherwell he had some difficult days financially. Moving to Govan made life a little easier and as pastor in Perth he was responsible for the building of the new church in Milne Road. An adverse vote in Perth saw Les and Gladys move with their four sons to Hull and then to Dewsbury where he had a very fine ministry. Finally he moved for some years to Dunfermline where he founded the Silver Liners. His final church was Irvine. His fine pulpit and Bible ministry was much under-rated, perhaps because of prejudice against his Brummie accent. It was always a privilege to be in Les and Gladys's home and share in the laughter which was so characteristic of the family. I have above me as I write two wood-carved pictures of the College, which Les did during a period of ill health and gave to us when we left the College in 1966. These have gone with us as treasured memories of the love and affection which he and Gladys expressed so liberally. He was indeed the first of a splendid group to enter the ministry from the Smallheath church.

Leslie Roberts ... as I remember him
Hugh Rae

Leslie Roberts was the leader of the independent Holiness Mission in Ilkeston which affiliated with the Church of the Nazarene in 1945. He became a licensed minister and moved to the church in Blantyre, living for a time at Hurlet College. His wife, Clarice, died shortly after they moved into the new manse in Blantyre and some time later, he married Elizabeth Paterson, a widow with two children. After ordination he moved to the church in Chesterfield. I remember being in their home for lunch with John Crouch, Alex G. Jones and Cyril Frame while we were holding a tent mission in nearby Clay Cross. Les was cooking that day, and we sat down to a lovely meal while he drank a glass of water with a few drops of orange. The Lord had laid it on his heart to fast and pray for Mrs Emily Frame, who was then seriously ill, and he was in the forty-third day of his fast having lost 42 lbs. Later he was minister of the Morley church at the time when the uniting assembly of 1952 was held there, then in the Skegoneill church in Belfast, as the pioneer pastor in Dublin, and in Albany Street church in Edinburgh. His meticulous sermon file is now in the archives at the College. In later years he would give his report to the district assembly in rhyme. Elizabeth lived to be over 90 and Les till he was 87. They retired to Blantyre, but he continued to preach as honorary pastor of the

Motherwell church. Visiting the high-rise flats around the church, this octogenarian would encounter young couples co-habiting, and far from denouncing them, he would extend the love of Christ by offering to marry them.

Frank Webster... as I remember him
Hugh Rae

It was in 1950 that I first met Frank and Mary Webster. They were members of the Ilkeston church and had been influenced by the Independent Holiness Mission led by George Wooster and also by Leslie Roberts, the leader of the Ilkeston mission. Frank would be seen as a radical 'holiness' man right to the end of his life. But he was also a man of vision and courage. His first church was in Derbyshire Street, Leeds. There Mary and he gathered a group of young people around them, some of whom were to become his great supporters and workers when he responded to God's Spirit leading him to Cardiff. His preparation for ministry owed a great deal to the influence of his friend, Leslie Roberts, and the grounding which he had received in his formative years.

After a few years in Bargoed he felt a strong urge to plant a church in the city of Cardiff. No support was forthcoming from the district, but undeterred, Mary and he began to investigate the possibilities. Finally they stepped out in faith to establish the Church of the Nazarene in Cardiff. They contacted friends in Ilkeston and Leeds and suggested that they find employment in Cardiff and come to start the church. Two nurses from Leeds, one from Ilkeston and a joiner with his family responded to the call and they formed the nucleus of the church. Opposition came from an unexpected quarter. The parents of one of these young women appealed to the district advisory board, suggesting that their daughter had been influenced wrongly. But God was on Frank's side and he prevailed. The church was established and a lovely building built. After a number of years and much labour Frank again stepped out on his own.

His friendship with Nan and myself was very special and on his sudden home-call while in America we felt that we had suffered a very deep loss. If he had been given the financial support that he needed he would have been a fabulous church planter. His wife Mary and the girls were whole-hearted in their support. Whatever the final reckoning, Frank Webster was a man of courage and vision although perhaps sometimes a little impatient to get things done.

Glyn Thomas … as I remember him
Hugh Rae

To meet Glyn Thomas was to encounter a man of sterling faith and confidence in God. He was the epitome of the proverbial 'fiery Welshman', but his fire was that of a Spirit-filled life. Early in life he was deprived of his eyesight. He studied at South Wales College and became one of the outstanding ministers in the Calvary Holiness Church. His guide dog used to lie at his feet in the pulpit while he was preaching and one would not have been surprised if it has responded with a loud 'Amen'! The story is told that on one occasion, one of Glyn's guide dogs was with him at a meeting where the congregation rose to sing General Booth's great hymn, 'God of Elijah, hear our cry! Send the fire! Send the fire!' The poor dog went berserk trying to get his master out of the building!

When the Calvary Holiness Church united with the Church of the Nazarene in 1955, Glyn was in their only Scottish congregation, at Scotstoun in Glasgow. He was called to the Lisburn church where for some years he served faithfully with his dear wife in building on the foundation laid by his predecessor Albert Lown. He followed Leslie Roberts in the Dublin church and while there, Glyn and Annie Thomas hosted some of the musical team for the Samuel Doctorian crusade of 1968. Peter Lown, George Williamson and Tom Noble remember coming back to the manse at night and hearing Glyn Thomas chuckle as he led the way into the house, 'I suppose we had better put on the light for these poor sighted people.'

The Thomases retired to Leeds where Glyn continued his great prayer and preaching ministry. A truly sanctified man in whom the Spirit of the Lord dwelt.

David Tarrant… as I remember him
Hugh Rae

David and Joy Tarrant found themselves in the Derbyshire town of Ilkeston. They had been working in the civil service during the war and had been located in Llandudno. They were both committed

Christians and on their arrival in Ilkeston they found their way into the Ilkeston Holiness Mission which had recently united with the Church of the Nazarene. It was soon evident that they felt called to serve God and in due course Pastor Leslie Roberts introduced them to Rev George Frame. In 1946 they moved into the pastorate of the Church of the Nazarene in Carlisle which like the Ilkeston mission had recently united with the church. Their ministry in Carlisle was under difficult circumstances but they never complained.

In 1950 I was one of a team of students (along with John Crouch, Alec Jones, Cyril Frame) who visited the Cosham mission in Portsmouth which had recently affiliated with the Church of the Nazarene. We spent two weeks in mission as David Tarrant moved in as the new pastor. As in Carlisle, this was a new beginning for the mission. The Tarrants then moved with their four children in 1955 to Port Glasgow, a long established church, and David did some part-time teaching at Hurlet Nazarene College. Finally he pioneered a new work in Edinburgh where his vigorous evangelism saw the new church in Clermiston grow and flourish. In 1972 the north district elected him superintendent and in that role his administrative ability and love for souls were successfully combined. He served as chairman of the college board of governors and we were well guided in the important decision made in the late 70s and early 80s. He would have succeeded as leader in any office in the church. My last contact with him prior to his death remains a vivid memory of a man much loved and a leader ready to give his account to God.

William B. Kelly… as I remember him
Hugh Rae

It was in the early fifties that 'Bert' Kelly came into the ministry of the Church of the Nazarene and he served in what came to be known as the Donegall Road Church in Belfast. Bert and his wife Elizabeth had a family of five (two daughters and three sons). On the first occasion of our meeting, Nan and I were hosting a district fraternal at Hurlet. On this occasion the spouses were also included, and Bert and Elizabeth were encouraged to come and bring their five children. We had some fears as to how we could cope, but that meeting established a friendship that has lasted down through the years. Those children were so well behaved that it was a joy to have them. Nan was somewhat pressured in the catering for the fraternal and the one person who was always on hand to help in every area was that mother of five. As the years passed Bert Kelly served the church in places like Fenton, Gelderd Road (Leeds), Port Glasgow and Govan. He was often out in evangelistic work and was a man who preached with passion. We were at the funeral of another long-standing friend, Jim Williamson, when the news of Bert Kelly's home-call reached us. This pastor and this layman had both been vital parts of the work of the Kingdom.

David McCulloch ... as I remember him
Hugh Rae

The Church in Paisley produced some strong loyal families. Names like Crawford, Rennie, Stewart, Pollock, Thomson and others played an important role in this church. One of her sons who was a strong advocate for the message of holiness was David McCulloch, Snr. He had spent many years after the war working in industry and was a lay-preacher who was always in demand. His preaching was that of a gifted orator. But it was more than that: there was behind that gift a life that had been changed by the power of God. Finally in 1958 he was called to be minister of the church in Oldham. The College had moved in April to its temporary location in Stalybridge and early in 1959 he came once a week to my home to take studies. He was a good student of the Word but confessed that he found the demands of the ministry much more difficult than he had imagined. His daughter Marion worked in a solicitor's office and once every week she came to do secretarial work for me, a great help in the midst of the uncertainties of location. He was then called to the church in Twechar and it was there that I encouraged his son David to think of the ministry.

On the death of Randolph Murray, Zion Holiness Church in Birmingham, then an independent church, called David, and there his ministry was cut short by his untimely death from a sudden heart attack while in the pulpit. Both as a lay preacher and as a full-time, ordained elder, David adorned the doctrine of holiness and the ministry.

Bob Reaper... as I remember him
Hugh Rae

The church at Parkhead was blessed in the calibre of leadership in the Sunday school - Robert Bolton, Thomas Gray, Willie Gillies and others, and the church used to be filled upstairs and down with local children for the 'opening exercises'. In 1946 the work was taken over by Robert Reaper. The son of a Kilmarnock policeman, Bob Reaper was a man's man – big and strong, with an authoritative bearing and an infectious sense of fun. Just what a large Sunday school of children needs - no nonsense, but lots of fun! His interest in children was seen when a family arrived at the church door for a service. If he was the steward at the door, it was the children he greeted first, immediately winning the hearts of the parents. Despite the doubts of the more straight-laced (no doubt), he had a ciné camera and projector, and on informal evenings he loved to show Laurel and Hardy or Charlie Chaplin films, and used to record the annual Sunday school trip. Tom Noble and George and Alison Williamson were among the Sunday school children living in the south of the city whom he invited to 89 Kingsbridge Drive to coach them for the annual Bible exam, taking them to a café for hot peas and vinegar on the way home. On the occasion of my ordination, my mother-in-law, Nurse McPherson, arrived a little late. Bob Reaper was stewarding, and escorted her right down the pew behind Nan and myself. It was that thoughtfulness which endeared him to us all.

In 1951 he was elected chairman of the district Sunday school board and had a lasting influence on the other Sunday school superintendents. In 1952, he was elected a delegate to the general Sunday school convention, meeting in Kansas City, Missouri. (This was the general assembly attended for the first time by J.B. Maclagan, who stood on the steps at the entry to the auditorium and gathered a crowd round by playing his concertina and leading singing.) There was no air conditioning in those days and, sharing a hotel room at the Phillips Hotel, sleep was difficult when the temperature rose to over 100 degrees. At 3.00 a.m. we would lean out of the window to get some cooler air. Despite the heat, Bob insisted on wearing his kilt! Evidently it brought invitations to dine. Once in a restaurant in the heat of the evening, he stuck his finger inside his collar to loosen it. Unfortunately, since it was one of the paper collars worn at that time, it was so wet that it disintegrated in his hand, and he was left with a collarless tie hanging round his neck!

Dr Tanner ... as I remember her
Hugh Rae

Known as 'Polly Tanner' when she was young, Mary was the older daughter of Robert Tanner, a working man who tried to give his bright and hard-working daughter every opportunity. With the support and sacrifice of her parents, she was able to study medicine at Glasgow with a view to going to Africa to help Dr Hynd. She arrived in Swaziland in 1931, just in time to free the Hynds to go on their first furlough. The strain of the work and the responsibility of the whole hospital was very heavy however for a newly qualified single person, without the support of a marriage partner. She also had a serious car accident while she was there. At the end of her first term, she went to America for a while and then returned to Glasgow and set up in practice as a GP.

In October, 1952, the day after the union of the I.H.M. and the Church of the Nazarene, George Frame and Mary Tanner were married. George Frame's son, Cyril, then a student at Nazarene Theological Seminary, sent a telegram:
What a saving! What a manner!
A Scotsman's gone and framed a tanner!

(A sixpence was known in Scotland as a 'tanner'.) To drive with the Frames was an experience! She was not exactly a natural driver, but because of his eye-sight, he did not drive in town. The result was a team effort! In those days the switch for the indicator (or 'trafficator' as it was called) was at the centre of the dashboard, and while Dr Mary used to operate the driving wheel and gears, clutch and brakes, Dr George used to operate the indicator and tell her which way to go!

'Doc' (as her husband called her) was ever a realist with her feet firmly on the ground and she could sometimes hold her visionary husband in check. Once at a ministers' fraternal in Northern Ireland, Dr George was giving testimony one morning. He had felt quite ill the previous evening he said, but this morning, he had been raised up thanks to prayer. Dr Mary's quiet voice added quite audibly, 'Plus two pills!'

T. Crichton Mitchell ... as I remember him
Hugh Rae

Tom Mitchell came into the Church of the Nazarene through the ministry of J.B. Maclagan and often referred to himself as a 'Maclagan man'. I first heard him preach in the Govan Church of the Nazarene and was deeply impressed with his knowledge of the Bible, his great love and use of language, and his enthusiasm for Christ. Serving during the war in a non-combatant regiment, he developed his preaching skills and was a frequent visitor to the Doe Lea Mission in Derbyshire run by the Ison family.

At the end of the war he entered full-time ministry for a brief period in Ilkeston before being called to the church in Paisley. There he was a great influence in the lives of many young people to whom he was a true mentor. In 1954 he moved to Bolton, following Albert Lown, and subsequently to Thomas Memorial in Battersea. He then accepted a call to teach at European Nazarene Bible College in Büsingen. A natural teacher and a lover of books, he was loved and appreciated by his students. Dr Jack Ford invited him to British Isles Nazarene College in 1970, and he moved to Nazarene Bible College in Colorado Springs in 1976. Unnecessarily aware of his lack of formal higher education, he was in fact highly erudite, especially in church history and homiletics. Like one of his predecessors in the Paisley church, J.D. Lewis, he revelled in language and was an eloquent preacher.

John Crouch ... some memories
Hugh Rae

An ardent Christian train-spotter had won John Crouch and his friend Len McNeil to Christ. I think the train spotting was his means of evangelism. John entered Emmanuel Bible College after the war and after completing his diploma at Hurlet, he went as pastor to a church which we had at that time in Norwood in London.

We first met when I was a student at Glasgow University and he was at Hurlet. John, Alex Jones, Cyril Frame and I spent the summer of 1950 in campaign work. Our first mission was at Clay Cross near Chesterfield. We moved to Ilkeston where the dramatic manner of John's approach to evangelism sometimes left me breathless. He thought that we should hold an open-air at the market cross at 10.00 p.m. when the public houses and the local cinema were spilling out and arranged that Alex Jones would stand on the edge of the crowd and heckle the speaker. Alex did this so successfully that the crowd turned on the heckler and he had to leave hurriedly to avoid being beaten up! We never dared take him back with us. The crowd stood patiently as I spoke and John fearlessly took questions. We ended up going home after midnight. I don't think any of the crowds came to the mission, but the church people were encouraged. Our final weeks were spent in Cosham (Portsmouth) and so ended a remarkable summer and the beginning of a friendship which meant much to me.

In those days George Frame bought a large mobile vehicle which opened up at the back to reveal a piano, a pulpit and all necessary equipment for evangelism. John was undoubtedly the man for that mission but resources dried up and the vehicle was disposed of. John then joined the Eric Hutchings Revival Team where he served for a number of years. While engaged in this work he met and married Sheila. He became pastor in Dunfermline and then for some twenty-two years in Perth. John might appear rather solemn to some, but those who know him best could recall many times when his mischief overcame his reserve. On one occasion as a student at Hurlet he was out late and called the College to speak to his friend Alex Jones. Knowing (as he thought) that Dr Frame was gone, he assumed that the voice on the phone was that of Alex, pretending to be Dr Frame. After a brief time of comedy he suddenly realised that he was actually speaking to the principal! I am not sure how John explained that away.

E.E. Dean ... as I remember him
L.C. Shepherd

This reminiscence of the Rev E.E .Dean, who served as minister of the Totterdown Church (now the Knowle Church) in Bristol from 1954-61, was written by Mr Shepherd for Into the Unknown, *a history of the Bristol congregation.*

Our new pastor, his wife and daughters, Audrey and Beatrice, were quickly adopted by the fellowship. Mr Dean was newly ordained, having been a Methodist lay preacher while following his business career in life assurance. He had applied to the IHM in response to the call of God that he should enter the full-time ministry. At his interview he had made a favourable impression, being confident of having no fears of taking a risk by giving up his secular employment in middle life. His eager smile and warmth of personality were infectious. Here was a man whose confidence in God could not be shaken.

Mrs Dean was queen of the manse. Her ministry was marked by a gift for making apple pies. (There was a fine apple tree in the manse garden.) If ever a member of the congregation was absent through sickness, you could be sure Mrs Dean would be on the doorstep with a welcome apple pie!

Mr Dean was widely read. His favourite author was Robert Murray McCheyne whom he often quoted verbatim. In the pulpit his subject could sometimes inspire him to a high degree of excitement. Physically he had a spare frame, but when inspired, his rather hollow cheeks would flush with excitement as his voice rose. On more than one such occasion his Adam's apple lifted his clerical collar up and down, up and down, until it came adrift. Without the least embarrassment he snatched it off and continued without it. On another occasion it was not his collar but his false teeth which flew out and landed on the lap of one of the three Seward sisters sitting on the front row! Re-telling such incidents is no disrespect to Mr Dean. He enjoyed the joke as much as any one and his *sang froid* endeared him all the more to the congregation.

Brian Farmer... as I remember him
L.C. Shepherd

Reminiscence adapted from Into the Unknown

It was a happy moment when the Rev Brian Farmer accepted our invitation to become our minister in Bristol Totterdown church. We learned that before entering College, he had attended his home church in Birmingham with two close friends, and all three had a call to the ministry. The friends were the Rev Leslie Evans and the Rev Alex Deasley. Having graduated through the Nazarene College in the Glasgow years, Mr Farmer was well versed in Nazarene procedures. An innovation of his which proved of great benefit to our youth was 'The Pastor's Hour' every Sunday evening at the manse after the service. It did much to hold the group together, and bore fruit even in later years. His preaching ministry was characterised by his thought-provoking insight into God's word. A memorable title to one of his sermons was: 'The Cross is a Plus Sign.'

Like some people of a studious turn of mind, Mr Farmer was also a little absent-minded – sometimes with disastrous results! On one occasion he stood waiting to catch a bus deeply immersed in the book he was reading. To his dismay the bus swept straight past him without stopping. He looked up at the post by which he stood and discovered it was only a traffic sign!

On another occasion he went ten miles or so to visit our home at Portishead. Walking from the bus along the narrow lane to the house, he did not notice that the road had been tar sprayed and gritted. Connie [Mrs Shepherd] had recently had a new carpet laid in the front hall, and there was consternation when the pastor's footprints were clearly printed upon it! Fortunately the carpet suppliers were able to advise a simple treatment (using lard), and only the memory remained.

To put the balance right, Mr Farmer had a true pastor's heart. When Connie's father was recovering in hospital after surgery, near midnight there was an urgent summons requesting her to come immediately. She telephoned the pastor before leaving the house, asking for prayer support. This good man left his bed to be there to give comfort as they learned that her father had died suddenly and unexpectedly.

Chapter Nine

EDUCATION AND GROWTH

The End of an Era: Frame, Ford and Martin

By 1972, Dr George Frame had been district superintendent and a member of the general board of the Church of the Nazarene for thirty-two years, a record in the denomination. His first decade, the forties, had seen the founding of the College, and the second decade, the fifties, the unions with the I.H.M, and the C.H.C. The sixties had not seen any such major developments, but he had continued to promote home missions, rejoicing in the establishing of several new churches. The doubts and opposition he had faced in the forties faded away as a whole new generation arose who had never known any other district superintendent. In his last years in office, he was chairman of the general board's department of Foreign Missions and immensely proud of the contribution of the British missionaries. The British districts had supplied more missionaries proportionately than any other district in the denomination. At one point, since Americans were unable to go to Cuba, he had gone there to conduct the district assembly on behalf of the board of general superintendents, and had also visited the Cape Verde Islands and Russia.

To mark his retirement, the district advisory board organized a celebration in the MacLellan Galleries in the centre of Glasgow based on the popular television programme, 'This is Your Life.' Dr Samuel Young, also due to retire, came to conduct his last district assembly, and the Sharpe Memorial Church held an evening to celebrate the life and service of two of its most eminent 'old boys'. There was some delight that Parkhead church had given the denomination one general superintendent, two district superintendents, as well as eminent missionaries and pastors. W.A. Noble, who just remembered the Young family leaving for America in 1916 (only just), made a presentation to Dr Young.

George Frame lived a further seven years in retirement struggling manfully with the restrictions and indignities of advancing Parkinson's, but along with 'Doc' (as he affectionately called Dr Mary) attended Parkhead church and enjoyed being taken along to the youth holidays. Always on the side of the young and lively against the old and stuffy, his sharp mind and dignified bearing had dominated board meetings, district assemblies and rallies for a generation. Some found him an enigma and some might criticize him for being rather too sectarian, but he had certainly shaped the Church of the Nazarene in the British Isles and shown his sacrificial and enduring loyalty to the cause to which he had dedicated himself as a young convert sixty years before.

The district assembly of 1972 elected the Rev David J. Tarrant as the new superintendent on the fourth ballot. Many had expected the Rev Sydney Martin to succeed Dr Frame, and at the first ballot the vote was very close. However the election of David Tarrant, a younger man with great energy and excellent administrative skills, gave Dr Martin three more years at Sharpe Memorial which were among the best in his ministry. Eastern Nazarene College in Quincy, Massachusetts, recognized his preaching and pastoral ministry by conferring a D.D, on him. Under the leadership of his son, John T. Martin, the NYPS had launched an evangelistic effort in the late sixties. The South African evangelist, Ken Terhoven, had trained them in 'fishing' – going out into the streets and inviting young people hanging around there to an evangelistic café where there was live music, relevant testimonies and short, sharp evangelistic talks. Sitting round the tables, the church young people would discuss with the newcomers what they had heard, and many conversations ended in prayer, some in prayers of commitment. At the same time, some years of youth work through a company of the Boys' Brigade and through Girl Guides bore fruit. Young people attract young people, and the NYPS accepted the challenge of providing an alternative way of life for new converts every night of the week. It was held that this was essential to give urban young people a new community to belong to. The overall result of this demanding effort over several years under the next NYPS president, Ian Gillies, was remarkable growth. To become a full voting member of the NYPS, a young person had to have a clear testimony as a committed Christian, but the group of teens and young adults in NYPS membership at Sharpe Memorial grew from thirty full members to over a hundred in the final years of Sydney Martin's ministry.

The Sunday school had also seen a growth in numbers and (unlike many churches in the 1970s) there was a large and enthusiastic choir of all ages. With many second and third generation Nazarenes belonging to inter-linked church families, there was a rich resource of young and able people with deep roots in the church and a strong sense of commitment. In 1975, at the end of twenty-five years of a ministry centred on mature and challenging biblical preaching, Sharpe Memorial was at the point where, under the right leadership, it could become a much larger church with an effective ministry to a depressed area and across the city and beyond. After his retirement, Sydney Martin was widely used in America and South Africa and in 1981 was the 'model' preacher at a series of pastors' and leaders' conferences ('Palcon') held in all of the Nazarene Colleges in North America and finally at BINC in 1981. Ill health then required a quiet retirement, but he outlived several of his more robust and active contemporaries till called home in 2004 at the age of 93.

By 1972 Dr Jack Ford was also near retirement. His years as principal of BINC were not easy since the student revolutions of the 1960s had their impact even on theological colleges and there was a new impatience with traditional restrictions. The lowering of the age of legal majority from twenty-one to eighteen meant that colleges and universities were no longer *in loco parentis*. Students were adults and could no longer be treated as minors. There was a considerable loosening of old rules, moves were being made to end the segregation of the sexes in university residences, and old taboos in relations between the sexes were being challenged. But even as they became legally adults, students stopped dressing as adults! Young men, supposedly adult, with long hair, beards, side burns and the fashion for 'hippy' dress styles, bemused and even offended the 'short-back-and-sides' generation, shaped by years of conscription into the forces, for whom any interest in fashion was considered effeminate. And as for women's dress, long an area of comment among the more strait-laced, especially in 'holiness' circles, the mini-skirt was the ultimate denial of Christian modesty. But the revolution in dress was merely symptomatic of a deeper change of attitudes to authority, seniority and rules, and Dr Ford, the epitome of the English gentleman, found the egalitarian mood and the fashion for the so-called 'casual' rather hard to relate to.

Despite these social changes, however, BINC flourished. Mr Deasley insisted that he had to reduce his involvement in order to complete his doctoral studies under F.F. Bruce, the Rylands Professor of Biblical Criticism at Manchester and the leading figure in the renaissance of evangelical scholarship. But Dr T.C. Mitchell (whose scholarship had been recognized also by an honorary D.D. from Trevecca Nazarene College in Nashville) came to the College from European Nazarene Bible College and taught the lion's share of the curriculum. A third member who joined the teaching staff was the Rev Bill Rolland, a graduate of the College who had completed his B.D. degree at Nazarene Theological Seminary in Kansas City. As the young member of the academic staff, Bill Rolland took responsibility for recruitment and student affairs. He attracted American as well as British students, and with his wife Lois, a notable singer, took a company on tour round the churches presenting the dynamic musical, *Life!* This effectively communicated the message that the College was young, energetic and 'with it'. Rolland also started a drive to get church members to collect enough 'Green Shield' stamps with their purchases to buy a College minibus, and collected so many that with the excess he paid for the re-paving of the College drive! The enrolment rose higher than it had ever been.

Meanwhile Dr Ford co-operated with other church leaders in Manchester to form ECMA, the Evangelical Council for the Manchester Area. Each year he entertained Dr D. Martyn Lloyd-Jones to lunch at the College when the doughty Welsh Calvinist came to Manchester to preach to a large rally. He also worked with the movement led by national figures such as the Catholic peer, Lord Longford, and Mrs Mary Whitehouse, the leader of the National Viewers' and Listeners' Association, to oppose the spread of pornography. After his retirement in 1973, he had a very successful ministry in the Heysham church but his health collapsed as he moved to retirement in Keighley and he died in 1981. At his funeral, his old comrade-in-arms, Maynard James, gave him an eloquent and moving tribute.

The Return of Hugh Rae

The retirement of Dr Frame in 1972, Dr Ford in 1973 and Dr Martin in 1975 marked the end of an era, but just before he retired, George Frame initiated conversations with Hugh Rae about returning from Canada. Dr Rae was rightly determined not to be caught a second time in the same treadmill, and so laid down some reasonable conditions as to finance. Dr Ed Mann, the executive secretary of the department of education at the Nazarene headquarters in Kansas City, gave strong support, and an annual grant was fixed which ensured that the College had a firm financial basis for development.

Led by the new chairman of the board, T.W. Schofield, the governors voted to bring Dr Rae back,[1] and he took up office in 1973. With his experience of Christian higher education in North America, he determined to make some changes. Despite the hesitations of one or two governors, the old Bible College ethos, where all staff lived together with the students in one large house and students were expected to do 'manual' labour to keep costs down, was going to go. Fees would rise but students would be paid for work around the campus, and members of staff would live in their own homes off-campus. An affiliation with Canadian Nazarene College was initiated so that students could take the Bachelor of Theology degree validated by the Province of Manitoba. They would require British university entrance qualifications. Dr Harvey J.C. Blaney, a veteran professor from Eastern Nazarene College in Quincy, Massachusetts, came for a few years to be academic dean and organize the new curriculum and Mr Kent Brower, a farmer from Alberta who had completed an MA in biblical studies at ENC, came to teach New Testament and enrol as a doctoral student with F.F. Bruce. Just before these reinforcements came from New England and Canada, A.R.G. Deasley, having completed his doctorate, was appointed to teach at Canadian Nazarene College.

Dr Rae was also determined that the Nazarene churches in the British Isles would be fully consulted so that they would support the College and have a sense of 'ownership'. He visited the different zones accompanied by Dr Mann, laid his vision before the laity and participated in open discussion. In order to draw on all points of view,

---

1 The 'trustees' were now called 'governors', and the author had just been voted on to the board in place of his father, so that the board was now T.W. Schofield, H.E. Wood, L.C. Shepherd, P.W. Gentry and A.J. Lown from the south district; and D.J. Tarrant, S. Martin. J.E. Crouch, S. Cairns and T.A. Noble from the north district. There was only one negative vote in Dr Rae's election.

he also initiated the appointment of the 'commission on the ministry and the College' by the British Isles executive council. Since the primary purpose of the College was preparation for Christian ministry, the vision for the College had to be rooted in a common understanding of the nature of ministry and of education for the ministry. A workable commission of eighteen members was appointed chaired by the Rev Leslie Evans and including the College governors, the executive council, the district NYPS presidents, Dr Rae and Dr T.C. Mitchell from the College staff, one other elder and three other lay people. The resulting report in March 1976 made four recommendations about education for the ministry.

The Recommendations of the Evans Commission

The first called on the British Isles executive council to set up a selection panel for the ministry which was to interview all applicants in depth before they began their studies or ever met a district board of orders and relations. The selection panel was not to be concerned with academic assessment, 'but to understand the applicant's personality, to assess his Christian maturity, to consider his medical history, and to assess his gifts for personal relationships and his experience of Christian work, particularly within the Church of the Nazarene.' The panel was thus to give external, objective confirmation to a person's inner subjective sense of call, and to prevent obviously unsuitable applicants from wasting years and money in a course of study which would lead them nowhere.

The other three recommendations were for the College to carry out, and they applied, not to the Bachelor of Theology course, but to the College Diploma which most students still took. These were: to institute academic entrance qualifications lower than university entrance qualifications for the diploma course, to extend the diploma course from three years to four, and to build in a term of practical experience as student assistant to an experienced pastor in the fourth year as part of the student's education. The first of these met some resistance on the commission in case it prevented those called of God from entering the ministry. But that was more the view of a generation who had had little opportunity for high school education themselves, and the final consensus was that if God called someone to ministry, he would equip that person with enough ability to gain a few 'O' levels!

Whereas higher education had once been the preserve of the few, it was now being extended nationally to the many, and, in truth, a course of study without entrance qualification no longer had any credibility. The extension of the diploma course to four years gave more time to include a general education at the higher level (at least an introduction to history, literature, the social sciences), and for much more Bible study. The aim was to introduce students to the study of all the major parts of the Old and New Testaments. The fourth called for a whole new development in practical or pastoral theology, which (the report said) 'by its very nature can only be engaged in to a limited extent in a formal educational institution.'

Behind these recommendations lay the educational philosophy that theological education was not merely the assimilation of information from a text-book, but a dynamic living process:

> Theological education must involve the whole man, mind, soul and body, in prayerful wrestling with the Word of God and mind-expanding intellectual and spiritual discipline in the power of the Spirit. The result should be a man with such clarity and precision of thought and expression, such originality of mind, such warm-hearted and imaginative sympathy, such strength of purpose and such generosity of spirit as will make him an inspiring herald of the gospel and a wise counsellor of the flock of God. Training in techniques alone, though necessary, is not sufficient for a spiritual ministry.

Despite the underlying suspicion which still survived unacknowledged among some that theology was intellectually dangerous and that academics and spirituality were necessarily in conflict, this philosophy of education believed that there was and should be no divorce between the practical and the theoretical, no opposition between the spiritual and the intellectual.

It was agreed that from that point onwards no one would enter the Nazarene ministry in Britain completely by the home study course in the Nazarene *Manual*. Given the rising levels of formal education, a system of home study originating on the American frontier was clearly inappropriate for late twentieth century Britain. Those excused the full college course on grounds of maturity or experience, would complete the equivalent of at least one year at College. This could be taken by concentrated study over three summer terms. But no clear criteria were laid down as to which applicants could be excused the full college course, and the denominational home study course which still made up the remainder of their studies remained educationally unsatisfactory. An attempt was made later (in 1983) to remedy this remaining defect by setting up a British Isles examination board to produce more adequate syllabuses for study and provide better tuition, but this proved difficult to operate.

These measures attempted to produce a nationally integrated system bringing together the two districts and the College. Meeting each year at the selection conference, the district superintendents, the lay members appointed by the advisory boards, the College representatives and the representatives from the two district boards of orders and relations who formed the selection panel, learned to work together. During the first six years of operation, the panel interviewed sixty-four applicants and accepted forty-nine, a figure which might suggest that too many were being given the benefit of the doubt. But the continuing annual reports and counselling of candidates until they were ready to come to the board of orders and relations (later renamed 'the board of credentials') meant that more thorough oversight and guidance was given to all candidates during their years of preparation and study.

The same year that the Evans commission reported, T.C. Mitchell accepted an invitation to teach at Nazarene Bible College in Colorado Springs and Harvey Blaney returned to a long and active retirement in New England. They were replaced by T.A. Noble and Herbert McGonigle. Noble, a high school history teacher who had just completed a B.D. specializing in Christian Dogmatics (doctrine) under the Edinburgh theologian, T.F. Torrance, succeeded Blaney as academic dean and Mitchell as theology lecturer. As a young school-leaver, McGonigle had been encouraged to become a student at Hurlet Nazarene College by that irrepressible advocate of the cause, J.B. Maclagan, who was a visitor to his family farm near Enniskillen. He had by now been a Nazarene minister in Walthamstow, Uddingston and the Dewsbury Road church in Leeds, and had repeated Jack Ford's feat of attaining a University of London B.D. while in full-time ministry. He succeeded T.C. Mitchell as lecturer in church history, also undertaking teaching in Old Testament and homiletics and the doctrine of Christian holiness. But like his predecessor, T.C. Mitchell, his greatest enthusiasm was in the study of the Wesleys.

Kent Brower taught New Testament, lived on campus as 'dean of students'[2] and was College Bursar. Norma Wilson, a graduate of the College and of Nazarene Theological Seminary in Kansas City, became librarian, fulfilled teaching and administrative duties and was 'dean of women'. Bill Rolland taught classes in Christian Education and continued to promote recruitment. The group of six did not long remain together however. Rolland went to the States to pursue further studies and Brower, having completed his PhD with F.F. Bruce, loyally answered the call to teach at C.N.C. in Winnipeg when A.R.G. Deasley became professor of New Testament at Nazarene Theological Seminary. The College had a series of short-term lecturers in biblical studies over the next six years.

By that time the revolutionary changes at BINC were symbolized by the new chapel and dining room. The J.B. Maclagan Chapel was opened by Mrs Maclagan on 9th September, 1978 in the presence of the Lord Mayor of Manchester. Dr Ed Mann, the executive secretary of the department of education at Nazarene Headquarters, gave the dedicatory address and the Rev Dr David Maclagan, minister of St John's Church in Largs, brought a tribute to his father.[3] Dr Jack Ford preached at the service of praise which followed the official opening. Dr Raymond Hurn, the executive secretary of the department of home missions which had contributed to the cost, also came from Kansas City to participate. It had been agreed with the department that the chapel would also be used to plant a new church in Didsbury, and in

---

2 The closest British equivalent to this North American term is the 'warden' in charge of a student residence. But the dean of students had a pastoral role to non-residential students as well.

3 The Rev Hamish Maclagan, a minister of the United Reformed Church and a military chaplain, was unable to be present, but was invited to preach in the chapel shortly afterwards. He began by commenting that if his father was looking over the battlements of heaven and saw him in a Nazarene pulpit, he would say, 'Hamishsh haz arrivedd at lasstt!'

1984, the Rev Leslie Evans came at Dr Rae's invitation to be College Chaplain and to form a new congregation.

The Church Growth Think Tank

With the success of the Evans commission, the College administration thought that a similar exercise in consultation might point the way ahead for the whole denomination in the British Isles. The thinking behind the commission report saw the key to growth in the *quality* of the ministry offered in Nazarene churches. It was quite notable that where there was a sustained preaching and pastoral ministry of quality, as in Sharpe Memorial under Sydney Martin or the Victoria Street church in Sheffield under Leslie Evans, a solid congregation resulted, with families and a large group of young people. But throughout the denomination's history in Britain there had been too many small churches at the other end of the scale which never grew. These characteristically had a succession of short ministries, sometimes from young licensed ministers who came with enthusiasm, lasted only a few years and then passed on disillusioned, many leaving the ministry or the denomination. From the perspective of the College it seemed as if the pressure on district superintendents to find people to fill the gaps in so many small churches perpetuated the cycle of poorly prepared ministers and tiny struggling churches.

The appearance of the new 'Church Growth' movement seemed to offer a way to think more systematically about the whole problem and to replace short-term expedients with some long-term planning. 'Church Growth' thinking had arisen from the missionary experience of some Americans who had been educated in the newly burgeoning social sciences. Donald McGavran, based at Fuller Theological Seminary in Pasadena, California, was the formative thinker. Like all evangelicals, 'Church Growth' thinkers were committed to mission and evangelism, but whereas revivalism had seen the basic method of evangelism as the 'revival' or (in British terminology) the 'campaign' (special meetings held periodically by itinerant preachers), the Church Growth thinkers saw that 'mission' involved the whole life of the church. It was not enough to think individualistically of conversions at times of revival. One had to ask how a church grew as a body. Undeniably one had to speak of the work of the Holy Spirit: that was not disputed. But the real interest of the 'Church Growth' thinkers lay in the *human* conditions which favoured church growth, and that was where their social science approach became central. Social science rather than theology was to be the basis for the planning which should go into mission.

They soon developed a set of characteristics which could be shown to lead to growth. These included strong leadership, a growing local community with young families rather than an older declining one, a church programme to cater for all the family, and – most controversially – the homogeneous unit. This last condition for growth particularly applied to the 'planting' of new churches, requiring that the people being reached were of the same socio-economic and ethnic group. All of this implied that instead of just arriving wherever circumstances took them (like the trekkers in the 1930s), church 'planters' should carefully research the local community and have a carefully prepared plan. Churches needed to examine their growth rates and age structure, distinguish 'biological' growth from growth through outreach, know what their 'decadal' growth rate was, and so on. The statistical approach of sociology could thus be put at the service of the mission of the church.

In order to harness this new thinking to the cause of building the Church of the Nazarene in the United Kingdom, the College Administration arranged a church growth conference from 5th to 9th June, 1978. Dr Paul Orjala, the professor of missions at Nazarene Theological Seminary, Kansas City, was invited to be the main presenter, with the Rev Eddie Gibbs, the 'Church Growth' consultant of the British and Foreign Bible Society, to give a British perspective. Albert Lown and Frank Webster were also invited to present seminars as those who had successfully planted new churches in the United Kingdom, Lown in Lisburn and Webster in Cardiff. The British Isles executive council and district leaders, both ministers and laity, were invited to participate. The conference was not to be merely educational but to be (in the contemporary government jargon) a 'think tank'. Like the Evans commission, it was intended to produce concrete recommendations, and the 'principles' of Church Growth thinking, absorbed from preparatory reading and Orjala's presentations, were to be applied to the specific problems of the denomination in the British Isles. Dr Raymond Hurn, who was just introducing the American

Nazarenes to 'Church Growth', was so impressed that the British Isles church was ahead of the game that he came back to Manchester to participate.

The church growth conference was not the same unqualified success as the Evans commission. It had probably been unrealistic to think that new thinking and new strategies could be hammered out in one conference. One specific recommendation was acted upon by the south district, namely that new churches should be planted by a team, an older more experienced minister and a younger colleague. Colin Wood and Trevor Overton had already operated as a team with remarkable success in reviving the Carmoor Road church in Manchester, and were to be equally successful in planting a new church in Thetford in Norfolk. East Anglia was a totally new area for the denomination. But 'Church Growth' thinking continued to be a useful tool for the home mission enthusiast, David Tarrant, who was now district superintendent in the north district.

The Church Grows

In 1977 Tarrant reported that twelve church boards on the north district had invited him to discuss 'Church Growth' with them. In his report to the assembly in 1978, he bemoaned the fact that the late arrival of text-books had thrown a plan for 'Church Growth' seminars out of gear. He also bemoaned the 'sorry pattern' of the membership statistics. Ten churches had grown that year, but fifteen had decreased. And while a hundred 'new Nazarenes' had come into membership, seventy-eight names had been deleted from church rolls:

> What a tragedy that, after so much earnest soul-winning endeavour, we are left with a net loss of two for a year's operation, involving something like 65,000 ministerial man-hours, apart from the hundreds of thousands of hours freely given by our fine laymen. My brothers, I cannot believe that God called us into his grand service to achieve so little!

He drew attention to the fact that the Church of the Nazarene in Northern Ireland was growing, with an excellent decadal growth rate of 87.7%, while the Church of the Nazarene in Scotland and the northern counties of England was declining, with a 6% negative decadal rate. 'How long,' he asked, 'do we intend to let this slide continue?' The significant growth, he pointed out from the statistics, came not from established churches, but from new churches.

Two years later, at the assembly of 1979, the picture was much brighter. Not only did he commend the 'stimulating' Church Growth conference at the College in June 1978, but he reported that since then the north district had made a net gain of seventy-one members. This was the largest net growth for many years, and he wished that Dr Frame, who had just died, had lived to share the jubilation. Notably, the new church in Carrickfergus in Co. Antrim was going from strength to strength. Having been forced to leave the converted chicken hut where they had been meeting, they were now temporarily in a loyalist hall. The Lurgan church had doubled its membership under Raymond Spence's leadership.[4] He also noted that the north district was losing the Dublin church, which was soon to become the first church in the newly established home mission district of Eire.

In 1980 the growth continued, with a net gain of forty members in the north district. Forty percent of the gain came from two new churches, one in Shankill Road in the heart of Belfast and the other in the new town of Cramlington near Newcastle-on-Tyne. Dr Paul Tarrant, the district superintendent's son, was moving with his wife Cathy and family to Erskine, a new town on the south bank of the River Clyde, with a commitment to planting a church there. The net gain in members reported at the 1981 assembly was a more modest 18, but there were signs of new life in some older churches – Motherwell, Dromore, and Viewpark. In his 'retirement', the Rev Leslie Roberts was bringing new hope to the Motherwell church. In Dromore there had been a new start with the Rev Noel Somerville, and in Viewpark in Lanarkshire, following the death of Dominic Sichi, a resident who had kept the key of the property and had gone in regularly to pray for the church to re-open, the Rev Alan Mounce had been inducted to the revived congregation.

---

4 This was the oldest Nazarene church in Ireland and benefited also from the lay leadership of Sidney Cairns, for a time mayor of Craigavon, and from moving from an old upstairs hall in the town centre to a purpose-built church building in a new housing estate.

There was soon progress in the new town of Erskine. The Rev John Packard had succeeded Sydney Martin at Sharpe Memorial in 1975. He had had an excellent ministry in Hart Memorial church (the former Partick Bethel) where he attracted a group of young people to the elderly congregation and had built a beautiful modern building to replace the old mission hall. In the Parkhead church however not all had been able to accept the style and direction of his ministry, the congregation had been divided, and eventually about a dozen families were to leave for one reason or another. But in Erskine from 1980, he successfully gathered a new congregation meeting in the medical centre. There was also a new opening in the seaside town of Bangor where the Rev Kelvyn Adams was holding meetings. D.J. Tarrant was also greatly encouraged that the shortage of ministers might be about to end. 'All at once, it seems, the tide has turned,' he reported. 'Fine young men and women are hearing God's call to the ministry and are entering our College for training.'

By 1985, David Tarrant was reporting a growth rate of 20.5% over the previous decade. Five new churches had been founded during the quinquennium,[5] 1980-85 – at Shankill Road in Belfast, Erskine, Bangor in Co. Down, Cramlington, and Larne in Co. Antrim. Together with the church founded earlier in Carrickfergus, they accounted for 276 of the 322 net gains in members over the decade. Church attendances also showed growth during 1984-85, morning services rising by 2½% and evening by 3½%. He saw this as particularly encouraging when many British churches were abandoning evening services, adding: 'We must never do this.'

Two years later David Tarrant gave his final report, his forty-second as a Nazarene elder and fifteenth as district superintendent. Disappointingly, they had not been successful in taking the membership figure above 2,000, and worryingly, a new trend now established over several years was a decline in Sunday school enrolment and attendance. Nevertheless, over the last ten years of his fifteen years as superintendent, David Tarrant had seen greater growth

---

5 Normally, there is a quadrennium between general assemblies, but the assembly which should have been held in 1984 was delayed one year so that from then on the denomination would not be trying to book conference facilities in the year of the American presidential election.

than there had been since the 1930s and 1940s. This is all the more remarkable in that British church membership as a whole had entered a steep decline. Was this growth due to the application of 'Church Growth' thinking? Certainly the attention to statistics came naturally to Mr Tarrant, a former civil servant. And the strategy of growth through church 'planting' seems to have been crucial in boosting the figures for the district. But although statistics and 'scientific' thinking no doubt helped, and may possibly help to explain why the growth came in that decade and not earlier, they would have accomplished nothing without a strong sense of mission, sacrificial commitment, hard work, and a loving concern for those without Christ on the part of many people.

The south district did not show the same decadal growth rate over the same period. However, although it had had a larger membership than the north since the addition of the C.H.C in 1955, it struggled with a larger number of small churches and what T.W. Schofield saw in his report of 1979 as a 'chronic shortage of pastors'. Total district membership fluctuated above the 2,000 mark. The Thetford church was organized in 1979, the Emmanuel church in Skelmersdale in Lancashire came into the denomination in 1981. But two churches which had charismatic leanings (Longton in Stoke with 55 members and Hazel Grove in Stockport with 63 members) left the denomination in the 1980-81 year. In the following year, the minister of the Dewsbury church left for similar reasons and took twenty-seven members with him. But the Thetford church doubled its membership. Thetford continued to grow with fifteen new members in 1982-83, as did Oldham, Hull, and the Woodside church in Watford, and new churches were organized in Penycae in north Wales and in Taunton in the West Country.

The charismatic movement not only led to the loss of two congregations, and of half the membership of the Dewsbury church (and also of the young people of the Oldham church), but it also briefly re-ignited an old debate. In the U.S.A., charismatic influence in some churches led the general superintendents to formulate a statement which they made public at the general assembly of 1976 held in Dallas:

> It is our considered judgment and ruling that any practice and/or propagation of speaking in tongues either as the

evidence of the baptism with the Holy Spirit or as a neo-pentecostal ecstatic prayer language shall be interpreted as inveighing against the doctrines and usages of the Church of the Nazarene.

The statement was greeted with applause by the 35,000 Nazarenes in the stadium,[6] but some British ministers felt that this was unnecessarily harsh. Maynard James was particularly concerned since he saw it as a breach of the 'special arrangements' negotiated with the Calvary Holiness Church in 1955. In fact it had been recognized in 1955 that the position taken by James, Ford and the C.H.C. was not the 'official Nazarene attitude'. But they had been given freedom to hold those opinions and the statement that to do so was 'inveighing against the doctrines of usages of the Church of the Nazarene' seemed therefore to be a denial of an assurance which had been given. Further, the tone of the correspondence from the board of general superintendents to various British pastors was rather high-handed. But whether a 'hard' or 'soft' line was being taken on the issue of the gift of tongues, what the general superintendents rejected was 'any practice and/or propagation of speaking in tongues', and Maynard James did neither. There was actually agreement that it would not be allowed to become common practice or to divert attention from the view of the holiness movement that the gift of the Holy Spirit was primarily the gift of Christian holiness.

Despite the counter-attraction of charismatic churches in England in the 1970s and some losses, the NYPS flourished under the imaginative leadership of Warren Tranter, a merchant banker who expanded the old youth holidays into 'Breakaway'. These annual holidays for all the family, set in an English boarding school with its excellent sports' facilities (including even a golf course) and seminars for all ages, were advertised in the Christian press and attracted people from all denominations. Later, in the eighties, when he became pastor of the Woodside church where his father had served, an attractive building was built which was both functional and beautiful and there was a considerable growth in membership. David Thirkell and John Lilley pioneered a new church in Taunton in Somerset, a new area for the

6 It was later printed in the official Nazarene periodical, the *Herald of Holiness* (15th October, 1976, 4f.)

denomination, and it was organized in 1983. The fine little church building they had been using was sold to them for the very reasonable price of £4,000.

There was also advance in Sheffield when Bruce Lloyd, assistant to Leslie Evans at Victoria Street (and his son-in-law), became pastor of a new church in the Heeley district of the city. The trustees of St Peter's, an Anglican mission, were so delighted that the Nazarenes were coming to Heeley to take up the work of Christian mission that they sold the sizable property to them for one pound and gave their personal support to the new church. Leslie Evans moved to the College in 1984 as chaplain, also launching a new Didsbury congregation meeting in the J.B. Maclagan Chapel. In 1985 the patience of the Manchester church was eventually rewarded. The congregation traced its roots back through the Manchester Tabernacle of the IHM to Star Hall, and now, when compensation came from the city authorities for their old hall in Carmoor Road, they moved again under Dwight Swanson's leadership into a purpose-built hall-church, and became known as the 'Longsight' church.

The Changing of the Guard: 1984-87

If the early seventies marked the end of an era with the retirement of Frame, Ford and Martin, the mid-eighties saw a similar series of changes with the retirement of Rae, Tarrant and Schofield. T.W. Schofield moved first to a new post with the new department of world missions. At the general assembly of 1980, the old division whereby 'home missions' provided support for districts in white Anglo-Saxon and European areas while 'foreign missions' looked after everyone else was swept away. It was clearly now indefensible. But the new arrangement was no less curious. Now everything outside North America was to relate to the department of 'world mission', and to be divided into six 'regions', including 'Europe and the Middle East'. This included the United Kingdom, originally one of the three 'home' countries of the denomination. As the Church of the Nazarene was growing rapidly around the world, the department of world mission had already created the post of 'regional director'. These unelected officials, appointed from above, effectively retained authority over all districts of the church outside North America. In fact, the 'internationalizing' of the denomination really only shifted the boundary between the 'home' countries (now confined to North America) and the 'international' church, where the director of the department of world mission controlled everything through the centralized budget and the regional directors.

Appointing a British Nazarene as the first regional director in the European and Middle East region was a wise move in that it somewhat disguised the fact that the British Isles now came under what was still actually, despite the name changes, a department of 'foreign' missions. Such supervision was appropriate of course for mission districts which needed guidance and direction from the centre until they became self-supporting and grew their own mature leadership. But it was not clear how the unelected staff of the department of world missions had any authority in self-supporting, long-established districts such as those in the British Isles.

If there was to be such an appointment, however, Dr Schofield (having been made a Doctor of Divinity by Olivet Nazarene College in Illinois) was an excellent choice. He established the regional office in Bolton and new ties and contacts were created between the British Isles districts and the newer Nazarene districts in continental Europe and the Middle East. He initiated a summer school for pastors from the Arab lands each summer at Larnaca in Cyprus, staffed by lecturers from BINC and European Nazarene Bible College. The Rev John Haines of the Atherton church worked with the regional office to run these.

The first regional conference was held at Hanau in 1983, and that successfully brought together leaders from across the region. But even there, the British delegation reminded world mission staff of the slogan of the American Revolution: 'No taxation without representation.' The implication was that if a new tier of authority was being created between the district and the general church, then like district and general superintendents, regional directors ought to be elected. The ideal of 'representative government' had always been the basic principle of the Nazarene constitution: leaders ought to be elected 'from below'. The fact that no such regional directors had been centrally appointed for North America betrayed the fact that only the church outside of North America was the 'international' church. Far from this being true internationalization; the word 'international' was in fact being used as a polite euphemism for 'foreign'.

Hugh Rae retired as Principal of the College in 1986. By then the Th.B. was firmly established through the affiliation with CNC and the College had further demonstrated its academic competence by successfully preparing several students to pass the more rigorous examinations for the London University B.D. The Rev Chris Cope had joined the academic staff in 1981 to lecture in philosophy, the social sciences and Christian education. Dr Kent Brower returned as acting dean during Dr Rae's last year as principal, 1985-86. The Rev Herbert McGonigle had been elected district superintendent of the British Isles south district in succession to Dr Schofield in 1984, but resigned after a year and returned to the College, being then appointed by the board of governors to succeed Dr Rae as principal in 1986. The Rev David McCulloch was appointed to fill a crucial post the same year. Until he returned from missionary service in Guatemala to take a Master of Theology degree at Glasgow, there had been no one with both the pastoral experience and the academic qualifications to teach in the crucial area of pastoral theology. Gordon Thomas similarly returned from missionary service as a school teacher in Swaziland, took a master's degree in hermeneutics at London Bible College, and was invited to join the College staff.

In 1988, Kent Brower returned from CNC permanently to teach New Testament and succeed T.A. Noble as academic dean. After twelve years, Noble needed to complete his doctoral research and make up for lost time in his reading in his own area of theology which had been seriously inhibited by administrative responsibilities. Peter Rae, with qualifications in literature and education, became registrar. By 1988, the years of inadequate and temporary staffing were ended, and an academic staff had been brought together which made possible an application to the Council for National Academic Awards to allow BINC to graduate students with British degrees earned through its own approved curriculum. There were also changes in the College office with the resignation of the Bursar, Eleanor Brocklebank, and after a few years when Carolyn White acted as College Secretary, Denise Whittle became Bursar.

Schofield's resignation as district superintendent came in 1984, and after the one year served by Herbert McGonigle, the Rev John R. Packard, who had just come to the south district three years before to be minister of the Daubhill church in Bolton was elected on the fifth ballot. McGonigle succeeded Hugh Rae as Principal of the College in 1986. David Tarrant retired in 1987, and the north district assembly (meeting for the last time in the Parkhead church) elected the Rev John Paton, minister of the Carrickfergus church, to succeed him. A whole generation of ministers also retired in the mid-eighties: Geoffrey Palmer, Norman Robinson, Norman Salmons, Desmond Dixon, Andrew Spence, Ernie Eades, Ernie Dunn, Frank Webster, Len McNeil, and Leslie Hands, to be replaced by a whole new generation now graduating from the College. Mr Harry Wood also retired after twenty-five years as treasurer of the south district and was succeeded by David Barnes, a business manager in Bolton. In the north district, Mr Sam Boal of Parkhead, who had succeeded Norman McRitchie (son of the Rev Kenneth McRitchie) as north district treasurer, died shortly after retiring from college teaching and was succeeded by Iain Vosper of the Irvine church.

By the late 1980s therefore, as these changes in leadership took place, the Church of the Nazarene in Britain was seeing some membership growth despite the decline of the British churches at large, was establishing new ties with the denomination in Europe and the Middle East, and was developing a College which would prepare young men and women to give the kind of quality of ministry which could build healthy and solid churches giving long-term growth.

Dr Frame, T.W. Schofield and Sydney Martin in conversation after Dr Frame's retirement celebration. In the background are (l. to r.) Miss Jessie Rennie, Mrs Isobel Reynolds, A.J. Lown and Maynard James.

Jack Ford

Hugh Rae

The Board of College Governors (1978-82):
l. to r.: T.W. Schofield, L.C. Shepherd, Percy Davies, Leslie Evans, John Macdonald, Hugh Rae (front), Anthony Greenwood (behind), David Thirkell, John E. Crouch, D.J. Tarrant

The opening of the J.B. Maclagan chapel at the College (1978).
Colin Wood leads the hymn of praise. The platform party includes (l. to r.) L.C. Shepherd, D.J. Tarrant, Dr Rae (obscured), Mrs J.B. Maclagan, the Lord Mayor of Manchester, Dr T.W. Schofield, Dr Raymond Hurn and (not visible) Dr Ed Mann.

Harry Wood and Len Shepherd... as I remember them Hugh Rae

I first met Harry Wood at the district assembly in Morley in 1953, when the district was divided. Working all his life with the Bank of England, he was the ideal person to be elected treasurer of the south district, and held that office for twenty-five years. He was also elected that year to the Board of College Governors and first visited Hurlet College with Mrs Wood and their two sons, Rodney and Colin, in the summer of 1954. He was quiet and reserved and would sit and listen to discussion in the board until he would intervene to make a vital contribution to resolving the problem. His wise counsel was always given attention, not least because he spoke only when he had something significant to say. He served as church organist in Thomas Memorial well into his nineties.

Len Shepherd, a gifted artist, returned from the Royal Air Force and established a flourishing advertising company. He too was elected to the College Governors and served for twenty-seven years, latterly as secretary. He also chaired the selection panel set up following the Evans commission. He had an incisive way of reducing complicated discussion to a few simple sentences. Once when we returned home, we found a large piece of paper with a cartoon and the legend, 'Tiny Drop was here.' Our daughter Marjory said sadly, 'Oh! Mr Shepherd was here.' He had left his trademark. One of his most embarrassing moments occurred the first time he took his family to Scotland and the three young passengers in the back persuaded him against his better judgment to stop on the very busy road outside the blacksmith's shop in Gretna Green. When he moved off, a Scottish policeman stopped him, and yelled in his broad Dumfriesshire accent at this polite English gentleman, 'I know your type! I'm all right, Jack!' He eventually drove off, dumbstruck and red-faced – much to the glee of the three in the back seat. What an introduction to Scotland!

Tom Schofield ... some recollections Hugh Rae

Thomas W. Schofield is a graduate of Emmanuel Bible College, along with his wife Marion. Both were members of the church in Morley. Licensed in 1944, Tom Schofield had his first pastorate in Birmingham in the second of our two churches in that city. In 1945 he accepted the call to the church in Govan, Glasgow. It was early evident that he had the mark of leadership about him and when he was ordained in 1947 he had already established himself as a pastor and preacher. When the Church of the Nazarene and the I.H.M united in 1952, he received a call from Dewsbury, near his home town of Morley. His ministry saw growth, especially amongst the young people. After some years he was called to the Daubhill church in Bolton. While there, he saw growth and was responsible for the building of the present sanctuary. In 1967, on the death of the Rev J. B. Maclagan, he was elected to serve as district superintendent of the British Isles South District. He was appointed in 1984 to be the first regional director of the Europe and Middle East Region (later including India) and held that post until his retirement. The promise of those early days as a pastor was fulfilled in the many ways in which he served the church. His wife, Marion, was a quiet, behind-the-scenes supporter in all of his endeavours, and was superb as a hostess to the many visitors in their home. Olivet Nazarene University honoured Thomas Schofield with the degree of Doctor of Divinity.

When the Schofields lived at Hurlet, two sheep wandered into the grounds. With the help of Dr Frame, Tom rounded them up and gave them shelter overnight in the boiler house. Unfortunately, when he went to check on the sheep in the morning before contacting the farmer, he discovered that they were both dead. This is what happens when 'townies' live in the countryside!

Clifford R. Warman ... as I remember him
Leslie Evans

It was in 1966 that I first met Cliff Warman, for it was in that year the Evans family moved from Stoke-on-Trent to Sheffield, to begin what was to become the longest, happiest and most rewarding pastorate of my ministry. During that whole period of eighteen years Cliff Warman served as church secretary of the Victoria Street church.

Clifford Roper Warman was born on the 26th of March, 1909, in Bradford, Yorkshire. He was the first of the three children born to Allen and Emily Warman who both worked in the wool mill. Although the family was poor, the parents gave the children a happy and encouraging start, putting great emphasis on the importance of education. Clifford was offered a place at Hanson Boys Secondary School, but the acceptance of this opportunity meant considerable financial hardship for the parents, including going without spectacles and dentures. He excelled in sport as well as academic subjects and was selected for Bradford Boys soccer team. He also played cricket for the village club and when he was twenty-one, he opened the batting with Len Hutton, a fourteen year old who was just starting his distinguished career, which culminated as captain of the England team and later a knighthood.

After studying engineering at Bradford Technical College, Clifford received a B.Sc. as an external student of London University. He tried three times during the war to join the armed forces, but was told he was in a reserved occupation and was given responsibility for civil defence in the city of Sheffield, which had been heavily bombed in the Blitz. This was in addition to his other planning and civil engineering roles in this workshop city of half a million people, involved in making special steels, tools and machines, industries vital to the war effort. Active in these roles in Sheffield Town Hall throughout World War II, he was also engaged in much far-sighted replanning of the city in anticipation of post-war re-building.

During these war years he married one of his former secretaries, Ruth Mace, the daughter of a Church Army Captain. Ruth was to make a profound spiritual impact on her fiancé's life, for he started to attend church and made a full commitment to Christ in 1943, a year before they were married. After ten years as City Engineer, Chief Planning Officer, and Surveyor, Cliff retired in 1969, and was awarded the C.B.E. (Commander of the British Empire). He then accepted an invitation to lecture part-time in the Department of Civil Engineering at Sheffield University, where he spent thirteen years until he was seventy-three.

One of the first problems I faced as pastor was that the church building in which we worshipped was rented from the Catholic Apostolic Church on a half-yearly rental lease, which meant we had no security of tenure. With possible university development in that area, the Catholic Apostolic Church was faced with the threat of a compulsory purchase order. Cliff's faith and vision along with his wise counsel and negotiating skills helped us to secure our position in the purchase of the property.

By this time I had come to rely heavily on his judgment in many different directions, and to respect the Christian spirit which was so typical of him. A notable example of this attitude came during the period when the church congregation had grown, and we were desperately short of space for the activities we wished to develop. The church board decided to go ahead with the building of a balcony area, but for aesthetic reasons with which I had some sympathy, Cliff Warman was not at all keen to change the interior appearance of the church so radically. Once the decision was made, however, he threw himself wholeheartedly into the project, and his professional expertise was invaluable to us.

But it was as a Christian gentleman that he made the deepest impression on so many lives. All who knew him were aware of his sincere and deeply held faith and of his characteristic humility. A week after he had been to Buckingham Palace to receive his C.B.E., he was to be found struggling to deliver a heavy wardrobe to one of the needy members of the church. This required considerable physical effort, and I could not help but think of the contrast between Buckingham Palace the week before and the poor home we were now visiting. I don't think it even occurred to Cliff to think like that.

Clifford Warman died in November, 2002, in his ninety-fourth year. At his funeral service in Watford his son, Alan, spoke of his father's personal devotional life and read a letter from Frank Entwistle, who had served as Surveyor of Building Control under Clifford throughout his ten years as 'Chief':

> 'One morning, in a hurry to see the City Engineer, I burst into his office and interrupted his morning prayers before starting his day. I paused, apologetic, but as he continued I closed my eyes and joined him. Afterwards I apologised, and he kindly forgave me, as he did for many other things over the years. When I returned to my office, I thought what a marvellous way to start the day. So henceforth throughout my career, I started my day in the office, as he did, with prayer.'

Much more could be said of this fine layman who served in the former Calvary Holiness Church and later in the Church of the Nazarene. He lives still in the memories of those who knew and loved him, for the world is a greener, sweeter place because he passed through it.

Bill Barker ... some recollections
Leslie Evans

William Barker (or Bill as we all know him) became a member of the Calvary Holiness Church in Sheffield while Dr Jack Ford was minister there in the 1940s. He did not come from a Christian background and most of his family members were publicans. His conversion was sudden and dramatic. In 1943 he went to Sheffield market one evening and was attracted by the noise of an open-air meeting being conducted by Dr Ford. The preacher was a young man in soldier's uniform, Thomas Crichton Mitchell. When the appeal was made, Bill responded immediately and made a public commitment to Christ.

His conversion was a big disappointment to his mother who wanted him to become landlord of his late father's pub. Three days after his conversion the brewery company offered him the job but he turned it down. He almost lost Mildred too, the love of his life. An outgoing, bubbly personality, she was in a group of dancers and singers who entertained members of the armed forces during the war, and did not take at all kindly to the fact that Bill had become a Christian. However her love for Bill was so strong that she accepted the change and they were married in 1945. Mildred herself was converted under the preaching of Clifford Filer when the Calvary Holiness Church held a mission in Rotherham in 1947.

I first met Bill Barker in April, 1966, when I began my ministry in Sheffield. He was church treasurer, an office he held for thirty-four years, seeing six ministers come and go! With his sound judgment and practical wisdom, he could always be relied upon to foster love and unity in the church. I once heard him say: 'The Christ in me will agree with the Christ in you: but the self in me will disagree with the self in you.'

He has a quick sense of humour. He tells the story of a minister's son who would watch him count the offering every Sunday, till one day he said, 'It's not fair! My daddy does all the preaching and you get all the money!' On another occasion another little boy asked, 'Whose is all that money?' Without looking up, Bill replied, 'It's the Lord's.' After a few moments' thought, struggling with this new concept, the little boy asked, 'But who is going to give it to him?'

Bill really does trust in the promises of God. When I proposed to the church board that Bruce Lloyd would be an excellent choice as full-time associate pastor, I expected the question to be, 'But how can we afford it?' But the board discussed it and Bill gave it full support. Only once the decision had been taken did he raise the question, 'Now, how are we going to pay for it?'

Bill is one of those rare people who, when he prays, brings you right into the presence of God. Some years ago he prayed with a social worker who attended the Victoria Road church and was going through a very difficult time. She said afterwards, 'I have never heard anyone pray like that in my life. The hairs at the back of my head stood up as I listened to him talking to God!' More than all Bill has done in his long and faithful service is what he *is*. The church today is in desperate need of such men of spiritual quality.

Percy Davies... as I remember him
Clive Coleclough

Percy Davies (known to many of us as Uncle Percy) was born in the Cefn area near Wrexham inside the Welsh border on 31st December, 1914. He had two brothers and a sister, Lilian, who was about the same age and very close to him. When their father died in 1923, they moved from house to house in the village of Llay struggling to make ends meet. He was a bright boy, always top of his class, but there was no opportunity to go to grammar school, so he left school at fourteen and took a job in the local gravel works. Having signed up for twelve shillings and sixpence a week, he confronted the manager when they only paid him ten shillings! He got his full wage. Reaching the age when he could be employed in the mines, he managed to pass an eye test despite a deficiency in one eye, and started to attend evening classes and sitting exams.

Percy was a regular chapel-goer, and was attracted to another young man, Dave Wynne, whom he heard rebuking a man for blasphemy. After the argument which broke out, Percy arranged to meet Dave, and the friendship led to regular meetings for prayer and Bible study, and Percy became a firm believer through a tract Dave gave him called 'Christian Certainty'. The two proved themselves men of faith despite the jibes and insults of their work mates.

Along with Dave's brother, Eddie, they invited the Rev Maynard James to conduct a revival campaign in the village, and as a result the Llay Calvary Holiness Church was formed with Percy as the church secretary in 1940. They met at first in the British Legion hall, then for many years in an old hut in Shones Lane where forty-five would sometimes crowd into a space which should only have held half the number.

When Percy was twenty-nine, he married Megan Thomas and they were to have sixty years of happy marriage. By 1949, the church had secured a 999-year lease of land in Nant-y-Gaer Road and a new church building was built at the cost of £900. Percy acted as lay pastor for ten years from 1947 to 1957 so that costs and overheads could be met.

Through his studies, Percy eventually gained a first class manager's ticket and was qualified to be a colliery manager with the National Coal Board. He was appointed manager at nearby Gresford where there was a training centre, and in 1968 his work with the Coal Board took the family to Bolton. He was a member of the Gideons, supplying Bibles to schools and hotels and hospitals, and a life-long Sunday school teacher. One of my lasting memories is that he made time for his pupils not only on a Sunday but throughout the week. When everyone else was struggling to maintain numbers, Percy always had a large class. Many years later, his former pupils would ask about him with interest and fondness. He was a mentor to many and his commitment and wise counsel in times of difficulty will always be remembered by those who knew him.

Brian Farmer ... as I remember him
Hugh Rae

One of the Birmingham boys who heard the call of God was Brian L. Farmer. Brian was that well-spoken Brummie who had the bearing and approach of the Christian gentleman that he was. From his entering college at 18 till his untimely death aged 69, Brian was ever the example of a man of God. Quiet spoken, even appearing solemn, he had a sparkle and love of life and people which fitted him well to be a minister of the gospel. He married Joyce, his childhood sweetheart, and they had two daughters, Sharon and Alison. He was greatly loved as minister in Dunfermline and Barlanark and in 1955 he became district NYPS president. He moved to accept the pastorate of the Totterdown church (now Knowle) in Bristol and seemed set to have a good ministry there. Dissension amongst some members, which had nothing to do with him, saw him compelled to leave. This was a severe blow to Joyce especially, and left her with a great deal of trauma which influenced her in the following years. They moved to the church in Salford and for some twelve years gave that congregation some of the best pastoral and preaching ministry it could have. Called to Paisley in the mid-seventies, Brian exercised a ministry in that town which was far reaching. He studied for a degree in psychology with the Open University and put his studies to great use as a hospital chaplain. Such was the impact of his ministry in the town of Paisley that when the parish church of St. Matthew's was being closed the congregation offered the building and some considerable finance to the Church of the Nazarene. Our lives are richer for having shared in the life of this couple, Brian with his charming smile and Joyce with her down-to-earth integrity. They were easy to love.

John Paton... some recollections
Hugh Rae

John Paton hails from Blantyre, the birth place of David Livingstone. He was well known in this large mining village and was probably feared by some! He did his national service in the army and was a very successful horticulturalist (another name for a gardener). It was under the ministry of the late Alfred Milliken, pastor in Motherwell, that John was brought to the Lord. Not having been very interested in school, when he sensed God's call to the ministry, he felt that he was inadequately prepared. I was visiting in the home of Alf & Doris when John came to visit and before he knew what was happening he was sitting an entrance examination for college! I assured him that he could, if he would, make an acceptable student and - in God's mercy - a minister.

John was born with a mischievous twinkle in his eye, and this did not change when he became a new creature. He had two close friends in College, Frank Morley from Leeds and Jim Martin from London. One of those would have been bad enough but to have all three together gave life a lively twist! John was, however, always on the alert for an opportunity to witness for his Lord. The student residence, Hurlet Hall, was being built and when we all gathered in the dining room for morning tea and biscuits John would be found around the fire with the workmen witnessing for Christ. There was a chemist in the village of Didsbury who was Jewish, but John was such a witness that when the Billy Graham campaign was on in Manchester, the chemist came to one of the services. On one occasion Dr Jack Ford was in the local barber's shop in Didsbury. While the barber was cutting his hair he asked Jack where he worked. 'I teach in a college at the other end of Dene Road.' 'Oh! You mean Paton's College.' Well, what can one say?

Students always benefited from John's sense of humour. One student who was reluctant to do his personal laundry found his pyjamas one winter morning in a bucket of water in the middle of the lawn, frozen stiff! Another student was having difficulty getting the fire lit in the Aga Cooker. John helpfully suggested putting a little petrol in. The student poured some in, put the lid on the Aga, and then put a match to the fire. Needless to say, the lid blew off!

Who would have foretold the future of this devoted rascal? Leaving college he pastored churches in Dunfermline, Dundee, Lisburn, and Bolton. Finally he pioneered the work of the small congregation in Carrickfergus, and was responsible for building a beautiful sanctuary. It became the largest congregation on the north district, sending at least six or seven students to college most of whom are having exceptional ministries. On the retirement of Rev D. J. Tarrant, John Paton was elected district superintendent for the north district and later served as superintendent in the south district. But his great love was the pastorate and we were not surprised when he resigned from the superintendency to return to Carrickfergus to pastor for a few years before retirement. He suffered a severe loss when his wife Helen went to be with the Lord. His friends hoped that he might marry again and were delighted when he and Mair were united in marriage.

Herbert McGonigle… some recollections
Hugh Rae

Herbert McGonigle first came into contact with the Church of the Nazarene when the Rev J. B. Maclagan was preaching at the camp-meeting held in Buldorran near Enniskillen in Co. Fermanagh. He was at that point looking for God's guidance on entering the ministry and when Mr Maclagan told him about Hurlet Nazarene College this eighteen-year-old Irishman was admitted as a student in the autumn term of 1957. He was one of the class of students who were part of the move from Hurlet to Beech Lawn in Stalybridge, and then to the White House in Didsbury. When we finally arrived in Didsbury there was very little accommodation available. This made for some tension and when I began to make changes in the two low-ceilinged attic rooms, there was some discontent expressed. Rumour had it that the students were going to be put in these two unacceptable rooms. Herbert was one of the few who refused to be involved in the dispute. When it was all sorted out the students were to learn that these two rooms were really being prepared for the principal's two young children (who came to love them). That incident was indeed a mark of this man in his relationship to authority and in his personal relationship with me.

When he moved to minister in Walthamstow, he was boarding in the home of a Christian lady who was a widow with a sixteen-year-old son. I had a call one Sunday night from Herbert asking to come and talk with me. He found that he had fallen in love with his landlady. He and Jeanne were married and have had a happy and fulfilling marriage for over 40 years. They have two sons and Jeanne has been a constant source of encouragement in all his endeavours. His was among the first letters which I received expressing delight that I was returning to BINC in 1976. Having graduated with two theology degrees, he joined us on the academic staff in 1976 and (apart from a year's aberration as a district superintendent) he has spent the last 29 years there, becoming principal on my retirement.

A leading authority on Wesley, he can always tell you the exact time and date of most events in Wesley's life! He also collected over many years the largest collection of Wesleyana in private hands. His founding and leadership of the Wesley Fellowship has led to a string of booklets on the life and theology of John and Charles, and although he is now officially retired himself, he is director of the Manchester Wesley Research Centre in which the college, the university, the John Rylands Library and the seminary co-operate. His second passion is the bed of dahlias which he tends with loving care each year by the College lawn and tries to keep blooming for College Graduation in October.

Chapter Ten

THEOLOGY AND MISSION

Wesleyan Theology

The twenty years which complete this centenary history cannot be seen in the distant perspective in which we can now view the earlier decades. A full and definitive assessment of these years must therefore await a future historian. But bare statistics establish the fact that the most remarkable growth in the Church of the Nazarene in the United Kingdom in this most recent period has not been in the membership of the churches, but in the number of students at the College. That holds hope for the future, but it is a fact which requires some exploration. Understanding why this has happened may help to show the potential this has for the future of the church.

One line of inquiry to explain the growth of the College lies in the theological questions which the holiness movement was having to face by the late twentieth century. After all, no one is going to be committed to life-long sacrificial service to God through the Church of the Nazarene without the conviction that its message is true. Is it at all credible that this tiny upstart denomination, often led by people with little theological education, has a hold on an aspect of Christian truth which all the great historic traditions of the British church have missed? But the answer to that is that the Wesleyan tradition *is* one of the great historic traditions of the church. John Wesley would have to be included in any list of the most influential Christian leaders of modern times.

The appointment of Herbert McGonigle as principal of BINC in 1986 was symbolic in that his chief interest was in the historical study of the Wesleys, and the last quarter of the twentieth century saw a significant revival of interest in Wesley studies. This was foreshadowed in the British Church of the Nazarene by the ministry of that former Methodist, Sydney Martin, the influence of the Methodist Cliff College on several of its leaders, and the enthusiastic advocacy of the erudite T. Crichton Mitchell. But in the holiness movement in the United States (and indeed in American Methodism) there was also a revival of interest in Wesley as a theologian. The work of the American Methodist scholar, Dr Albert Outler, was crucial here. Outler began to argue in 1964 that Wesley needed to be taken seriously as a theologian, a novel thought in the world of academic theology where Wesley was dismissed as a 'pietist'. Methodists and pietists were regarded as those concerned with 'piety', that is, the life of holiness, not with theology. Outler's advocacy of Wesley led however to publication of the new multi-volume scholarly 'Bicentennial edition' of Wesley's *Works*, still in progress, and a whole new interest in Wesley as a theologian.

Also by the 1960s, there were developments in theology within the Church of the Nazarene. It has been argued that the early preachers and writers at the beginning of the twentieth century had a rather simplistic, black-and-white doctrine of Christian holiness, over-optimistic and sounding rather like a teaching of 'sinless perfection'.[1] But by 1940, H. Orton Wiley had produced his more scholarly and balanced three-volume work of systematics, *Christian Theology*, in 1945 a graduate seminary had been established beside the Nazarene denominational headquarters in Kansas City, and some more balanced and qualified presentations of the doctrine had explored the limitations of holiness, the 'imperfections of the perfect'.[2] In the mid-1960s, the theologians of the American holiness movement, led by Dr Richard S. Taylor of Nazarene Theological Seminary, formed the Wesleyan Theological Society, and began publication of the *Wesleyan Theological Journal*.

It was in this journal, and at the invitation of its editor, Richard Taylor, that Herbert McGonigle fired the first shot in a battle which was to change the holiness movement. His article, 'Pneumatological

1 See Mark Quanstrom, *A Century of Holiness Theology: The Doctrine of Entire Sanctification in the Church of the Nazarene* (Kansas City: Nazarene Publishing House, 2004), the published version of a doctoral thesis completed at the University of St Louis.

2 Quanstrom cites here such works as Richard S. Taylor, *A Right Conception of Sin* (Kansas City: Beacon Hill, 1945) and William S. Deal, *Problems of the Spirit-Filled Life* (Kansas City: Beacon Hill. 1961), and also (relevant to the British context), J.D. Drysdale's admission in his foreword to the book by the I.H.M. layman, Henry Brockett, *Scriptural Freedom from Sin* (Tunbridge Wells: C. Baldwin, 1939) that some presentations of the doctrine of holiness had been 'extravagant'.

Nomenclature in Early Methodism,'[3] reminded the world of the holiness movement of what they had long forgotten or ignored: that there were certain key differences between Wesley's doctrine of Christian holiness and that of the later nineteenth-century holiness movement. Many nineteenth-century Wesleyans, influenced by those 'new school Calvinists', Charles G. Finney and Asa Mahan, had interpreted the experience of the apostles on the day of Pentecost as being what Wesley described as 'entire sanctification'. But Wesley himself had made no such equation. He did not identify the apostles' 'baptism in the Spirit' on the day of Pentecost as their 'entire sanctification', and he rejected the idea that entire sanctification should be called 'receiving the Spirit', since the Christian 'received' the Holy Spirit at the new birth.

This may well seem a rather abstruse point to the ordinary Christian, 'theological' or 'academic' in the sense of being theoretical and irrelevant. But in fact the theological questions intersected with some very practical ones. The Finney-Mahan emphasis on Pentecost and the 'baptism of the Spirit', taken together with the 'altar theology' of Phoebe Palmer (the so-called 'shorter way' to holiness), served to highlight the drama and excitement of the public 'altar call' which was the invention of American revivalism. This modern development of American culture gave liturgical shape to an increased emphasis on the great 'crises' of the Christian life. By contrast, Wesley's pastoral wisdom had encouraged his early Methodists to 'go on to perfection' only in the context of the regular, practical, down-to-earth, week-by-week sharing of experience in the Methodist bands and classes. His teaching that Christian perfection, while entered into in a moment by faith, came at the end of years of seeking and discipline was now replaced by a kind of 'instant holiness'. The historical recovery then of this difference in perspective between the 'classic Wesleyan' view and the view of the nineteenth-century American holiness movement with its 'Pentecostal' and 'altar' language had practical implications for methods of evangelism and for the pastoral question of how young Christians were to be encouraged to 'go on to perfection'.

---

3 Herbert McGonigle, 'Pneumatological Nomenclature in Early Methodism,' *WTJ, 8* (Spring, 1973), 61-72.

But in Britain this raised particular cultural questions. From D.L. Moody's visits in the 1870s up to the Billy Graham crusades of the 1950s, American revivalism had been highly influential across the British evangelical movement and beyond. Particularly for Nazarenes, the Maynard James 'revivals' of 1930s came to form for many Nazarenes the 'myth' (that is to say, the model or shaping story) of how churches should be planted and how it 'ought' to be. There was a constant longing for such 'revival', an outpouring of the Holy Spirit. The 'revivalistic' form of the Wesleyan tradition then – expressed in the altar call and the emphasis on the crisis of the Pentecostal baptism of the Spirit – was fairly familiar and culturally relevant.

But the influence of American revivalism in Britain waned in the last quarter of the twentieth century. British secular culture became suspicious of American religion in general and revivalism in particular, especially the use of sales techniques and the manipulative use of emotionalism and sentimentality by tele-evangelists.[4] Did the private counselling approach of the Wesleys and their emphasis on the life of disciplined service and 'gradual sanctification' as the essential route to 'entire sanctification' suggest pastoral practice more in keeping with British culture than the open drama and emotion of the 'altar call'?

But beneath the cultural question of the place of American revivalism in Britain, the difference between the two forms of the Wesleyan-holiness tradition raised *theological* questions and questions of biblical interpretation. Did Nazarene doctrine have a firm basis in scripture? Did scripture explicitly teach a 'second blessing'? How did the doctrine of Christian holiness relate to the doctrine of the Holy Spirit, highlighted now by the charismatic movement, or the doctrine of original sin? Was original sin actually 'eradicated' as the Nazarene articles of faith declared, or was such a bold and unqualified claim not bound to lead to overblown and spiritually dangerous claims to 'sinless perfection'? The articles of faith were amended in the 1960s by the

---

4 A conversation with the late Dr Jack Sanders, president of Nazarene Theological Seminary, driving in his car in Kansas City in 1982, revealed to the author that Dr Frame had come to the conclusion that the altar call was not appropriate in British culture. He had debated this in the 1960s with Sanders, then minister of the Skegoneill Avenue church in Belfast, and Sydney Martin.

general assembly of the denomination to introduce various qualifications and clarifications, but these by no means answered all the questions.

But the recovery of Wesley's own teaching gave promise that behind the superficial and cultural matters of circumstance, there was a solid core of his doctrine which was based in scripture and discovered in genuine experience. It was not a matter of 'magical' moments of spiritual crisis which solved all one's problems at a stroke, but of a patient seeking, a 'zealous keeping of all the commandments' (to quote Wesley), a growth in grace which finally brought one to that point where God purified the heart by the infilling with the Holy Spirit. Since the Spirit is the Spirit of love, the Christian's love for God and neighbour was thus 'perfected', not in the sense of having 'arrived' spiritually at *final* perfection, but in the sense that it was whole and undivided. This heart of Wesley's doctrine (along with a critique of many of the inadequate ideas of the later holiness movement) was presented supremely by Mildred Bangs Wynkoop, the 'theologian in residence' at Nazarene Theological Seminary in the 1970s, in her book, *A Theology of Love.*[5]

The recovery of Wesley and the exposition of the heart of his conception of 'Christian perfection' by Wynkoop (along with others)[6] may not have directly affected student recruitment at BINC! But it did help to persuade a generation of thinking teachers there that the narrow stereotypes and false exegesis which had too often characterized the holiness movement were not truly representative of the Wesleyan tradition. And without those teachers, the growth of the College could not have happened. They were persuaded that while John Wesley may not have been a front-rank systematic theologian, he had to be respected as a highly skilled classicist and scholar whose doctrine of

---

5 Mildred Bangs Wynkoop, *A Theology of Love* (Kansas City: Beacon Hill Press, 1972). One of the contrasts drawn by Dr Wynkoop was between a 'magical' idea and a 'moral' or ethical understanding of sanctification.

6 Such as George Allen Turner, *The Vision Which Transforms* (Kansas City: Beacon Hill, 1964) and Leo Cox, *John Wesley's Concept of Perfection* (Kansas City: Beacon Hill, 1964). Wynkoop's advocacy of a 'relational' rather than 'substantial' conception of Christian holiness was also taken up by H. Ray Dunning in his systematic theology, *Grace, Faith and Holiness* (Kansas City: Beacon Hill, 1988)

Christian holiness was based (unlike the teaching of Palmer and Mahan) on a close knowledge of the Greek text of the New Testament and of the tradition of the ancient catholic church. That gave a basis for believing that the Wesleyan understanding of Christian holiness (which was the reason for the existence of the Church of the Nazarene) could be expounded and preached not only in frontier or small-town America, the home of revivalism, but in the more sophisticated and sceptical culture of post-Christian Britain and Europe.

The College's Academic Standing and Growth

A second context for understanding the growth of Nazarene Theological College (the new name adopted on 1st September, 1990) is the evangelical renaissance in Britain since the Second World War. Liberal theology dominated the British scene both before and after the war, but the founding of London Bible College, the increasing strength of Inter-Varsity Fellowship (which became UCCF, the Universities and Colleges' Christian Fellowship) and the growing strength of evangelical biblical scholarship through the example and encouragement of Professor F.F. Bruce of Manchester, Professor I. Howard Marshall of Aberdeen and others, and the ministry of many leading evangelical preachers such as Dr Martyn Lloyd-Jones and the Rev John Stott, led to a renaissance of evangelical Christianity and of evangelical theology in Britain. But since this was largely led from the universities and not the grass roots, it rejected the obscurantist fundamentalism which disfigured much of American evangelicalism. From the 1960s there was also the growth of the charismatic movement in the Church of England and elsewhere. An enormous increase in Christian books for the intelligent reader published by Inter-Varsity Press, Paternoster, Hodder and Stoughton, and various other evangelical publishers, testified to the growing constituency of reading and thinking Christians. Even though total national church membership was declining from the 1960s, the evangelical constituency within that was growing.

Evangelical theological colleges were also growing. LBC (which more recently became LST, the London School of Theology), Spurgeon's College, All Nations' Christian College, and the Anglican Colleges, St John's, Nottingham and Trinity in Bristol, all became degree-granting institutions.[7] The Nazarene College aspired too to that status, and with its experience in preparing students for the Canadian ThB and the London BD, and with its newly completed full-time academic staff, it was ready to take that step. Its reputation had also been enhanced by the prestigious academics who accepted the invitation to give the Didsbury Lectures. These lectures had been inaugurated at the College in 1979, when F.F. Bruce agreed to give the opening series of four lectures and arranged a link with Paternoster Press which has since published the series annually. I. Howard Marshall of Aberdeen (a fellow-student at Cambridge with Dr Deasley), James Atkinson of Sheffield, T.F. Torrance of Edinburgh (Dr Noble's professor) and C.K. Barrett of Durham all accepted invitations to lecture, and with a line-up of such eminent professors, the future of the lecture series was assured.

This background in the renaissance of evangelical Christianity and evangelical colleges became particularly relevant once the College was approved by the Council for National Academic Awards in 1990. First, in January, the College was approved as an institution worthy to be granted associate status, then (in February) came the approval of the college's proposed BA degree, and finally (in December) the approval of a one-year MA degree for graduates in 'Aspects of Christian Holiness'. The work of the staff in preparing for this was led by the new Dean, Dr Kent Brower, and the documents he submitted were regarded as models of their kind. That year the College took in fifteen undergraduate students to give a total enrolment of fifty-three, thirty-four of whom were full-time and nineteen part-time. Eighty percent were Nazarenes. But the approval of CNAA degrees now made the College attractive to prospective students in evangelical churches across the conurbation of greater Manchester and beyond. A new publicity and recruitment drive led by Gordon Thomas targeted this new constituency, and by 1992, the College was reporting an enrolment of seventy-two students, forty of these full-time and thirty-two part-time.

---

7 The oldest of the 'Bible colleges', the Bible Training Institute, which became Glasgow Bible College and then united with Northumbria Bible College (previously the 'holiness' Lebanon Bible College) in Berwick-on-Tweed to form the International Christian College, has also more recently become a degree-granting institution.

That year, however, since the government was abolishing the CNAA, the College became an affiliated College of the University of Manchester, a development which increased its attraction without threatening its independence. By 1994, the year of the College's golden jubilee, there were ninety students (forty-seven full-time and forty-three part-time) including those on the MA course and those doing PhD research. Two years later in 1996, there were one hundred and sixty-two students (including sixty-four MA or PhD students, mainly part-time). Two years later again, in 1998, the College reported 193 students, an increase of 141 per cent in five years. Nazarene students were now in the minority, but despite the small membership of the denomination in the United Kingdom, the increase in Nazarene students was 41 per cent to a total of fifty-seven. In 1999 the first PhD students gained their doctorates.

The academic staff was further strengthened when the Rev David Rainey came from Canada in 1996 to replace Dr T.A. Noble, who was called to be professor of theology at Nazarene Theological Seminary in Kansas City, and Dr Peter Rae came back from Canadian Nazarene College to be registrar, eventually succeeding Dr Brower as dean. Dr Dwight Swanson returned after some years at the Nazarene College in Europe and the seminary in Philippines, to teach Old Testament. An imaginative course of education for church youth workers also added to enrolment, and the Rev Deirdre Brower was added to the academic staff. In 1997, Emmanuel Bible College, Birkenhead, founded by J.D. Drysdale, decided to unite with Nazarene Theological College. The principal, the Rev Victor Edwards, a graduate of Emmanuel and a former Nazarene missionary in Argentina, and Mr John Isherwood, came to teach on the Didsbury campus. The funds which came from the sale of Emmanuel College helped to build the 'Emmanuel Centre', much needed to house the library and class-rooms for the oversized student population, and a centre for overseas missions. It was opened in 2005. The union with Emmanuel also brought a new focus on world missions.

The College did not continue to expand at the same phenomenal rate, but the increased enrolment has been maintained and it continues to grow gradually. In 2005, 246 students were reported, 88 of these being Nazarenes. By meeting the demand for evangelical theological education in the north-west of England and beyond, the College is obviously a more economically viable institution and more attractive to students from its own Nazarene constituency, and has become one of the larger theological colleges in Britain. Further, despite the much greater financial resources of the eight Nazarene Colleges in the United States, who average 2,000 students each and are almost all now designated 'universities', Nazarene Theological College in Manchester is ironically the only one which can offer supervision of research leading to a PhD. With over fifty Nazarene Bible Colleges, theological colleges and seminaries around the world, the Manchester College can therefore offer a unique service in preparing their future lecturers.

A farther background to the growth of the College is the growth of higher education generally. Whereas only a tiny minority of school-leavers went on to college or university earlier in the century, by the end of the century it was well over forty percent. The Manchester BA, taken at Nazarene Theological College, can qualify a student for employment in teaching or indeed in a wide range of professions. But it was not forgotten that the College had been founded originally to prepare students for the Nazarene ministry, and that remained its primary *raison d'être*.

Packard and Paton

At the same time in the mid-eighties when the College had at last put together an academic staff to allow it to begin to approach the CNAA, John R. Packard had become district superintendent of the British Isles south district and John Paton of the north.

John Paton was district superintendent for five years in the north district, from 1987 to 1992. The slow growth in membership continued and in 1992 he reported that over the previous decade there had been 1,172 members received by profession of faith, but taking into account the loss from death and removals, the net gain was 246. But once again, that modest increase has to be seen in the context of the continuing catastrophic decline of all the major denominations in Britain. That decline was not characteristic of Northern Ireland, however, and much of the gain was there. New buildings were opened in Cramlington near Newcastle and in the Shankill Road in Belfast. The church buildings in Irvine and Troon were renovated and enlarged and a modern brick building put up in Erskine where the Rev Geoff Austin was now minister.

The most notable acquisition of property was in Paisley where the Nazarene congregation took possession of a magnificent red-sandstone church building in a prominent position facing across an open space to the medieval Paisley Abbey. St Matthew's Church was a parish church of the national Presbyterian Church, the Church of Scotland, which for several decades had been managing a process of decline by merging congregations and closing buildings. At first the rationale for this had been the rationalization of church buildings in areas which the three Presbyterian denominations had been in competition in the nineteenth century. St Matthew's Church had originally been a congregation of the United Presbyterian Church, in whose constitution the local congregation owned the building. When the Presbytery insisted that St Matthew's unite with another parish church, the congregation (after fighting this all the way to the general assembly in Edinburgh) decided to *give* the magnificent building, notable for its *art nouveau* architecture, to the nearby Nazarene congregation along with a fabric fund of £20,000.

Some of the Nazarenes were unsure about this move for Albert Lown had built a highly serviceable modern brick building which they filled comfortably, but that building was sold to a youth organization for £80,000. The Nazarene congregation, led by the Rev Brian Farmer, then attracted a grant of half a million pounds to renovate the St Matthew's building, much to the delight of both conservationists and Nazarenes! The Paisley congregation also gained about forty members of St Matthew's who wanted to continue to worship there, but these were all elderly, and the sudden rise in membership statistics would be short-lived. Soon after receiving the gift of the building, the Paisley congregation hosted a campaign with the Rev Samuel Doctorian during which the old building was packed to capacity and many responded to the challenge of the gospel.[8]

---

8 In 1990, Samuel Doctorian had his credentials as a Nazarene elder reinstated by the north district assembly and transferred to California where he was now resident.

John Paton's years as the north district superintendent also saw the passing of some notable figures. Dr David Hynd, CBE, paid his last visit home in 1990 at the age of 95 on his way to receive an award in the United States, and at short notice the Parkhead church was filled with people from across the district to greet the veteran missionary. He died the next year, having been a member of the Parkhead church since 1916 and a missionary member since 1925, and the minister of Sharpe Memorial, C.H. Wood, went to represent the church at his funeral in the Sharpe Memorial church in Swaziland along with Dr T.A. Noble. British Nazarenes contributed to a fund to establish a Hynd scholarship at the College to enable African post-graduate students to study there. That same year, the Rev John T. Henson was laid to rest in the picturesque Dumfriesshire village of Durisdeer, and the next year, the Rev Leslie Hands, originally from the Birmingham church, passed away. Both of these had given life-long and sterling service as dependable and compassionate pastors in several churches. In 1993, Dr Albert Lown died after a long and productive ministry, having spent his very active years of 'retirement' visiting the United States as a preacher much in demand.

In the south district, J.R. Packard's seven years as superintendent saw new churches organized in Brixham (Devon), King's Lynn (Norfolk), pioneered by the Rev Don Mentch, and Cleethorpes, Humberside, led by the Rev Frederick Grossmith. Nineteen college graduates were placed in churches as older ministers retired. The congregation in inner-city Salford had to demolish the old church they had renovated, finally beaten by dry rot, but re-built on the same site. The congregation in Dewsbury Road, Leeds, led by the Rev David Montgomery, left their old mission hall to become the South Leeds church. Both built serviceable buildings for work in urban areas. During these years the number of members of the British Isles south district grew to 2,232 by 1991. Dewsbury (Raymond Busby), Thetford (David Leeder), Woodside church in Watford (Warren Tranter), Llay (Charles Hagenrader from Nazarene Bible College in Colorado Springs), Knowle church in Bristol (Alan Mounce) and Didsbury (Don Maciver) showed particularly healthy growth. Sunday school ministries, led by David Morrell, reported in 1992 that twenty Sunday schools had increased attendance by ten per cent.

With the fall of the Berlin Wall in 1989 and the series of revolutions which swept the communist bloc culminating in the collapse of the Soviet Union in 1991, several churches engaged in charity missions to Eastern Europe. Under the Rev Fred Grossmith, the new Cleethorpes church supported Rom-Aid, a charity organizing aid for Romania. The committee on Christian Action at the district assembly also showed an awareness of national and social concerns, commenting in 1987, for example, on abortion, the AIDS epidemic, the Obscene Publications Bill, divorce, and a local government bill to prevent the use of public funds to promote homosexuality.

T.W. Schofield retired as regional director in 1990 to be succeeded by an American, Dr Franklin Cook, and the regional office moved to Gottmadingen in southern Germany and later to Büsingen. But the south district hosted the regional conference at The Hayes Conference Centre in Swanwick in 1991. Maynard James died on 21st May, 1988, and at the assembly of 1992, the deaths of Stanley Tranter and Thomas Ainscough, retired missionary to Argentina, were also reported.

John Packard's years as district superintendent were also marked by controversial issues, notably those he raised in his assembly reports in 1988 and 1992. In 1988 he criticized the new regionalization, and in 1992 spoke of being 'weary and battle-scarred in the fight for holiness', not with those outside the denomination, but with those within. The subsequent rather confused debate which centred on the role of the College was ably chaired by the general superintendent, Dr Jerald D. Johnson. A few weeks later, in June 1992, largely at John Packard's request, the college arranged a second church growth conference for selected leaders from north and south districts with Dr Martin Robinson of the British and Foreign Bible Society. This excellent conference gave a new strategic vision for advance, but its impact was lost when John Packard resigned shortly afterwards. Since it was so soon after the annual district assembly, the board of general superintendents asked the Rev John Paton to move to the south district and appointed the Rev C.H. Wood as north district superintendent in his place.

Paton and Wood

Colin Wood had been at the Parkhead church since 1980 and on his appointment as district superintendent, ratified by election at the next district assembly, he decided to remain there and appointed four 'senior elders', Philip McAlister of Carrickfergus for the Ulster zone, David Thirkell of Troon for the west of Scotland, John E. Crouch of Perth for the east of Scotland, and James C. Martin of Cramlington for the northern counties of England. This was discontinued however after two years, and Mr Wood was enabled to perform his dual role with the help of an assistant minister. When Richard Porter filled that role, he led the Sharpe Memorial Church in tackling the drug problem which had become rife in the Parkhead area. Later, Ian Wills was assistant and engaged in evangelism using an adapted version of the Alpha course. Alpha, in contrast to American revivalism, unites evangelism with teaching and brings people to belief through the experience of belonging to a discussion group over a number of weeks. It was also used in Uddingston, Hart Memorial (Partick), Clermiston in Edinburgh and in a new church planted in Houston in Renfrewshire not far from Erskine.

The Rev Brian Farmer and the Rev John Crouch retired after long ministries in Paisley (now St Matthews) and Perth (now Trinity). John Crouch had grown up in Speke Hall (now Clapham Junction church), going to college at Emmanuel College in Birkenhead, and was committed to the primacy of preaching. He had succeeded the Rev James McLeod as district secretary and now handed that post on to the Rev Geoff Austin. Under Crouch, the Perth congregation moved out of their building in Milne Street (built on land with only a twenty year lease!) into Trinity Church, another solid stone building vacated by a congregation of the Church of Scotland. An imaginative restructuring put a new floor across the building between the wings of the gallery and provided rooms and a hall underneath for youth work.

Brian Farmer had been one of a group of lads trained to preach in the streets of Birmingham by the Rev Robert Deasley in the 1940s. He set a record as the longest-serving Nazarene minister in the British Isles, having served without a break for forty-five years. He had gone into his first church straight from his studies at Hurlet Nazarene College and had served in Dunfermline, Barlanark (Glasgow),

Totterdown in Bristol, Salford, and finally, for twenty-four years, in Paisley. His qualification in psychology, taken while in the ministry, had enabled him to develop a significant ministry in pastoral counselling, and his chairing of the district committee on 'Christian action' had given the district informed guidance on a range of contemporary ethical questions. Sadly, both Brian and Joyce Farmer died within a few years of retirement.

Among other losses, both in 1994, were the retired missionary, Mary McKinley of Swaziland, and unexpectedly, the not-yet-retired missionary, Frank Howie of Mozambique. In 1999, the district assembly remembered the life and service of the Rev Leslie Roberts, who had continued to give pastoral supervision in the Motherwell church until his death at the age of 87. In 2001, the Rev James Graham, retired missionary to Malawi, passed away and the district also mourned the loss of its retired superintendent, the Rev D.J. Tarrant. Mr Tarrant had been very active in retirement, and when the general superintendents refused to leave the safety of the United States during the Gulf War, he chaired the district assembly of [1991] with undiminished wisdom and clarity of mind. His sermon to the assembly on 'perfect love' in action in the local congregation, simultaneously theological and practical, was one of the best any district assembly ever heard. Another severe and unexpected loss was the sudden and tragic death of the district treasurer and administrator, Iain Vosper, knocked down by a car while representing the district at the Christian Resources Exhibition in Belfast.

The rising membership of the 1980s and the early 1990s was followed by a disappointing decrease. Colin Wood was able to report that in 1992-93, the assembly year in which he succeeded John Paton, the membership of the British Isles north district had at last passed 2,000. But in the succeeding years it dropped steadily until a small increase in 2005 brought it to 1866. Despite a courageous rear-guard action by the Rev Peter Ferguson, the Barlanark church had succumbed several years previously to the severe vandalism, violence and social problems which were affecting the housing estates in Glasgow. And the Ardmillan church in Edinburgh (originally Albany Street) had to be closed.

But a second church, the Bethany congregation led by the Rev Irene Wallace, was formed in Lisburn in October, 1995, and (the same year) preparatory work began in the village of Houston in Renfrewshire. The Rev Claire Fender of Carlisle was appointed district youth pastor, and various social ministries flourished in the LINC centre in Belfast, the Family Ark centre, the Lighthouse ministry in Stockton-on-Tees and the Raffles project in Carlisle. More recently, the Houston church has since flourished under the ministry of the Rev Trevor Hutton, while in the church in Bangor, Co. Down, the Rev Ken White has seen notable growth, and a new start has been made in Larne, led by the Rev Philip McAlister.

Social and political action was also undertaken by Brian Souter, the Perth layman who founded the very successful Stagecoach bus company along with his sister, Anne Gloag. Souter was one of the leading figures nationally in Scotland in opposing the ending of 'Clause 28' by the government, a piece of legislation which the previous government had intended to prevent the promotion of homosexuality in schools. The Souter Foundation financed a private poll. The foundation also stood behind a project to provide sheltered housing for elderly members of the denomination (and of other churches) by building Strathclyde House in Skelmorlie, providing apartments with a view out over the scenery of the Firth of Clyde and open lounge areas for community life. A scheme to give college graduates further preparation as assistant ministers was also supported.

The McAlister Commission, appointed by the British Isles Administrative Board in 1997 to review the Evans Commission, reported to district assemblies in 1999. Chaired by the Rev Philip McAlister, it affirmed that the normative route to prepare for the ordained ministry was through the college, but abolished the British Isles Examination Board and Selection Panel. These were to bring the British arrangements into line with the requirements of the new International Course of Study Advisory Committee (ICOSAC).

The north district refused to have anyone from the department of world mission regional office chair the district assembly in 2001.[9] In his

9 The Rev John Haines from the regional office of the 'world missions' department chaired the south district assembly.

annual report the district superintendent expressed his disappointment that the resolution passed the previous year, that the general superintendent in jurisdiction should chair the assembly as required by the Nazarene *Manual*, had apparently 'fallen on deaf ears'. But he welcomed general superintendent emeritus Dr Jerald D. Johnson to the chair.

Nazarene involvement in chaplaincy ministries increased with the Rev Caroline McAfee serving in the Northern Ireland Hospice, the Rev Ann Findlay serving as a hospital chaplain in Dundee, and the Rev Thomas Goodwin serving in the Royal Navy. Tom Goodwin was particularly in Nazarene prayers when he served in HMS Chatham in the Persian Gulf during the British and American invasion of Saddam Hussein's Iraq in 2003.

In the south district, a community project, the Grapevine Centre, was launched by the Heeley church in Sheffield, and became a registered charity in 1994. John Paton appointed Deirdre Brower as youth pastor, also giving her the pastoral care of the small group at Southmead in Bristol. Serving also with the region and on the general council of the NYI, she was elected general president of the Nazarene Youth International in 2001 and preached in South America, India, Europe and North America at large youth congresses. Here she broke through the 'glass ceiling', being the first woman (and the first from outside North America) to be general NYI president. She also took on the leadership of a team ministry in the Longsight church in inner-city Manchester which flourished as a multi-ethnic congregation embodying holiness as inclusiveness.

The south district membership figures reached a peak of 2,233 in 1994, and thereafter declined year by year. The shortage of ministers for many small churches continued to be a problem, but John Paton wisely noted in his report in 1997 that the college was a channel but not a source for ministers. 'The truth is as it has always been,' he said, 'that we can only get out of the college what we send to college.' But in Sheffield, under the leadership of the Rev Stuart Reynolds, the Victoria Street church started a new church at Dronfield through a phone ministry, and the Rev Peter O'Brien served as their first minister. The Victoria Street church also moved out of their historic old Gothic building in the city centre to a pub in a housing area which they 'converted' into Norfolk Park Church of the Nazarene. Zion Holiness Church in Birmingham, an independent congregation, was led by their minister, the Rev Brent Long, into union with the denomination in 1995.

The district suffered the loss of a number of retired ministers: Frank Webster, the redoubtable pioneer of Cardiff, Fred Upton, Alfred Milliken, George Brown, John Jones, Stanley Shields, Ron Thomas, and William Russell. The Rev Ron Thomas was one of the last of the ministers of the Calvary Holiness Church, and had given sterling service in several difficult areas, particularly in Shankill Road in Belfast during the 'troubles'. (Later, in 2003, the death of the Rev Fred Grossmith was also reported). Several stalwarts retired. The Rev Len McNeil, a graduate of Emmanuel Bible College, had ministered in Halstead in Essex (where H.R. Brockett was in the congregation), in Cosham, and then long-term in Ashton-under-Lyne, where he led the congregation out of the old mission hall into a converted bank building in the town centre. He also retired as district secretary to be succeeded by the Rev Barry Hall. The Rev Raymond Busby was a graduate of Hurlet Nazarene College who had gone on to take further degrees in theology and education, and after lecturing in a college of education, had built up the congregations in Port Glasgow in the north district and in his home church of Dewsbury in the south district. The Rev Attill Arnold was the exception to the rule that the denomination had generally failed to reach people from the holiness churches in the West Indies who had settled in Britain. But unexpected losses to the pastoral ministry came with the death of several active ministers – Alan Mounce of Totterdown, Bristol in 1995, Paul Johnson in 1996, Sadiq Bhatti in 1998, Bill Nuttall of Clapham Junction church in 1999, and Dan Merchant of Ilkeston in 2001. The Rev Alan Longworth of Thomas Memorial also had to retire through ill-health, and although he made a remarkable recovery, was not able to take a church again. But in 2002, in the year John Paton retired as district superintendent, he suffered the most severe personal loss in the death of his wife, Helen.

Mission in the New Millennium

At the south district assembly of 2002, the Rev Clive Burrows was elected district superintendent on the second ballot. A graduate of the college and of the University of Lancaster, he had been a missionary in Papua New Guinea, had taught at European Nazarene Bible College and been minister of the Woodside church in Watford and the Didsbury church in Manchester. The following year an audit of church rolls led to a decrease of 261 in the membership of the district, followed the next year by a farther 110. But there was no point in keeping on the roll the names of those who had clearly departed and were not likely to return. While names might be removed with reluctance, membership rolls had to be honest. But there were hopes of new work in Coventry through sports ministry, and a thorough review was undertaken of the structure and operation of the district. There was the possibility too of a special project for London, taking up an issue which had first been raised in the 1950s. In 2004, Clive Burrows had the unique distinction for any district superintendent in the British Isles districts of being re-elected by a unanimous vote of the assembly.

In 2004, Dr David McCulloch succeeded Herbert McGonigle as principal of the Nazarene Theological College, but Dr McGonigle continued with the part-time teaching he had done throughout his years as principal. But by now the college was faced with the challenge of finding new, suitably qualified lecturers within a decade from the ranks of British Nazarenes before retirement began to reduce the contribution of those who had taken the college to its high standing.

At the conclusion of a century of corporate life and ministry then in 2006, the Church of the Nazarene in the United Kingdom faces a second century full of challenges. What can be learned from the past to guide her in the future? Enormous social and cultural changes separate us from the world in which David Thomas stepped out and George Sharpe was thrust out. But there have also been theological developments in the Wesleyan tradition. Can the ongoing study of the scriptures and the deeper understanding and recovery of the Wesleyan heritage help the church to shape her mission in a way that will be more effective in the new century? How will theology and mission interact?

EPILOGUE AND PROLOGUE

A history such as this is not merely an antiquarian exercise. It should stimulate thanksgiving of course for the commitment and sacrifice of those who have gone before us. But it also raises questions to ponder, and these should lead to deeper understanding. That deeper understanding of the past should issue in turn in a more practical wisdom in facing the challenges of the future.

Questions

The most fundamental question for the Church of the Nazarene in the two British Isles districts is whether they have a mission in this country in the twenty-first century. For all Christians it is self-evident that the Church of Jesus Christ has a critical role for the future of the nation. The moral and social problems issuing from the turn of the tide in the 1960s are gathering pace. The breakdown of the family is all around us with all the incalculable effects which that is going to have on the next generation of families. Co-habitation has become socially acceptable in society at large, divorce is common, and even promiscuity is almost accepted as the norm. Vandalism and gang warfare plague many housing estates and inner-city areas. Crime has risen to levels which would have appalled the people of the early twentieth century and drugs are widespread among the young. 'Binge drinking' has become common and drunkenness is affecting work efficiency and family life. The old temperance movement has gone.

The media meanwhile indulge in salacious gossip and sexually explicit programmes and publications while rejoicing in the freedom they have won from censorship and restrictive taboos. Sunday schools have declined dramatically and the vast majority of families have now lost all contact with the church and are almost totally ignorant of the Bible or the Christian gospel. It is true of course that commentators in all ages have bemoaned the deterioration of their times, even at the height of the church's influence in the Edwardian era! But a sober study of social trends supports the generalization that the social and moral advances of the nineteenth century which followed the evangelical revival have now gone into reverse. So there can be no doubt that the United Kingdom is once again a mission field and the role of the church is critical.

But what about the Church of the Nazarene? Does the emphasis on Christian holiness which was so much part of the dominant evangelical ethos of 1906 still have relevance in 2006 and in succeeding years? And did the British Church of the Nazarene embody that holiness any way? And is it not too small in any case to be significant? There are no doubt many different views and perspectives, but some reflections may be a starting point for discussion.

Compared with the Church of the Nazarene around the world, it is true that the denomination in Britain has grown very little. In the United States the three groups who came together to form the denomination in 1907-08 numbered only 10,000, but a century later the American membership has grown to over 600,000. The growth in other areas of the world has been even more remarkable. The membership of 3,000 on the 'mission fields' when George Sharpe became a missionary superintendent in 1923 is now moving on to a million, spread across the five continents and about 150 countries. But here we need to note that the Church of the Nazarene shares in the general pattern for the global Christian church, that whereas the church is strong in North America and growing steadily and often dramatically in the two-thirds world, it is declining catastrophically in post-Christian Europe. Only evangelical churches are growing in Europe, but they only do so by swimming against a vast cultural tide. The British Isles districts of the Church of the Nazarene have mirrored that pattern. The fact that they have grown at all is worthy of comment and is a tribute to the sacrifice and sheer hard work of many of its members. But the apparent decline of the last decade calls for concern. And why has it not grown more?

Some Responses

One factor which loyal Nazarenes often refuse to consider is the name of the denomination. Since the name does not appear to be a hindrance in the 'New World' or the two-thirds world, why should it be a problem here? But that is to become so shaped by the cultural horizons of the international Church of the Nazarene as to fail to hear the resonances and undertones of British culture. In Europe, unlike the multi-denominational world of America or the rest of the world, the assumption that Christians should all belong to one (national) church remains (even in this post-Christian age) a basic cultural assumption. To be a Baptist or a Presbyterian or Methodist in England or an

Episcopalian in Scotland is to be odd. But at least these names have a history and a cultural resonance. Well-informed people know what they mean. But the name, 'Church of the Nazarene', conveys nothing to the ninety percent of the British population who have never heard of it, and it arouses suspicion, sounding like a strange sect or cult to many.[1] It is impossible to speculate accurately about this, but it is highly probable that had the name incorporated the word 'Methodist' or the word 'Wesleyan', the denomination in Britain would have been much larger. Certainly the Church of the Nazarene in the United Kingdom needs to avoid sectarianism and to work at building up its relationship with all God's people in every church, but especially evangelical Methodists.

A second factor which presents itself is the structural problem present particularly since the unions of the 1950s. What has appeared to be a chronic ongoing shortage of ministers may instead be seen as an unrealistic expectation as to how many Christians will be gifted for the preaching and pastoral ministry. Perpetuating the existence of small churches in very difficult situations by placing inexperienced or half-prepared pastors in them has led over decades to the loss of literally hundreds of disillusioned people. And even in the healthy churches, it is not that they have failed to win converts: the statistics show hundreds who have joined the churches by profession of faith. But what cries out for examination is the number of those who have been lost, who have gone to other denominations or been removed from the roll after making a shipwreck of their faith.

There will always be those who lose their faith, sadly, but why have members in good standing moved to other denominations? Many have simply moved to areas where there is no Nazarene church, and a small denomination will suffer from that more than others. Some churches have sometimes been stuck in a rut so that parents have reluctantly reached the conclusion that a small group of loyal elderly members cannot provide the context for winning their growing children to the

---

1 Dr Sydney Martin once received mail addressed to 'The Chief Rabbi, Church of the Nazarene'! The author heard the prominent Dutch theologian, Hendrikus Berkhof, in an after-dinner speech in Leiden in 1989, say how welcome the Church of the Nazarene was in the Netherlands. 'But,' he said, 'You will have to change your name!'

faith. The converse has also been true. Others (including many brought up in the church) have grown in their faith and understanding to the point where the revivalistic preaching and worship seem repetitive and superficial and fail to feed them the strong meat they need. The British Isles districts have always had thriving youth work, but the lively services that appeal to youth may appear to be a kind of stuck-adolescence to the thinking adult. It is notable that, although there are notable exceptions, many of the children of the leading ministers and lay people have gone as adults to other denominations. A church that seems to exist only to reach those outside and for 'milk' Christians can very often fail to cater to the needs of 'meat' Christians who are hungry for a fuller diet of teaching and more thoughtful worship. It never succeeds in getting beyond being an evangelistic 'mission' to becoming a fully fledged 'church'.

That of course is rather ironic. One would have expected that the focus on Christian holiness would have led to a concern not to keep on repeating the 'simple gospel', but to balance evangelism and care for the immature with the care of those who (as the writer to the Hebrews puts it) are 'pressing on to perfection'. Perhaps the problem here is the very idea given to the holiness movement by Phoebe Palmer that there is a 'shorter way' to 'perfection'. Nothing presumably could do more spiritual damage than encouraging young Christians to claim prematurely a level of Christian experience and deliverance from sin which they do not have the maturity or self-knowledge to understand. That is going to result either in severe disillusionment or life-long hypocrisy.[2]

More Questions

And have the British Nazarenes actually embodied the holiness which they proclaim? What are we to make of preachers of holiness who engage in rivalries, or who have a reputation for proclaiming their own achievements, or are difficult to live with, or are over-sensitive about their standing or lack of formal qualifications? And what is the implication of the fact that proportionately just as many Nazarene ministers have had to leave the ministry through moral failure as in any

---

2 Compare the comments of Dr Wes Tracy in his introduction to H. Ray Dunning, *A Layman's Guide to Holiness* (Kansas City: Beacon Hill, 1991)

other denomination? And does holiness consist merely in acts of piety – prayer meetings and open airs and going to church? Where are the acts of charity and mercy, the 'good deeds' which cause an unbelieving world to give glory to our Father in heaven? Do the holiness people stand out for feeding the hungry and clothing the naked and caring for the poor and marginalized?

More Responses

The first response to these questions is that it is always highly risky to preach and teach about Christian holiness! It is much easier and safer to proclaim how much of a sinner you are, and that Christians are 'not perfect, only forgiven.' But if one is really convinced that the New Testament declares a measure of deliverance from sin, one is obliged to declare it and – by the grace of God – to embody it. Secondly (as John Wesley argued), a thousand false witnesses cannot discredit one true one. The existence of hypocrites in the church does not devalue the witness of one true saint. And although there have been unbalanced fanatics and happy extroverts who have falsely claimed a holiness they did not exemplify, there has equally been a host of quieter witnesses whose faithful and consistent lives have testified to the sanctifying work of the Holy Spirit.

Thirdly, although the twentieth-century welfare state has taken care of many needs which previously fell to the churches, and even though many evangelical Christians shied away from the 'social gospel' early in the century, there has in fact been a ministry of 'charity and mercy'. Throughout the century, the people in this history were deeply involved in supporting the ministries of healing and teaching as well as the ministry of preaching being exercised by their missionary representatives in the Transvaal and Swaziland and Mozambique, in India and Papua New Guinea and a dozen other mission fields. And as the twentieth century ended, a recovery of concern for 'compassionate ministries' led to expeditions to Eastern Europe, work among addicts and several community projects.

Learning Lessons

But there are a number of lessons which can be learned from all this. First, the deepening understanding of Wesley's teaching can alert us to the fact that too often Christian holiness has been taught in a way that is simplistic and misleading. There needs to be a greater awareness of the paradoxes of Christian holiness, what Wesley called 'the imperfections of the perfect'. That is difficult to grasp, for the very concept of 'perfection' in Western society is of an absolute final flawlessness. But the biblical concept which Wesley was expounding was 'perfect *love*' or a 'pure *heart*', that is, full-hearted, unreserved, unconditional love, but not flawless performance or faultless character. Reading this history carefully certainly makes us aware of the flaws and failings of the leaders of the British holiness movement. But what cannot be questioned is the sacrificial commitment to what they believed was the call and leading of God. They embody the paradox of being those who have 'tasted the powers of the age to come', but are still living within 'this present evil age.' While they were focused on the will of God as they saw it, and had declared to Him their total consecration, and were filled with His Spirit so as to love Him with all their heart, soul, mind and strength, yet they lived within the fallen body with fallen minds so that their understanding of His will was always limited and sometimes even wrong. Their total consecration did not magically remove flaws of character. In our sophisticated and sceptical age therefore it is vital that those who proclaim Christian holiness should embody it. But to embody it means to be deeply aware of, and openly honest about, how far they fall short.

Secondly, the deepening understanding of Wesley's teaching can alert us to the fact that 'there is no holiness but social holiness.' When Wesley wrote that, he was not thinking about social action or social reform. He was thinking of the 'social' holiness of the Methodist 'society'. The later holiness movement, shaped by nineteenth-century revivalism, concentrated its preaching so much on the need for the *individual* to be fully consecrated and to 'die out' to sin and to love God with all the heart, soul, mind and strength, that it tended to lose sight of the fact that 'perfect love' is only possible within the community of the church. 'Love' is by definition *relational*. And it is only within the matrix of loving relationships within a healthy fellowship (*koinonia*) of Christian brothers and sisters that 'perfect love' is possible.

Now in fact the practice of the holiness movement was better than its preaching. Whereas legalism and hell-fire preaching was sometimes used to drive individuals to seek individual inner sanctification, in fact what attracted most people to Nazarene churches was the rich fellowship, the mutual support and the sense of belonging. As Mrs Rae said to her son after her first visit to the Nazarene church in Troon in 1929, 'Hugh, these are my people!' People did not characteristically join a Nazarene church because they believed the doctrine: they believed the doctrine because they belonged to the church! The doctrine of 'perfect love' was embraced only once they had experienced the mutual love of the fellowship.

This is a lesson which can stand the Church of the Nazarene in good stead in the 'post-modern' age. Whether in fact we are passing out of the 'modern' age into the 'post-modern' age needs to be treated with a certain amount of scepticism. But it does appear to be true that there is a trend towards celebrating the community which is replacing the focus which 'modernity' had on individualism. On these grounds the American Methodist theologian Henry Knight has argued that the Wesleyan tradition is in a better position to evangelize than those Christian traditions which have laid more emphasis on apologetics and rational persuasion.[3] That would suggest that to be effective for Christ then in post-modern, post-Christian Britain, the Church of the Nazarene must not present holiness as judgmental legalism, nor as antiseptic individualistic piousness, but must *embody* holiness in inclusive communities of 'perfect love' which image the very inner love of the Holy Trinity.

Of course all the talk about 'inclusive communities' can all too easily become cosy sentimentality. While true Christian holiness is not judgmental and censorious, it is nevertheless redemptive. And redemption only comes through the judgment of the cross. It involves a deep repentance, a dying to sinful self-centredness which can only come about through identifying ourselves with the death of Christ. While Nazarene churches must *embody* the holiness of Christ, it is not their own holiness they proclaim - but *His*. A church can only be truly filled with the Spirit of Christ and truly holy if it is centred not merely on an abstract doctrine or ideal of 'holiness', nor on itself as a 'holiness movement', but on Christ crucified. He is the only source of true Christian holiness.

---

3 Henry H. Knight, *A Future for Truth: Evangelical Theology in a Postmodern World* (Nashville: Abingdon, 1997)

The most effective churches in the twenty-first century will surely be those who grasp the significance of that text on the handbills distributed in Parkhead on 30th September, 1906, to invite people to the new church:

> "We preach Christ crucified... Who of God is made unto us Wisdom, and Righteousness and Sanctification, and Redemption."

Select Bibliography

Atkinson, J. Baines, *The Beauty of Holiness* (London: Epworth, 1953)
An older but scholarly biblical theology of Christian holiness by a Methodist

Bangs, Carl, *Phineas Bresee: His Life in Methodism, the Holiness Movement, and the Church of the Nazarene* (Kansas City: Beacon Hill, 1995)
A carefully researched biography written by a leading American church historian who also wrote the standard biography of James Arminius

Banks, Rhoda, *Stanley Banks: First My Friend* (Manchester: OMS, 1992)
The daughter of J.D. Drysdale wrote this life-story of her husband, Stanley Banks, who succeeded his father-in-law as principal of Emmanuel Bible College, Birkenhead

Banks, Stanley *et al*, *The Right Way: A Symposium of Teaching on the Way of Holiness* (London: Oliphants, 1964)

Barker, J.H.J, *This is the Will of God: A Study in the Doctrine of Entire Sanctification as a Definite Experience* (Winona Lake, IN: Light and Life Press, 1956)

Bebbington, David, *Evangelicalism in Modern Britain* (London: Unwin Hyman, 1989)
The standard work on British Evangelicalism: see esp. Chapter 5, 'Holiness unto the Lord', 151-180.

Bebbington, David, *Holiness in Nineteenth-Century England: The 1998 Didsbury Lectures* (Carlisle: Paternoster, 2000)

Bedwell, H.K, *Black Gold: The Story of the International Holiness Mission in South Africa 1908-1936* (Cape Town: Cape Town Times, c. 1936)

Brockett, H.E., *The Riches of Holiness: A Testimony and Message* (London: Marshall, Morgan &Scott, [1936]; 2nd ed. Kansas City: Beacon Hill Press, 1951)
Autobiographical testimony to Christian holiness by an I.H.M. layman.

Brockett, H.E. *Scriptural Freedom from Sin* (Tunbridge Wells: C. Baldwin, 1939)

Brower, Kent, *Holiness in the Gospels* (Kansas City: Beacon Hill Press, 2005)
A new scholarly study of the basis in the Gospels (often neglected) for the doctrine of Christian holiness

Chadwick, Samuel, *The Call to Christian Perfection* (London: Epworth Press, 1936)

Chadwick, Samuel, *The Way to Pentecost* (London: Hodder & Stoughton, 1932) Reissued by Cliff College Publishing 1996.

Chambers, Oswald, *My Utmost for His Highest* (London: Simpkin & Marshall, 1930)
The devotional classic by the leader of the League of Prayer, still selling thousands of copies. Numerous other books of Chamber's talks were published by his widow. See *The Complete Works of Oswald Chambers* (Grand Rapids: Discovery House, 2000)

Chapman, J.B., *A History of the Church of the Nazarene* (Kansas City: Nazarene Publishing House, 1926)

Cook, Thomas, *New Testament Holiness* (London: Epworth Press, 1958)
A re-publication of a classic by the first principal of Cliff College

Crossley, E.K., *He Heard from God* (London: Salvationist Publications, 1959)
A biography of Frank Crossley of Star Hall, Manchester, by his daughter

Deasley, A.R.G., *Doctrines Are Different* (Kansas City: Beacon Hill, 1961)

Deasley, A.R.G., *Marriage and Divorce in the Bible and the Church* (Kansas City: Beacon Hill, 2000)

Deasley, A.R.G., *The Shape of Qumran Theology* (Carlisle: Paternoster, 2000)
Professor Deasley's Didsbury Lectures

Doctorian, Samuel, *From Calvary...: The Story of Samuel Doctorian* (London, 1963)

Drysdale, J.D., *The Price of Revival* (Edinburgh: Oliphants, n.d.)

Drysdale, J.D & L.M., *"Emmanuel" 25 Years After* (Birkenhead: J.D. & L.M. Drysdale, 1933)

Drysdale, J.D. *Holiness in the Parables* (London: Oliphants, 1952)

Dunn Pattison, Mary W., *Ablaze for God: The Life Story of Paget Wilkes* (London: Japan Evangelistic Band, 1936)
A hagiography, but of one who was genuinely a *hagios* (saint).

Dunning, Norman G., *Samuel Chadwick* (London: Hodder & Stoughton, 1933)
With a foreword by David Lloyd George

Fawcett, Arthur, *The Cambuslang Revival: the Scottish Evangelical Revival of the Eighteenth Century* (Edinburgh: Banner of Truth Trust, 1971)
Dr Fawcett's Glasgow PhD in which he examines the revival of the 1740s in Cambuslang near Glasgow – one of a number of local

'awakenings' in Britain and the American colonies in which George Whitefield played a prominent part.

Ford, Jack, *In the Steps of John Wesley: The Church of the Nazarene in Britain* (Kansas City: Nazarene Publishing House, 1968).
Dr Ford's London doctoral thesis is the standard work on British Nazarene history up to 1955.

Ford, Jack, *What the Holiness People Believe* (Birkenhead: Emmanuel Bible College, 1955)

Frame, George, *Blood Brother of the Swazis: The Life Story of David Hynd* (Kansas City: Beacon Hill, 1952)
A 'missionary book' life-story written in popular journalistic style.

Gentry, Peter W., *The Countess of Huntingdon* (Peterborough, Foundery Press, 1994)

Gentry, Peter W., *Revival Cameos* (London: Evangelical Press, 1985)

Girvin, E.A., *Phineas F. Bresee: A Prince in Israel* (Kansas City: Pentecostal Nazarene Publishing House, 1916)
Written immediately after Bresee died: see also the scholarly biography by Carl Bangs

Gorman, Hugh, *Requiem for a Rebel* (Kansas City: Beacon Hill, 1980)
The testimony of a wild Belfast 'fella' who was converted in the Donegall Road Church of the Nazarene and who became a Nazarene pastor and evangelist in the U.K. and Canada.

Govan, J.G., *In the Train of His Triumph: Reminiscences of the Early Days of the Faith Mission* (Edinburgh: The Faith Mission, 1946)

Govan-Stewart, I.R., *Spirit of Revival* (Edinburgh: Faith Mission, 1938)

Govan-Stewart, I.R., *When the Fire Fell: The Outcome in the Life of John George Govan* (Edinburgh: The Faith Mission, 1961)
A biography of John George Govan by his daughter.

Grossmith, Fred, *The Cross and the Swastika* (Worthing: Henry E. Walter, 1984)

Grubb, Norman, *Drysdale – Prophet of Holiness* (London: Lutterworth, 1955)
A biography of J.D. Drysdale by one of the initiators of Inter-Varsity Fellowship who was the son-in-law of C.T. Studd, succeeding him as director of W.E.C.

Harris, Reader, *The Beatitudes* (London: P.L. Publishing Depot, 1912)

Harris, Reader, *Is Sin a Necessity?* (London: Partridge & Co., 1896)

Harris, J. Rendel, *Aaron's Breastplate* (London: National Council of Evangelical Free Churches, 1908)

Harris, J. Rendel, *The Life of Francis William Crossley* (London: James Nisbet & Co., 1900)

Hills, A.M., *Fundamental Christian Theology* (Pasadena: C.J. Kinne, 1931)
The first systematic theology written by a Nazarene, but not accepted as officially representing the stance of the denomination

Hills, A.M., *Holiness and Power* (Cincinnatti: Revivalist Office, 1897)

Hills, A.M., *Scriptural Holiness and Keswick Teaching Compared* (Manchester: Star Hall, c. 1912)

Hooker, Mary R., *Adventures of an Agnostic. Life and Letters of Reader Harris, Q.C.* (London: Marshall, Morgan & Scott, 1959)
A biography of Richard Reader Harris by his daughter

Hynd, David, *Africa Emerging* (Kansas City: Nazarene Publishing House, 1959)

James, Maynard G., *Facing the Issue* (Burnley: Pilgrim Publishing House, 1948)

James, Maynard J., *I Believe in the Holy Ghost* (Nelson: Coulton & Co., 1964))
With a commendation by fellow-Welshman, Dr D. Martyn Lloyd-Jones

James, Maynard, *When Thou Prayest: Plain Talks about the Devotional Life* (Kansas City: Beacon Hill, 1963)

James, Paul J., *A Man on Fire* (Ilkeston: Moorley's, 1993)
A biography of Maynard James by his son. Although clearly showing deep admiration for his father and identification with his views, Paul James has not written a mere 'hagiography', but a genuine biography which is honest about the old saint's shortcomings.

Jessop, Harry E, *Foundations of Doctrine* (Chicago: Chicago Evangelistic Institute, 1949)

Jessop, H.E., *The Heritage of Holiness* (Chicago: Chicago Evangelistic Institute, 1950)

Jessop, H.E., *We the Holiness People* (Chicago: Chicago Evangelistic Institute, 1948)

Jones, Charles E., *Perfectionist Persuasion: The Holiness Movement and American Methodism 1867-1936* (Metuchen: Scarecrow, 1974)

Jones, Mrs D.B. and her sons, *David Jones. Ambassador to Africans* (Kansas City: Beacon Hill, 1955)

Jones, E.M., *Our Spoke in the Wheel* (London: I.H.M., n.d.)
An early account of the I.H.M. missions in southern Africa by Mrs Emily Jones

Laird, Rebecca, *Ordained Women in the Church of the Nazarene* (Kansas City: Nazarene Publishing House, 1993)
This contains a chapter on Dr Olive Winchester, the first woman to be ordained in Scotland

Lambert, D.W., *Heralds of Holiness* (Stoke-on-Trent: MOVE, 1975)
A collection of short biographical sketches by D.W. Lambert, a Methodist who lectured at Cliff College and then founded Lebanon Bible College, a missionary training college in the 'holiness' tradition which became Northumberland Bible College and united with Glasgow Bible College (originally the Bible Training Institute) to form the International Christian College in Glasgow.

Lown, A.J., *A Pastor's Pot Pourri: From Pulpit and Pen* (Keighley: Briggs, 1989)

Lown, Albert J., *From Dreamer to Deliverer* (Kansas City: Beacon Hill, 1959)

Lown, Albert J., *Mastering our Moods* (Kansas City: Beacon Hill, 1967)

Lown, Albert J., *Portraits of Faith: Meditations from Hebrews 11* (Kansas City: Beacon Hill, 1981)

Lown, Albert J., *Your Purse and You* (Kansas City: Beacon Hill, 1960)

Mahan, Asa, *The Baptism of the Holy Ghost* (London: Elliott Stock, c. 1876)

Mahan, Asa, *Christian Perfection* (London: Primitive Methodist Book Room, c. 1840)

Martin, Sydney, *The Gospel of Power: The Message of Paul for Today's World* (Kansas City: Beacon Hill, 1973)

Martin, Sydney, *Thessalonians, Timothy, Titus*, Vol. 10 of *Beacon Bible Expositions* (Kansas City: Beacon Hill, 1977)

Martin, Sydney, *Living with Fire* (Kansas City: Beacon Hill, 1983)

McCasland, D.C., *Oswald Chambers: Abandoned to God* (Grand Rapids: Discovery House Publishers, 1993)
A modern, well-researched biography of the leader of the League of Prayer who is best known for the devotional classic, *My Utmost for His Highest*

McGonigle, Herbert Boyd, *Sufficient Saving Grace: John Wesley's Evangelical Arminianism* (Carlisle: Paternoster, 2001)
A major work on Wesley's theology by the former principal of Nazarene Theological College in Didsbury.

McLean, J.B. (ed), *Faith Triumphant: A Review of the Work of the Faith Mission 1886-1936 by Those Who Have Seen and Heard* (Edinburgh: The Faith Mission, 1936)

McRitchie, K.M., *Overcoming Life's Handicaps* (London: Marshall, Morgan & Scott, n.d.)
A book by one of the early Nazarene ministers in Scotland

Mitchell, T. Crichton, *Charles Wesley: Man with the Dancing Heart* (Kansas City: Beacon Hill, 1994)

Mitchell, T. Crichton, *The Wesley Century (1725-1825)*, Vol. 2 of *Great Holiness Classics* (Kansas City: Beacon Hill, 1984)

Mitchell, T. Crichton, *Meet* Mr *Wesley: An Intimate Sketch of John Wesley* (Kansas City: Beacon Hill, 1981)

Mitchell, T. Crichton, *To Serve the Present Age: The Church of the Nazarene in the British Isles* (Kansas City: Beacon Hill, 1980)
A well-written 'missionary book' giving a popular account of British Nazarene history up to 1980.

Noble, T.A., *Tyndale House and Fellowship: The First Sixty Years* (Leicester: IVP, 2006)
This history traces the development of Tyndale House, the biblical research library in Cambridge founded by F.F. Bruce and others, and the associated Tyndale Fellowship for evangelical scholars and theologians, in which several of the academic staff of NTC have been active.

Palmer, Phoebe, *Entire Devotion to God* (London: Salvationist Publishing and Supplies, n.d.)

Parker, J. Fred, *Into All the World: The Story of Nazarene Missions through 1980* (Kansas City: Nazarene Publishing House, 1983)

Parker, J. Fred, *Mission to the World: A History of Missions in the Church of the Nazarene through 1985* (Kansas City: Nazarene Publishing House, 1988)

Peckham, Colin N., *Heritage of Revival* (Edinburgh: The Faith Mission, 1986)

Peters, J.L., *Christian Perfection and American Methodism* (New York: Abingdon, 1956)

Pollock, John, *The Keswick Story* (London: Hodder, 1964)

Purkiser, W.T., *Called unto Holiness*, Vol. 2 (Kansas City: Nazarene Publishing House, 1983)
The first volume was written by Timothy L. Smith

Quanstrom, Mark, *A Century of Holiness Theology* (Kansas City: Nazarene Publishing House, 2004)
A published doctoral thesis tracing the evolution of the doctrine of Christian holiness in the Church of the Nazarene through the twentieth century.

Rae, Hugh, *Scholarship on Fire: A Personal Account of Fifty Years of the Nazarene College in Britain* (Salford: Agape Press, 1994)

Ravenhill, Leonard, *Why Revival Tarries* (Minneapolis: Bethany Fellowship, 1962)

Sharpe, George, *Addresses on Holiness* (Glasgow: A.L. Burnett, n.d.)

Sharpe, George, *A Short Historical Sketch of the Church of the Nazarene in the British Isles* (Glasgow, 1926)
Although no publisher or date is given, this brief history was written in 1926 (acc. to page 54).

Sharpe, George, *This is My Story* [Glasgow: Messenger, 1948]
An unfinished autobiography covering Dr Sharpe's early life and published soon after his death.

Shepherd, Len, *Into the Unknown* (Bristol: Knowle Church of the Nazarene, 1999)

Smith, Allister, *The Ideal of Perfection* (London: Oliphants, 1965)

Smith, Hannah Whitall, *The Christian's Secret of a Happy Life* (London: Nisbet, 1906)

Smith, Timothy L., *Called unto Holiness* (Kansas City: Nazarene Publishing House, 1962)
A history of the Church of the Nazarene up to 1932 by a leading church historian who was a professor at John Hopkins University

Swanson, Dwight, *The Temple Scroll and the Bible: The methodology of 11QT* (Leiden: Brill, 1995)
Dr Swanson's PhD thesis on the Qmran Community

Taylor, Mendell, *Fifty Years of Nazarene Missions*, Vols. 1-3 (Kansas City: Beacon Hill, 1952)

Taylor, Paul and Mellor, Howard, *Travelling Man: a Tribute to the Life and Ministry of Rev Dr Arthur Skevington Wood* (Cliff College & Wesley Fellowship, 1994)

[Thomas, D.L., and Milbank, W.S.], *David Thomas, Founder of the International Holiness Mission* (London: International Holiness Mission, [1933])

A biography with tributes from members of the Thomas family and the I.H.M. published shortly after David Thomas's death. The book is anonymous but most of the writing seems to have been done by David Lowth Thomas (his son) and W.S. Milbank.

Wiley, H. Orton, *Christian Theology*, Vols. 1-3 (Kansas City: Nazarene Publishing House, 1940)

A traditional 'systematic theology' by president of Pasadena College (now Point Loma Nazarene University) adopted as the 'official' Nazarene stance in the 1940s.

Winchester, Olive M., *Christ's Life and Ministry* (Kansas City: Beacon Hill, c.1932)

Winchester, Olive M., *Crisis Experiences in the Greek New Testament* (Kansas City: Beacon Hill, 1953)

Winchester, Olive M., *Moses and the Prophets: A Brief Survey of the Old Testament* (Kansas City: Beacon Hill, 1941)

Winchester, Olive M., *The Story of the Old Testament* (Kansas City: Beacon Hill, 196?)

Wilkes, Paget, *Sanctification* (London: Japan Evangelistic Band, 1931)

Wilkes, Paget, *The Dynamic of Faith* (Edinburgh: Oliphants, 1922)

One of several 'dynamic' books by the founder of the Japan Evangelistic Band

Wood, A. Skevington, *Love Excluding Sin: John Wesley Doctrine of Sanctification* (Stoke-on-Trent: Wesley Fellowship, 1986)

Wynkoop, Mildred Bangs, *A Theology of Love* (Kansas City: Beacon Hill, 1972)

Pamphlets

Anon., 'A Souvenir: Fifty Years' Ministry' (London, 1957)

A brief history of the first fifty years of Thomas Memorial Church of the Nazarene, previously the Battersea Tabernacle of the I.H.M.

Anon., 'Golden Jubilee 1931-1981', (Bolton, 1981)

Barnes, David, 'A Pipe Dream: The History of the Organ of the Bolton First Church of the Nazarene' (Bolton, reprinted, 2003)

Collins, Florence M., '75 Years On' (Uddingston, 1984)

Collins, Stephen (ed), 'Church of the Nazarene Lisburn: The First 50 years' (Lisburn, 2004)

Cunningham, John R., '29 Years After' (Dundee, 1968)

Farmer, Brian L., 'Paisley Church of the Nazarene 1909-1984: A 75th Anniversary Review' (1984)

Anon., 'Sharpe Memorial Church of the Nazarene, 1906-1996: Ninety Years at Parkhead – A Celebration' (Glasgow: Sharpe Memorial, 1996)

Goff, G.M., 'A Church on the March, 1935-1985: Church of the Nazarene, Govan, Handbook for the 50th Anniversary' (Glasgow, 1985)

Hynd, David, *Bremersdorp Mission Station* (Bremerdorp, Swaziland, 1944)

Hynd Samuel W., *A Pictorial History of Manzini Nazarene Mission (1925-1975): Fifty Years of Service to Swaziland* (Florida, South Africa: Nazarene Publishing House, 1975)

Johnson, David and Lawton, G.W. (eds), 'Ye Shall be Witnesses: Church of the Nazarene, the Tabernacle, York Street, Oldham, 1932-1972' (Oldham, 1972)

Lown, Albert J., 'The Story of Trekking' (n.d.)

M'Caw, S.E. and Winterburn, M., *The Manchester Tabernacle of the International Holiness Mission: A Survey of 25 Years' Work, 1919-1944* (Manchester, 1944)

Merchant, Dan, 'Centenary Celebration, 1895-1995, Fiftieth Anniversary 50 Ilkeston' (Ilkeston, 1995)

Traces the history of the congregation over a hundred years, fifty of those as Ilkeston Church of the Nazarene.

Miles, Ivan, 'Megain Memorial Church of the Nazarene: Fifty Years of the Church of the Nazarene in Ballymacarrett' (Belfast, 2001)

Payne, Ronald, 'History of the Church of the Nazarene in Irvine, 1931-2001' (Irvine, 2001)

Perry, David E., *et al*, *Church of the Nazarene, Victoria Street, Sheffield: Golden Jubilee, 1938-1988* (Sheffield, 1988)

Rae, Andrew, 'Come and Celebrate Our Church's 75th Birthday' (Troon, 1983)

Rae, Hugh (ed), 'One Man's Vision: A History of the Church of the Nazarene Twechar 1935-2000' (2000)

Rae, Hugh, 'The Church of the Nazarene's Ninety Years in Paisley' (1999)

Rae, Hugh, *The First 90 Years: Trinity Church of the Nazarene, Perth* (Perth, 1999)

[Solly, E.], 'Centenary Celebration 5th-6th Oct. 1985 – Church of the Nazarene, Clapham Junction' (London, 1985)
  Traces the history of Speke Hall and the League of Prayer through to the Clapham Junction Church of the Nazarene

Valentine, S.R., 'Called unto Holiness: The Church of the Nazarene, Keighley, 1934-1994: Diamond Jubilee Souvenir' (Keighley, 1994)

Weatherill, J.R., '100 Years: Celebrating a Century of Service 1886-1986' (Leeds, 1986)

Unpublished Dissertations

Allam, Beryl P., 'The Outreach and Mission of the Holiness Movement in the British Isles in the Twentieth Century with particular reference to Holiness Trekking, the League of Prayer, the Faith Mission Pilgrims and Holiness Conventions,' B.A. dissertation, University of Leeds, 1990.

Fewkes, G.N., 'Richard Reader Harris 1847-1909: An Assessment of the Life and Influence of a Leader of the Holiness Movement,' MA dissertation, University of Manchester (Nazarene College), 1995

Whiteford, Jean Cameron, 'A Holiness Church in Scotland: The Origins and Development of the Church of the Nazarene, 1906 to 1950,' MTh thesis, University of Glasgow, 1996.

Wood, Colin H., 'Personalities and Powers: Crises in the British Holiness Movement, 1934-1976', MA dissertation, University of Manchester (Nazarene College), 1996.

Periodicals
Africa Calling: the magazine of the I.H.M. in Africa

Holiness Herald: the magazine of the British Isles district of the Church of the Nazarene

Holiness Mission Journal: the magazine of the I.H.M. published in London

Holiness Today: the new name for *The Herald of Holiness*, published in Kansas City

The Flame: the magazine of the C.H.C., still published independently

The Herald of Holiness: the denominational magazine of the Church of the Nazarene, now renamed

The Other Sheep, magazine of the WFMS, later the NFMS, then the NWMS

The Way: the abbreviated title of *The Way of Holiness*

The Way of Holiness: first published by Star Hall, then the name of the Nazarene district magazine

Tongues of Fire: the magazine of the Pentecostal League of Prayer

The Link (previously *BINC Link*): the news-sheet distributed by Nazarene Theological College

World Mission: the new name for *The Other Sheep*, now incorporated in *Holiness Today*

Journal
European Explorations in Christian Holiness

Index
of Personal names, local churches, and mission stations.

Printed in Great Britain
by Amazon

75255007R00203